MARTIN CLASSICAL LECTURES

VOLUME XXIX

The Martin Classical Lectures are delivered annually at Oberlin College on a foundation established by his many friends in honor of Charles Beebe Martin, for forty-five years a teacher of classical literature and classical art in Oberlin.

THE ART OF
BACCHYLIDES

ANNE PIPPIN BURNETT

PUBLISHED FOR OBERLIN COLLEGE BY
HARVARD UNIVERSITY PRESS
CAMBRIDGE, MASSACHUSETTS,
AND LONDON, ENGLAND
1985

The Greek texts have been reproduced photographically from *Bacchylidis,
Carmina cum fragmentis* (Bruno Snell; Herwig Maehler, ed., 1970) by
permission of BSB B. G. Teubner Verlagsgesellschaft, Leipzig.

This book is printed on acid-free paper, and its binding materials
have been chosen for strength and durability.

Library of Congress Cataloging in Publication Data
Burnett, Anne Pippin, 1925–
The art of Bacchylides.
(Martin classical lectures ; v. 29)
Includes indexes.
1. Bacchylides—Criticism and interpretation.
2. Bacchylides—Translations, English.   3. Odes—
History and criticism.   I. Title.   II. Series.
PA25.M3   vol. 29 [PA3943.Z5] 937 s [884ʹ.01] 84-10764
ISBN 0-674-04666-8 (alk. paper)

For my first teacher of Greek
W. Kendrick Pritchett

I would like to thank the faculty and the students of Oberlin College for the welcome I enjoyed among them in the Spring of 1977.

CONTENTS

THE ART OF BACCHYLIDES

INTRODUCTION

In the year 1898 even the dullest classical journal seethed with excitement because the poet Bacchylides had just risen from his grave and become audible. He had been without a tongue for centuries, a voiceless ghost that inhabited 107 nonsequential lines (69 fragments), and he had seemed a dull and commonplace phantom because the words that did survive had been chosen by imperial grammarians for their sententious gravity, if not merely to illustrate points of usage. It had been impossible to sense the flavor of Bacchylides' song and little enough had been known about the man, though ancient critics had listed him among the greatest of Greek poets. He had come from the island of Ceos (Strabo 10.5.6; Suda, *s.v. Bakchylides*) and had lived in exile in Lacedaemon (Plut. *de exil.* 14); he was the nephew of Simonides (*Et. Mag.* 582.10) and a professional rival of Pindar's. He had a reputation in antiquity for charm, elegance and fluidity—"from his tongue came sweet delicacies" was the way a Hellenistic poet put it (*AP* 11.571)—but nevertheless from the fall of the Roman empire he had been only a name.

Then, in 1896, the great Egyptologist Sir Wallis Budge was approached by a man who wanted to sell a sizeable papyrus roll containing several columns of Greek uncials.[1] The dealer was not known to Budge and his story of having found the roll in a ransacked tomb, between the feet of a broken mummy, was not entirely convincing, but somehow the find seemed important. Outbidding his rivals, Budge bought the papyrus roll for a "preposterous" price, and then found that he would have to defy the British Consul, fool the Egyptian Service of Antiquities, and outrun a customs cutter if he was to get his purchase home to the British Museum. With a native friend, an ulster, and a crate of oranges to be used as a decoy, he put together a Hitchcockian scenario of switched trains and clandestine embarcations, and finally he sailed in triumph from Suez with what seemed to be a small package of photographs while angry officials searched through the pile of trunks he had left behind at Port Saïd. It was a sensational way for a classical poet to enter the modern world.

The papyrus had been broken when he first saw it, and Sir Wallis had cut it into sections in order to disguise it, so that what reached England at last were some 200 scraps. Fourteen of these were of good size, however, and their content was easily recognized as Greek poetry, then swiftly identified as Bacchylidean because twenty-four of the lines already known made their appearance here and there in the fragments. (When the work of editing was finished, 14 of the 69 book fragments were accounted for.) One of England's finest papyrologists, Frederic Kenyon, went to work at once to sort and reassemble the bits and pieces of papyrus, finding evidence, in all, of one thousand three hundred and eighty-two lines, about a thousand and seventy of which were perfect or easily restored. In an unbelievably short time he reconstructed twenty poems of considerable length, six of them nearly complete, and these were published as soon as possible.[2] It was the appearance of this initial edition in 1897 that filled the learned periodicals with Bacchylidean reverberations.

A Teubner edition followed in 1898,[3] Jebb published his magisterial presentation in 1905,[4] and in this first decade of rediscovery an astonishing quantity of further work was done. The Bacchylidean dialect was analyzed (it is more Doric and less Aeolic than Pindar's) and his metrical practices were observed (they are less complex and less free than his rival's are). Notes were written on Homeric echoes, on the victors' families, and the dates of certain contests; cult titles were investigated and mythic references were illustrated from vase paintings and from other early literature. And best of all, the combined learning of Britain, Europe, and North America engaged in the teasing game of reading unreadable lines and restoring lost words and phrases. It was a splendid moment for all amateurs of antiquity and yet these journals of '98 and '99 convey an excitement that is not warmed by delight. The find was a great one, the *editio princeps* was incomparable, and the philological problems were appetizing, but nevertheless no single one of those who fell to work so joyously seemed to have taken much pleasure from the actual poetry that had been recovered from its long entombment.

An Italian scholar greeted Bacchylides with these words:[5] "Certainly we find no rush of inspiration in these songs, no bold flight of fantasy, no ardent imagery, no profundity of new and unexpected thought, such as we find in Pindar." And meanwhile in France, in the *Journal des Savants* for January 1898, Henri Weil was just as invidious: "There is no doubt that he fails of the elevation, and also of the depth, of Pindar. The soaring wing was refused him, and he never should have compared himself, as he does somewhere, to an eagle." In Germany Wilamowitz regretfully wished that the discovery might have been made three hundred years earlier, in 1597, when taste was less highly developed and men still enjoyed Anacreontics and simple ballad-like songs.[6] In support of these fresh opinions, the lukewarm judgments of certain ancient critics were revived, and the correct view soon came to be that one far preferred the sublime Pindar, even at his most oppressive, to the frivolities of this new-found fellow of his.

Because he composed the same kinds of poetry as Pindar, Bacchylides quickly became the special property of the Pindarists and in their hands he was treated even less sympathetically. If his unfamiliar epinicians in some detail resembled the well-known ones of his rival, it was always Bacchylides who was accused of imitation; but on the other hand, wherever his songs strove for their own effects, they were reproached for not living up to the mode and style of the great Theban master. Indeed, the students of Pindaric poetry almost succeeded in burying Bacchylides all over again, for their partisan criticism persuaded specialists in other realms that the newly found poet was "like Pindar only worse," and consequently many students of antiquity never made his acquaintance at all.

Fortunately, however, the world is not made up exclusively of classicists, and in 1961 Robert Fagles of Princeton brought out a new translation of the poems of Bacchylides.[7] His version was a noble one, elegantly introduced by Adam Parry, and through it the work of Bacchylides was made attractive and available to a larger public. Poets and students of comparative literature began to enjoy a Greek poet they had not known before, but nevertheless the original negative vote of the turn-of-the-century scholars has continued to carry weight among classicists. Because of the post-Bundy vogue of the victory ode, Bacchylides is better known now than he was twenty years ago, but the pleasures that he has to offer are still being refused, on the grounds that they are overfelicitous and therefore suspect. Individual Hellenists sometimes confess in private to a weakness for his lyrics, but only a handful of recent scholars have given ungrudging attention to him. A group of Americans are the first to come to mind—Jacob Stern, Mary Lefkowitz, P. T. Brannan, C. P. Segal—each of whom has studied some aspect of Bacchylides' poetry with a friendly recognition of its worth. All of them, however, have limited themselves to separate and well-defined problems such as the images, the Homeric echoes, the verbal style, or the epinician structure of a given ode.[8] No one, so far as I know, has written fully about the Bacchylidean compositions taken as a whole, or about the poetic impulses behind them.

An appreciation of the the poetry of Bacchylides depends upon an understanding of the genre that he worked in. Consequently I shall begin by describing the magical power that resided in a group of dancing performers, using Ode 17 as an example of Bacchylides' manner as he exploited the latent religiosity of his chosen mode. Next I shall consider one kind of danced song, the epinician kind, exposing a set of ethical problems that confronted all makers of victory odes; here I mean to use Ode 3 in order to reveal a typical Bacchylidean response to this challenge. Then I shall focus on just one of the conventional elements of choral song, the fiction, seeking its function in praise poetry and observing Bacchylides' purpose and technique in the narrative parts of Odes 13, 9, and 11. Finally I shall call attention to an attitude towards his fictions that Bacchylides shared with the Attic tragedians, discovering it in Odes 18, 16, and 5. In every section the subject will be Bacchylides' peculiar reaction to generic opportunities and demands, but after practices common to all choral poets have been discussed, the poet's own temper and technique will be emphasized—most especially his instinct for the largest meanings of myth and his sense of tragic irony. I shall be, throughout, less disciplined and more subjective than my predecessors (whose work I intend to plunder but not to resume), because I approach all of these topics as an unabashed admirer of Bacchylides' famous felicity.

1. THE CHORAL MODE

Thanks to Budge and Kenyon and Jebb (thanks also to the anonymous man who took the "preposterous" price) we have today pages of print that are called the odes of Bacchylides. We do not, however, have what the poet made, for he was an impresario, not a writer of pages, and what he created was a series of ephemeral performances. The lines that are read with at best a single speaking voice were meant to be sung, not read; they were meant to be sung by many mouths in unison, and what is more they were meant to be depicted by the gestures and figures of many hands and feet. Mind, ear, and eye were all addressed, for the choral ode was apprehended not merely as sense and sound but as spectacle as well, and in actual production it mixed melody, poetry, movement, color, and costume while it borrowed further complexities from the ritual hubbub of the festival of which it was a part. Above all, each such production had the excitement of the unique, for it was an event that would never be witnessed again. The words alone could be preserved, while all the rest perished with the exit of the dancers and the last notes of the lyre or the flute.

When possible, the poet trained the singing dancers of Greek choral song himself, guiding them as a helmsman would a ship. Nevertheless, a fiction of spontaneity was always maintained, for in this kind of performance the many participants represented the many members of a community freely engaged in a shared gesture. The poet might put his name to his work, or make his singers sing "I" in the sense of "I, the poet of this chorus," but he also made them sing "I" in the sense of "I, Theseus," or "I, Heracles," thus causing the tongues of his group to be forever putting on disguises and casting them off again. Frequently the singers imitated a cry of fear, a shout of victory, a prayer, or a long speech from a story being told, and they also mimed imaginary actions with the movements of their dance, but they were nevertheless wholly unlike tragic performers because they never separated and they never strove to maintain an illusion. Instead, the whole group switched modes in unison just as it did characters, moving easily from invocation to narrative, from reflection to histrionics, from incantation to wise exhortation, and drowning every artful assumption of dramatic individuality in an overall voice that was unified, multiple and public—society in sung communication with itself.

The origins of this complex and rigorously conventional poetic performance are lost in the unrecorded time when Hellenic society was first organizing itself. The Greeks themselves said that they danced in imitation of the Olympian gods, who danced when Apollo brought them the lyre, but dancing of some sort must have gone back to the times when men first began to collaborate in the hunt. Dance was the most direct and economical route to ecstasy and ecstasy is necessary, as any people with a shaman knows, to courage and strength as well as to truth and the higher forms of cleanliness.[1] What is more, singing dancers do not work just upon themselves, and ecstasy need not be their only end, for their activity may also be directed outward toward the daimonic world that is approached, sometimes even controlled by magical means. In this realm a band of singing dancers has a special efficacy since many voices obviously have more effect than one when calling upon a nonhuman power, while many hands and feet make the rite more binding when the actions of sympathetic magic are performed. Much of magic depends upon repetition,[2] and the plurality of a chorus provides a multiplied simultaneous repetition of puissant patterns of gesture and sound. Their numbers enforced their demands, and even in a postmagical world the communal songs of the choruses were always—especially by contrast to the single-voiced "interior" lyrics of a monodist—the poetry of power.

The Greek choral lyrics that survive admittedly have nothing of savagery about them and not much of ecstasy either. All of them come from a time when religion had so nearly replaced magic that the practices of cult were almost purged of sorcery, and consequently they contain much more of praise and thanksgiving than they do of manipulation or duress. They worship and magnify powers conceived of as gods, but even these later songs show a functional kinship with the primitive magical performance because they still try to alter the relationship of nature to the supernatural.[3] They continue to voice a need that is communal and they still try to make something happen. The primitive community had called out to its spirits or daimones, asking them to repeat and reconfirm their former actions—"As the hunt was good last season, so let it be again!" or "As the plague ended before, so make it end today!" The later choral songs differed from these calls in that they were not inspired by a particular exigency but belonged instead to a regular calendar of worship, but it was in truth the same old thing that they did, for the archaic and early classical performances were still trying to draw divine power into the human sphere and to reactivate it in a favorable way. Choruses in the sixth and fifth centuries danced fertility for brides and grooms, as well as for orchards, vineyards, and tilled fields. They sang and danced the seasons through their course, and ensured with their performances placation for dangerous gods and hilarity for gracious ones. They sang and danced when girls came of age or young men's military service was over, and also in order to revitalize heroes and solemnize funerals.[4] The chorus, indeed, came to symbolize all the human achievements that made men more like gods and less like beasts (who could only dance when they were bewitched); this is why the painter of the Francois vase stationed a line of dancers in balancing opposition to a centaur battle, and why Bacchylides brought a wild boar into the dancing places of Calydon, when he wanted to figure a breakdown in human culture.

These enlightened singers of the archaic period did not try to coerce the gods with magic, but there was nevertheless still a touch of sorcery in some of their practices. The old prayer formula, "As you did once, do now again!" rested on the idea that the past in a sense dominated even the gods, since they could not change it and actually had to conform to it. What *had been* was clearly a source of power, and it gave man a kind of leverage in his dealings with heaven. Past moments in which divine presence or influence had been manifested were filled forever with an elixir of efficacy, just as a blasted tree forever contained something of the lightning bolt, and their force was still available. Choral song could recreate an old event by means of mimicry and then, since the gestures of the multiple chorus still contained a bit of their primitive authority, the demonic force of the original moment could be danced into the present ceremony. In this way, while it offered a pleasing and worshipful spectacle to the gods, the archaic chorus also pressed upon the supernatural world by means that were almost magical to obtain what it sought—the immediate presence of an active divine influence.

Obviously this choral practice of recreating a bit of the past depended upon a special sense of time. We tend to think of time as a series of units arranged in a line (one end of which is clear, the other indiscernible), wherein only the final item is real. The moments along this line are wedged tightly between their predecessors and their successors and though they may survive as causes of present phenomena they cannot break away from their own before and after, or be brought to life again. Choral lyric, on the other hand, saw time as a pool in which past events sank aimlessly but never ceased to be. Any agitation could bring a fragment of yesterday up from below, and what the dancers did was give this pool of time an artful, ritual stir. A voice, a gesture, even sometimes a silence could be made to detach itself from its old context and rise for an instant to the surface of today, lively and whole.[5] And since the archaic past included legend as well as history, engulfing what we call fiction as well as what we call fact, the stock of ancient moments was almost infinite. Myths, however, recalled the times when men were most open to demonic influence, and consequently mythic moments were the most commonly chosen for revival by the celebrating community.

A fabulous beast might die, or Io might cry out, in the midst of a worldly festival at Syracuse or Athens, as a combination of magic and mimic artistry danced them into the present. At the same time, however, the present celebration had to be subtly detached from its own specific hour and locality if it was to receive this extratemporal infusion, and to achieve this the singers used a technique that was as old as sorcery— self-description. The girl singers of Alcman's *Partheneion* spent half of their song depicting their own performance, as if the visible present were a story to be told, and, in this way, they made of their own ceremony an event that had some of the truth and durability of myth. Not all choruses were as full of themselves as this one, but even in the austere epinician odes the male chorus, performing in the Dorian mode, would sing about singing in that mode,[6] much as the witch who cut her herbs into the fire chanted, "I cut my herbs into the fire." Self-description was the witch's way of liberating her gesture from its bondage to the actual and the quotidian, so that it could operate outside the daily laws of causation, and the choral dancers who imitated her attempted to do much the same thing. Singing of themselves, they sacralized their own movement and their own sound, for they were to be the medium through which power that was not human would pass into the present company.

Whatever their effect upon the unseen audience of divinities, it is easy to understand the effect that such songs had upon the ordinary crowd of celebrating citizens. The spectator saw dancers whom he knew, wearing costumes that he had perhaps seen before; they were a part of his life, but he heard them describe themselves and their performance with the same music that described matters from another world and another time, and meanwhile in the dance these neighbors were instantaneously heroes or monsters or even gods. Such a spectator watched while his own familiar and tangible present became indistinguishable from a world that was strange and timeless.[7] His own incidental presence at a festival lost its fleeting and random quality, for it was recorded as it occurred, memorialized and translated into art, and at the same time the past came to him as a freshly felt sensation.[8] A bit of it was lifted from remembered accounts, embodied, and given the air of improvization that life itself generally has, and then it was offered directly to him. All of which meant that the spectator at such a performance became a kind of communicant who celebrated the real presence of daimonic power as it inhabited the mythic past.

I will not apologize for this mystical way of talking because only with this or some similar reconstruction of the aim of choral lyric can we explain its most striking characteristics. The most obvious of these and to moderns often the most troublesome is its way of handling what we call its "fictions." Choral performances usually contained references to stories, and scholars have written about the "narrative style" of this or that poet, but nevertheless it is almost universally felt that these songs do not tell their stories properly and Wilamowitz was fond of assuming, whenever he could, that they had been left unfinished. This is because the so-called mythic section characteristically has no beginning, middle or end, nor does it first knot, then loosen its difficulties. In fact, it does not narrate at all, for it does not lay out a continuous account or explain why or how its events have occurred. The accepted sequence and processes of causation and time are often disturbed as the passage takes shape; incidents appear out of chronological order, and the chain of events breaks off unexpectedly, often just where no listener would have let a bard or a story-teller stop. And finally, these odd fragmented fiction-bits frequently emphasize a deed or a word that will be neutralized or even negated in the continuing uncut version of the saga that everyone carries in his head. Such practices would be serious flaws in the work of an epic entertainer, but they are generic to choral poetry and they are easily understood when we realize that here the myth was not a form of embellishment or a story told for its own sake. Myth, in choral lyric, is a source of essential *dynamis* or power.

Consider the *Partheneion* of Alcman, the oldest Greek choral song to survive.[9] It comes from the fabled Sparta of luxury that existed before strict reforms made it "Spartan,"[10] and it was meant to be performed by ten pretty girls who were well known to the city. With their leader, they carried a gift at dawn to a goddess of the dawn[11] in a real or metaphorical race,[12] and at some point in their progress they sang this song. The text is fragmentary and there are many mysteries about it, but two things at least are certain. One of these is that the performance was divided equally between the evocation of a mythic moment and the description of a present performance. And the other is that the song, in its second half (the portion we can read), purged itself of banality by lending an air of fiction to its own visible and audible moment. It is as if the present were what was being summoned up by magic as the girls sing of their own gestures and those of their leaders, sing out their own names, sing even of their costumes and ornaments (66-69),

> snake-bracelet of gold, Lydian crown,
> playthings for girls with violet eyes . . .

They are turning themselves into poetry and even these trappings are no longer mere objects but music and memorable song. And then their song too is transformed, objectified and distanced as the girls sing of their own singing (85–88);

> girl that I am I sing in vain
> like the small owl from the barn-beam
> and yet I long to please
> the Lady Aotis.

This of course is conventional mock-modesty, and elsewhere (28 ff.) the chorus is ready to compare its present voice to that of the Sirens,[13] though they are goddesses, much as it is ready to enhance its present speed by a comparison with the horses of dreams (46 ff.). Indeed, they almost make celestial bodies of themselves in a passage that perfectly expresses the mythification of the actual (60 ff.):

> The rising Pleiads rival us
> as through the ambrosial night we run
> bearing a robe that shines like Sirius[14]
> to the goddess of the dawn.

Such was the festival—one in which girls could tease and flaunt their jewels and their accomplishments[15] while they disengaged themselves from everyday time. Whoever the dawn goddess was, and whatever her connection with other Laconian cults, she was obviously expected on this occasion to be pleased by lightness and laughter and feminine "playthings."[16] The song's self-portrait makes this a joyous celebration filled with motion, delight, and the expectation of day, but nevertheless its ruined first half proves that Alcman added a measure of mythic violence and blood to this ritual hilarity. He chose to have his chorus sing of the sons of Hippocoön, all of whom were killed by the Dioscuri and a wounded Heracles in an ugly punishment for some ugly crime of theirs.[17] Even with its details unspecified, the episode seems shockingly inappropriate to the day's golden bracelets and Lydian crowns, for one would have thought that the notion of mass slaughter would certainly offend a goddess who fancied this fastidious chorus. Alcman thought differently, however, and he charged the present with this death-filled moment from the past by means of an incantatory list of names. As each Hippocoöntid is cited with his epithet another maimed body seems to join the heap that the three heroes have made, and worse yet this list confounds itself with its opposite, the list of dancers that follows in the second half of the song. The result is that the ten scented girl-names of the present, when they come, echo the ten blood-soaked masculine names of the mythic past with an effect that is clearly contrived and markedly baroque.

Why did Alcman bring the sons of Hippocoön into his song for the dawn goddess? Obviously his intention was in part ethical, for with this story he could set an example of active blasphemy (the Hippocoöntid crime, whatever it was exactly, was tantamount to storming heaven and attacking female divinities, 16 ff.) over against the active piety of the present day.[18] The mythic male action, offering violence, serves as a contrary definition of the actual female gesture of offering a gift to a goddess, and so by reverse analogy the mythic punishment suggests that the present community will be rewarded for today's reverence and praise. At the transition point, when the song turns from past to present, the girls sing (36–39),

> There is a punishment that comes from god,
> but he is blessed who
> unlamenting, intertwines his days with cheer,
> and I sing Agido . . .

This is not, however, a cautionary lesson in which bad boys get into trouble while good girls go to a party. The contrast of blasphemy and piety is offered to the self-consciously civilized minds of individual members of the mortal audience, but meanwhile the performance as a whole has mixed past dying with present dancing, gathering a great pile of corpses into the beauty of the dawn. By so doing, it has offered the blood of the slain men to whatever is savage in the goddess of the dawn, and it has also introduced the awesome spirit of the avenging heroes among the community of worshippers. Heracles and the Twins were instruments of god, part god themselves when they killed the ten young men, and the names of their victims, like the names of places that gods have visited, still hold some of their *dynamis*. Chanted by the chorus, those names bring the force of primitive *aretē* into the early morning springtime of this happy Spartan feastday.[19]

Another example of the choral revival of indwelling mythic force can be found in the lines about Danaë that come from a choral song by Simonides, the uncle of Bacchylides.[20] We do not know what the festive occasion was; we do not even know if the chorus was female, since male performers could deliver long speeches in a female persona (as they do, for example, in Pindar's *Pythia* 4). The theme of submission and deliverance, and the image of the child within the box both suggest that this chorus means to praise a divinity interested in birth—Leto, Artemis, Hera, or Eilythia—but they might also have wished to please Dionysus the Deliverer.[21] The place of performance is equally uncertain but at any rate somewhere, in some rich Greek city, a chorus was set to dancing, and after an introductory stanza or so (probably about the present celebration) the singers made reference to the daughter of Acrisius and then they mimed this passage about the princess and the baby at the bottom of the sea (543 *PMG*):[22]

> Against the decorated chest
> the wind breathed rage
> and pounding sea and fear laid siege.
> Tears wet her cheek; she put her arms
> round Perseus and whispered, "Child,
> what grief I have, and yet you sleep
> with quiet heart inside this cheerless
> brass-bound box, locked up
> in close blue gloom and deep unbroken night.
> The weight of waves that shift
> above your head is all in vain,
> for you don't care! You don't hear
> the voices of the wind but,
> warm within your purple shawl,
> you stretch at ease and show me
> beauty's face in yours. If fear
> were truly fear then it would strike you too
> and when I spoke you'd turn
> that perfect ear . . .
> But sleep, I beg you, child!
> Sleep, sea, and this unfathomed evil, sleep!
> Let some shift of purpose come,
> Father Zeus, from you
> and if I pray too boldly here,
> asking more than is my due,
> forgive me!"

These lines do not tell the story of Danaë or even recount one chapter from her tale. There is no continuity and no resolution in them and the end—for Danaë's prayer was in all probability the end at least of the mythic section—does not round off the event pragmatically. Mother and child are still locked in their chest underneath the sea when the passage closes, and so if we hear this fragment as many scholars do, simply as a scrap of story—the perversely narrated fragment of a Perseus saga—we are troubled by its lack of resolution and its problematic connection with a public festival. The immediate situation is one of terror and the lines seem to ask the spectator to feel an answering and unassuaged terror hardly suitable to an occasion of public festivity. If, however, we recognize in the Danaë passage the evocation of a moment when something divine entered the world—if we see it as a choral attempt to capture a bit of supernatural energy—then its truncated form becomes functional, and its appropriateness to a ceremony of worship is manifest.

Instead of telling a tale, Simonides has here made a living tableau so that even we, centuries later and merely staring at a page, can see the strangely luminous child and hear the whispered words of the frightened girl. Our perceptions are controlled by those of Danaë—hers of course by the poet—and like hers they take a special hourglass form, as all understanding and emotion is forced to pass through one tiny aperture. Conscious with Danaë's consciousness, the spectator becomes aware first of the angry elements and the vast enclosing sea; next of the wooden box within the sea; then of the child within the box; then of his face upon the shawl; and after this he looks at nothing except the abstract idea of beauty and tranquility. From this point of finest concentration Danaë's mind then leads the spectator out in a splendid, symmetrical explosion—out of the box, up from the sea, beyond all elements to the widest reach of all where there is another (but the same) tranquility, that of Father Zeus. Like her, the spectator has been forced by poetic means to look at the child and see god.

Simonides was an intellectual poet, influenced by the rationalism of the late sixth century, and part of what he has arranged here is a philosophical lesson about the nature of reality. Fear, in the fragment's opening (*deima*, 4), brought with it a conviction that "the fearful" (*to deinon*, 18) was a concrete and independent fact, and if ever anyone had reason to think so Danaë did, in her chest. Nevertheless, the notion of subjectivity insinuates itself as soon as she turns to Perseus, almost in anger at the contradiction between his state and hers. She sees that darkness, imprisonment, even the weight of the sea (note the almost oxymoronic quality of *hyperthe . . . batheian* at 13–14; the deepest part of the sea is still above their heads), all can disappear when the child refuses to perceive them. Then she understands that it is the same with fear. Her terror belongs only to herself; it cannot frighten the baby in her lap, and so it loses its objective existence. If Perseus can sleep, then evil might likewise retire (note how the *kakon* of 22 rings against *kalon* of 17), and wind and sea may rest as well.

Such is the demonstration that is offered to the spectator's mind, but Danaë's experience is religious as well as intellectual. To the sleeping child, disaster is indistinguishable from bliss and his quiescence leads his mother (and her audience) to a second, more transcendent recognition. The baby has beauty's countenance,[23] testifying with his face to an existing good, and he likewise testifies with his flesh to the miraculous strength of god, for there would be no Perseus if Zeus were not able to cross any barrier and enter any enclosure. Danaë remembers through him that there is no sea so deep, no darkness so thickly shadowed, no box so strongly locked that Zeus may not penetrate it, for the proof of this proposition lies sleeping in her lap.[24] As soon as the child's unlistening ear has extinguished her complaint, the beauty of his face makes her directly aware of god and so of the possibility of prayer. In that it comes from the child, Danaë's prayer comes also from Zeus and consequently it contains within itself a promise of his coming favorable response. Through the child, Danaë has been taught to ask, and ask in the right way, for the "shift of purpose" that Zeus has always intended.[25]

All of which means that it is not fear, but fear's dissolution that the dancers depict in this passage. They have conjured up the sudden flood of irrational psychic energy that followed upon Danaë's recognition of the power of god, and they have mimed the arrival of hope in a place where hope could not possibly come. The moment in the chest is in Christian terms a moment of grace, for it is one in which a god's strength helps a mortal to worship that same strength. Such an instant, thus reconstituted, would be appropriate to any cult occasion, and (if the choral magic has worked) this particular festival, whatever it was, will have been transformed. Thanks to Simonides and the dancers it will be filled now with the supreme Olympian force that can control weather and the sea and cause a sunken chest to rise again and be opened on a saving shore, while it can also make a child, and cause a woman to pray.

2. THESEUS' DIVE

It was the function of choral poetry to introduce a bit of demonic power into a rite or festival, and so the performers would often mime an event that had been touched with supernatural force. The idea was to activate a moment so numinous that some of its electricity could be tapped for the present ceremony—providing of course that the gods were pleased with the song. The thing could be done in twenty lines or two hundred, but the essential trick was always the same since the singers had first to remake the moment so well that its indwelling spirit was aroused, then draw its force off quickly, before it had time to dissipate. It was a process that Bacchylides understood to perfection, and it can be observed in an extended form in a song that is called "The Noble Youths" or just "Theseus." The piece is placed among the dithyrambs as number 17,[1] but the prayer at its close proves that it was a song for Apollo, meant to be danced on Delos. There is no formal opening or invocation, however, and no narrative preface. Instead, the listener is abruptly put in contact with an event already under way—one that occurs in the middle of the Cretan Sea.

A'   1 Κυανόπρωιρα μὲν ναῦς μενέκτυ[πον
            Θησέα δὶς ἑπτ[ά] τ᾿ ἀγ᾿λαοὺς ἄγουσα
            κούρους ᾿Ιαόνω[ν
     4 Κρητικὸν τάμνε{ν} πέλαγος·
    5 5 τηλαυγέϊ γὰρ [ἐν] φάρεϊ
            βορήϊαι πίτ᾿νο[ν] αὖραι
            κλυτᾶς ἕκατι π[ε]λεμαίγιδος ᾿Αθάν[ας·
     8 κνίσεν τε Μίνωϊ κέαρ
            ἱμεράμπυκος θεᾶς

10 10 Κύπ'ριδος [ἄ]γ'νὰ δῶρα·
        χεῖρα δ᾽ οὐ[κέτι] παρθενικᾶς
        ἄτερθ᾽ ἐράτυεν, θίγεν
    13 δὲ λευκᾶν παρηΐδων·
        βόασέ τ᾽ Ἐρίβοια χαλκο-
15   θώρα[κα Π]ανδίονος
16 16 ἔκγ[ο]νον· ἴδεν δὲ Θησεύς,
        μέλαν δ᾽ ὑπ᾽ ὀφ'ρύων
    18 δίῃα[σ]εν ὄμμα, καρδίαν τέ οἱ
        σχέτ'λιον ἄμυξεν ἄλγος,
20 20 εἰρέν τε· ,,Διὸς υἱὲ φερτάτου,
    21 ὅσιον οὐκέτι τεᾶν
        ἔσω κυβερνᾶις φρενῶν
    23 θυμ[όν]· ἴσχε μεγαλοῦχον ἥρως βίαν.
     1 ὅ, τι μ[ὲ]ν ἐκ θεῶν μοῖρα παγκρατὴς
25   ἄμμι κατένευσε καὶ Δίκας ῥέπει τά-
        λαντον, πεπρωμέν[α]ν
     4 αἶσαν [ἐ]κπλήσομεν, ὅτ[α]ν
     5 ἔλθηι· [σ]ὺ δὲ βαρεῖαν κάτε-
        χε μῆτιν. εἰ καί σε κεδ'νὰ
30   τέκεν λέχει Διὸς ὑπὸ κ'ρόταφον Ἴδας
     8 μιγεῖσα Φοίνικος ἐρα-
        τώνυμος κόρα βροτῶν
    10 φέρτατον, ἀλλὰ κἀμὲ
        Πιτθ[έ]ος θυγάτηρ ἀφνεοῦ
35   πλαθεῖσα ποντίωι τέκεν
    13 Ποσειδᾶνι, χρύσεόν
        τέ οἱ δόσαν ἰόπ'λοκοι κά-
        λυμμα† Νηρηΐδες.
    16 τῶ σε, πολέμαρχε Κνωσίων,
40   κέλομαι πολύστονον
    18 ἐρύκεν ὕβ'ριν· οὐ γὰρ ἂν θέλοι-
        μ᾽ ἄμβροτον ἐραννὸν Ἀο[ῦς
    20 ἰδεῖν φάος, ἐπεί τιν᾽ ἠϊθέ[ων
    21 σὺ δαμάσειας ἀέκον-
45   τα· πρόσθε χειρῶν βίαν
    23 δε[ί]ξομεν· τὰ δ᾽ ἐπιόντα δα[ίμω]ν κρινεῖ.''
     1 τόσ᾽ εἶπεν ἀρέταιχμος ἥρως·
     2 τ]άφον δὲ ναυβάται
     3 φ]ωτὸς ὑπεράφανον
50   4 θ]άρσος· Ἀλίου τε γαμβρῶι χόλωσεν ἦτορ,
     5 ὕφαινέ τε ποταινίαν
     6 μῆτιν, εἶπέν τε· ,,μεγαλοσθενές

7 Ζεῦ πάτερ, ἄκουσον· εἴ πέρ με νύμ[φα
8 Φοίνισσα λευκώλενος σοὶ τέκεν,
55 9 νῦν πρόπεμπ᾽ ἀπ᾽ οὐρανοῦ θοάν
10 πυριέθειραν ἀστραπάν
11 σᾶμ᾽ ἀρίγ'νωτον· εἰ
δὲ καὶ σὲ Τροιζηνία σεισίχθονι
φύτευσεν Αἴθρα Ποσει-
60   δᾶνι τόνδε χρύσεον
15 χειρὸς ἀγ'λαὸν
ἔνεγκε κόσμον ἐκ βαθείας ἁλός,
17 δικὼν θράσει σῶμα πατρὸς ἐς δόμους.
18 εἴσεαι δ᾽ αἴκ᾽ ἐμᾶς κλύηι
65   Κρόνιος εὐχᾶς
20 ἀναξιβρέντας ὁ πάντω[ν με]ọ̣[έω]ν."

B′   67 1 κλύε δ᾽ ἄμεμπτον εὐχὰν μεγασθενὴ[ς
Ζεύς, ὑπέροχόν τε Μίνωϊ φύτευσε
τιμὰν φίλωι θέλων
70 4 παιδὶ πανδερκέα θέμεν,
5 ἄστραψέ θ᾽· ὁ δὲ θυμάρμενον
ἰδὼν τέρας χέρα πέτασσε
κ'λυτὰν ἐς αἰθέρα μενεπτόλεμος ἥρως
8 εἶρέν τε· ,,Θησεῦ τάδ᾽ ἐ⟨μὰ⟩
75   μὲν βλέπεις σαφῆ Διός
10 δῶρα· σὺ δ᾽ ὄρνυ᾽ ἐς βα-
ρύβ'ρομον πέλαγος· Κρονί[δας
δέ τοι πατὴρ ἄναξ τελεῖ
13   Ποσειδὰν ὑπέρτατον
80   κλέος χθόνα κατ᾽ ἠΰδενδρον."
ὣς εἶπε· τῶι δ᾽ οὐ πάλιν
16 θυμὸς ἀνεκάμπτετ᾽, ἀλλ᾽ εὐ-
πάκτων ἐπ᾽ ἰκ'ρίων
18 σταθεὶς ὄρουσε, πόντιόν τέ νιν
85   δέξατο θελημὸν ἄλσος.
20 τάφεν δὲ Διὸς υἱὸς ἔνδοθεν
21 κέαρ, κέλευσέ τε κατ᾽ οὖ-
ρον ἴσχεν εὐδαίδαλον
23 νᾶα· μοῖρα δ᾽ ἑτέραν ἐπόρσυν᾽ ὁδόν.

90 1 ἵετο δ᾽ ὠκύπομπον δόρυ· ϲόει
νιν βορεὰς ἐξόπιν πνέουσ᾽ ἀήτα·
τρέσσαν δ᾽ Ἀθαναίων
4 ἠϊθέων ⟨—⟩ γένος, ἐπεὶ
5 ἥρως θόρεν πόντονδε, κα-

95   τὰ λειρίων τ᾽ ὀμμάτων δά-
κ᾽ρυ χέον, βαρεῖαν ἐπιδέγ᾽μενοι ἀνάγκαν.
8 φέρον δὲ δελφῖνες {ἐν} ἁλι-
ναιέται μέγαν θοῶς
10 Θησέα πατ᾽ρὸς ἱππί-
100   ου δόμον· ἔμολέν τε θεῶν
μέγαρον. τόθι κ᾽λυτὰς ἰδών
13   ἔδεισε⟨ν⟩ Νηρῆος ὀλ-
βίου κόρας· ἀπὸ γὰρ ἀγ᾽λα-
ῶν λάμπε γυίων σέλας
105 16 ὧτε πυρός, ἀμφὶ χαίταις
δὲ χρυσεόπ᾽λοκοι
18 δίνηντο ταινίαι· χορῶι δ᾽ ἔτερ-
πον κέαρ ὑγροῖσι ποσσίν.
20 εἶδέν τε πατ᾽ρὸς ἄλοχον φίλαν
110 21 σεμνὰν βοῶπιν ἐρατοῖ-
σιν Ἀμφιτρίταν δόμοις·
23 ἅ νιν ἀμφέβαλεν ἀϊόνα πορφυρέαν,
113 1 κόμαισί τ᾽ ἐπέθηκεν οὔλαις
2 ἀμεμφέα π᾽λόκον,
115 3 τόν ποτέ οἱ ἐν γάμωι
4 δῶκε δόλιος Ἀφ᾽ροδίτα ῥόδοις ἐρεμνόν.
5 ἄπιστον ὅ τι δαίμονες
6 θέλωσιν οὐδὲν φρενοάραις βροτοῖς·
7 νᾶα πάρα λεπτόπρυμνον φάνη· φεῦ,
120 8 οἵαισιν ἐν φροντίσι Κ᾽νώσιον
9 ἔσχασεν στραταγέταν, ἐπεί
10 μόλ᾽ ἀδίαντος ἐξ ἁλός
11 θαῦμα πάντεσσι, λάμ-
πε δ᾽ ἀμφὶ γυίοις θεῶν δῶρ᾽, ἀγ᾽λαό-
125   θρονοί τε κοῦραι σὺν εὐ-
θυμίαι νεοκτίτωι
15 ὠλόλυξαν, ἔ-
κλαγεν δὲ πόντος· ἠΐθεοι δ᾽ ἐγγύθεν
17 νέοι παιάνιξαν ἐρατᾶι ὀπί.
130 18 Δάλιε, χοροῖσι Κηΐων
φρένα ἰανθείς
20 ὄπαζε θεόπομπον ἐσθλῶν τύχαν.

1 str.   The dark-prowed ship, with bold
            Theseus and fourteen more Ionians,
            the sheen of youth upon them,
            cut through the Cretan sea.

The bright sail caught
　　the full north wind
　　that armed Athena sent
and in his heart King Minos felt
　　an itch of lust, love-crowned
Aphrodite's sacred gift.
　　He did not check his hand
　　but let it stroke
　　the girl's white cheek
　　and she cried out, for she was Eriboea,
　　bronze-armed Pandion's child.
And Theseus saw it all.
　　Beneath his brow
his angry eye rolled dark,
　　a sordid pain tore at his heart
and, "Son of Strongest Zeus," he called,
"You guide an unclean thought
　　within your mind.
A hero curbs his violence!

ant.　　What regal Moira ratifies
　　　　as mine from god—what Justice
　　　　weighs out as my fated share
　　I will fulfill, when
　　it may come, but you must check
　　　　the outrage you intend!
　　　　Perhaps the child of Phoenix
　　(she of lovely name) did lie with Zeus once
　　　　under Ida's crag, did give you birth,
　　a strong man among men; yet I
　　　　was born to wealthy Pittheus' child
　　　　who slept beside
　　　　Poseidon Water-Lord
　　　　and got as gift a golden crown
　　　　from blue-locked Nereids.
So, Captain of the Cnossians,
　　I now demand from you cessation
of this violence. I would not choose
　　to see the holy light of dawn
if insult came from you
to any of this company. I'd sooner show you
　　what this hand can do.
All to come is shaped by god."

ep. So the spear-skilled warrior spoke
and his contemptuous pride
struck all on board with awe.
But then the heart of Helius' kin
grew angry, and he spun a dreadful plan
in his response. "Almighty
Father Zeus," he prayed, "hear me! If
the white-armed girl of Phoenix bore me
as your son, then send a sign:
a darting fire-tressed bolt
of lightning from the sky! And if
   in truth it was to earthquake god
   Poseidon that the maid of Troezene
   bore you, then you may bring
this golden finger ring of mine
   up from the salt sea!
Dive, and pay a visit to your father's halls—
but first observe how well
   he listens to my prayer,
the thundering son of Cronus, sovereign of all!"

2 str. And strongest Zeus did hear the perfect prayer,
   did sow the seeds of overweening
   honor for King Minos,
that the son he loved might be admired by all:
he sent a lightning bolt. And when the warlike hero
   saw the portent he had called for
   he pointed to the high fair sky
and spoke. "Theseus, you
   are witness to the signal gift
Zeus sends me. Dive now
   into the roaring sea. No doubt
   your father, Lord Poseidon
   Cronus' son, will make your deed's fame
spread far across the timbered land."
   He spoke; the other's
spirit did not shrink. He took his stand
   upon the rowing bench
and made his dive, the kindly
   brackish wave receiving him.
Amazement filled the heart
of Zeus' son; he gave command
   to run the strong-built ship before the wind,
but Moira had another course in mind.

ant.   The racing keel sped on, northwind
          rushing from the stern,
          and all that godlike group
of young Athenians trembled as
their hero leapt into the sea.
          Tears fell from tender eyes
          that watched this rough necessity
but sea-bred dolphins came
          and swiftly carried Theseus
to his hippic father's realm.
          He stepped into the hall
          of the divinities and there he saw
          the fabled girls of Nereus
          and was afraid, for lights
          leapt from their shining limbs
like sparks, and strands of gold
          wound through their hair
in diadems as, circling in their play,
          they danced on sea-wet toes.
He saw as well his father's wife,
august, wide-glancing Amphitrite,
          mistress of the lovely house.
She wrapped a purple cloak about him,

ep.   then placed upon his uncut curls
the perfect rose-dark wreath
that on her wedding day
sly Aphrodite once gave her to wear.
Nothing that the gods desire
should be beyond the faith of thinking man!
He showed himself beside the ship's
light prow, and oh he checked
the Cnossian king's plans now
as he rose up, unwet, out of that sea,
a marvel to them all! The godly gift
          clung shining to his limbs
          and bright-robed Nereids
          with festive newmade melody
cried out in praise; the Sea
          sang too, and close at hand the godlike
sweet-voiced youths intoned Apollo's song.
O Delian one, let dancing Cean men
          rejoice your heart and grant to us
a godsent portion of good things.

Only in its last three lines does this Cean chorus mythologize its present moment; for all the rest of the song it is engaged in the opposite process of making a mythic moment present, repeating Minos' insults, miming the distress of the Athenians, dancing the Nereids' dance. But why this particular moment? Theseus, of course, is precisely appropriate to the occasion of the Delian performance because according to official aetiology he led the very first crane dance[2] and the original paean at Delos (Plut. *Thes.* 21; Paus. 9.40, 3–4).[3] He had landed there with his rejoicing company after the escape from the labyrinth, and he had consecrated the statue of Aphrodite that Ariadne had given him, establishing her shrine in Apollo's *temenos.* The burgeoning Theseus legend had made the whole story famous by the end of the sixth century, but it is a story that Bacchylides, in this song, has chosen *not* to tell. Instead he has produced an episode that comes before the adventure of the labyrinth, a girl who is not Ariadne, a goddess who is not Aphrodite, and Athenians who are not rejoicing, but who are dedicated to death.[4]

Furthermore, though the chorus obviously means to entertain its present festival audience while it delights the god it would praise, these urbane intentions do not explain the song's distinctive narrative qualities, all of which can be classified as breaches in the ordinary rules of the story-telling art. The fact is that the story of Theseus' undersea visit, appropriate or inappropriate, is not properly *told* at all, for the song sets up fictional expectations, then leaves them unsatisfied. The singers begin with a challenge[5] but never let us know whether the challenge was met; they send their hero off to visit his father and never let him find him; they make two men quarrel, then show neither resolution nor victory between them. Early in their tale a girl cries out,[6] engaging all our attention, but she is never mentioned again.[7] And halfway through, a ring is cast into the sea, likewise never to be heard of more.[8] The singers linger over preparatory moments, then race past their crucial scene; they pay more attention to irrelevant water sprites than they do to the queen of the sea, and worst of all, when this choral narrative is broken off, the physical condition of all the principals is exactly what it was at the start. The hero is still alive, but the Athenians are also still at sea, still being carried as victims toward the labyrinth, and in the self-defined world of story-telling for its own sake nothing has occurred, since Minos is still master of the fates of everyone on board.

The tale has been rich in poetic magic, offering enchantments like the "sea-wet toes" of the Nereids, but its central narrative miracle—the wonder that a Hecataeus or a Herodotus would have dwelt upon—has been almost suppressed. Theseus disappeared into the water, the ship sped on before a following wind, and then Theseus reappeared at a point far to the south of the position of his dive, astonishing Minos who thought him probably drowned and certainly left behind. All this we are expected to understand, just as we are expected to understand the purpose of the voyage and the dangers that wait at its end, for the essential fictional questions of why and how and what happened next are exactly the ones that this chorus does not propose to face. They refuse to treat their episode as a free-standing anecdote with a beginning, an end, and a "point," and they likewise refuse to treat it as a "chapter" in the continuing saga of Theseus. Instead they detach a single event, emphasizing its discrete nature by locating it in the lost time of a journey at sea,[9] and then they use their voices, hands, feet, and bodies to bring it to life again.

The Bacchylidean performers sing sometimes like bards, sometimes like lyric balladeers, and sometimes like actors in the theatre, but the episode that they recreate has a sense of immediacy that triumphs over all the artful conventionality of the choral form—triumphs even over the printed page and minds accustomed to language of a very different sort. Various causes contribute to its extreme vitality, but most obvious is the song's insistence upon motion, and the way its speed has been matched to the unrelenting speed that permeates the event. The ship that "cuts" the sea in the first lines is given a renewed impetus at the beginning of the second strophe, but the ceaseless wind has never allowed it to pause in its race towards Cnossus and the Minotaur,[10] and the poet has used brief metrical phrases and short rhetorical statements to create an impression of rapid and irresistible approach to that place. Even in the tranquil depths of the sea all is in motion, dolphins are "swift" and Nereids whirl, and the uninterrupted rush of this frame means that the central actions become abstract problems in motion, like jumping up on a down elevator. Everyone on the ship is in one sense passive since all are borne along by the ever-present wind while decisive action lies ahead in the labyrinth. In another sense, however, every action performed here is discontinuous and pure, existing as it does in a bit of useless time and in a space that defies definition. And this is exactly how the singers present the actions they recount, for they use a series of violent verbs to revive the intensity of these floating interim gestures that can never play themselves out. The wind "falls" (6), lust "scratches" (8), Eriboea "shouts" (14), the eye of Theseus "whirls" (18), and pain "tears at" his heart (19). The lust of Minos becomes as actual as a beast, and Theseus' answering emotion moves like a living thing as it changes from anger to a courageous, contemptuous pride (49–50) in the course of his chorally rendered speech. What is more, we are also made aware that this restless ship with its balanced cargo of vigorous passions has caught the active attention of an inordinate number of divinities, for Athena fills its sail (7), Aphrodite invades its captain's heart (10), Zeus aims his thunderbolt towards it (71), and Moira plans the progress of its journey (89).[11]

The ship is a swiftly speeding point of focus for daimonic forces and the song causes everything that occurs on or near it to be touched by the marvelous. The purely physical miracle of Theseus' submersion in one spot, emergence in another, underlies the whole account, but what the listener is asked to witness is a series of related marvels, arranged in a special order and marked for his notice. First there is the purely psychological wonder of the captive hero's arrogant assertion of equality with his captor, and this the young Athenians (like a tragic chorus) marvel at, so that the audience shall marvel too (*taphon*, 48). Next there is the primitive and fundamental miracle of the lightning bolt that, coming in answer to Minos' prayer, marks him almost as a wizard even as it shows him to be authentically the son of Zeus. It is called a *teras* (72) and is plainly a supernatural, not a natural sign, but the audience is not asked to wonder or indeed to have any response at all, for as the poem continues the plunging bolt of lightning is upstaged by the plunging body of Theseus. That marvel fills even Minos with wonder (*taphen*, 86),[12] and the audience is further instructed in the emotions that it should feel by the despair and lamentation of the watching Athenians (*tressan*, 92; *dakru cheon*, 96). At the end of the second strophe the marvel of Theseus' psychic and physical energy has encompassed and surrounded the heaven-sent miracle, but the roster of wonders does not stop with the dive, for others follow that are neither human nor quite divine. The dolphin escort is hardly remarked (though it serves to perpetuate the sense of speed even in this instant when we have left the speeding ship: *megan thoōs*, 98), but the fairy-tale prodigy of the phosphorescent mermaids is actively described as fearful by Theseus' fear. After them come the unwithered roses, which seem at first to be a wonder of the same sort, part of a merely fantastic vision meant to dazzle a child-like audience. Nevertheless, they appear as the donation of Amphitrite,[13] and the song exalts them as a wedding gift from one goddess to another, making them proof that every wonder here is finally Olympian in origin. That might seem to be instruction enough, but since the ultimate marvel is about to occur, the chorus stops its narrative, changes its voice, and in almost didactic fashion calls its spectators' attention to the final display of wonders. "Prepare yourselves for the incredible," they say in effect, "for what we have just told you is as nothing in comparison with what we are about to report!" (117–18). Theseus appeared beside the ship: there is the physical wonder of the tale. The abandoned man-overboard baffled the intentions of the evil captain: there is the psychological pleasure of the fiction. Both of these fairly ordinary matters we are asked to note in passing, but the chorus hastens on to the ultimate triple miracle for which all the others have been mere preparation. Theseus came up from the sea unwet;[14] he came up wearing a purple robe; he came up accompanied by singing Nereids. This is what pride, lightning bolt, dive, dolphins, undersea choruses and unwithered garlands together have produced. The creation of this wonder is what has shaped the singing of the song.

Though it does not provide the usual narrative satisfactions, the Theseus song thus offers pleasures of another sort. The spectator marvels as abstract human passion combines in a rush of motion with an almost tangible divine power to make things that cannot happen happen. At the same time, however, he is led into other responses that are far less simple, for this song also offers something other than pleasure. Any choral performance could, with its repeating melodies, establish unstated connections between the images or concepts of its mirroring stanzas, and this was a potential that Bacchylides loved to exploit. In the present case we can observe how he uses the triadic form not only for a kind of unemphatic instruction but also for the more primitive purposes of bringing one revived moment to bear directly upon another.

Take for example the "plan" of Minos. It is fabricated in the first epode and put into action with Minos' prayer (53 ff.); it is frustrated in the second epode and put out of commission with Theseus' reappearance (119 f.), the two passages being in responsion. That is an obvious piece of triadic design; less obvious is the pattern that involves Moira. The miracle that the gods have arranged to check Minos requires that the ship's course be perfectly adjusted to the course that Theseus takes under the sea. It depends, in other words, upon the Moira of line 89. She takes over the actual governance of the ship at the close of the second strophe, and in this position she forms a pair with Amphitrite, since that goddess manipulates the robe in the same lines of the antistrophe. These two are thus necessarily among the daimonic agents whose will is present in Theseus' reappearance, and logic puts with them the Athena who fills the sails and the Poseidon who sits invisible at his wife's side. Aphrodite must also be in their company since she not only inaugurated the entire episode but set her seal upon it by allowing her wreath to rest upon Theseus' head. What then of Zeus? Are we being told that all these divinities combined against him, and frustrated his will along with the plan of Minos? Again, the music gives the answer, for the first mention of Zeus' thunderbolt (in Minos' prayer) prepares the melody for the glory of Theseus: the words "a fire-tressed bolt, a clear sign," are sung to the same melodic line as "he came from sea unwet, a marvel to all" (56–7; 122–23). Evidently Zeus, with his thunderbolt, meant that Minos should be conspicuous (70) but also that Theseus should appear as the central figure in a miracle of his own. His lightning is explicitly the "sign" (57) of Minos' paternity, but it is also the signal for Theseus' dive, according to Minos' words (75–6), and more significantly, according to the poem's structure. Zeus casts his bolt in the first syllables of the fifth line of the second strophe (71), and Theseus casts himself into the sea in the first syllables of the fifth line of the antistrophe (94) and to this same melody Athena has already cast wind into the ship's sails (5). In these ways the music assures us that everything here is in harmony with Zeus' fiery will.

A careful manipulation of words and concepts about divine gifts acts to reinforce the sense of heavenly design that the song has imposed with its structure. Minos receives two such gifts—the gift (*dora*, 10) of lust from the Cyprian,[15] and the gift (*dora*, 76 = 1. 10 of str. 2) of lightning from Zeus. Then in the central undersea scene Theseus also receives two—the wreath that derives from Aphrodite (*dōke*, 116), and the robe conferred by his father's queen (112). The dubious value of the first of Minos' gifts casts a shadow of doubt upon the second, since it proves that these infusions of heavenly electricity can be misused or misprized and are to be welcomed as good only when men have given them a positive ethical form. The two gifts that originated with Aphrodite are blatantly offered for comparison, for what Minos receives is a bestial passion (it "scratches" and is not *hosios*; 8, 21) that earns him blame and makes him less than a hero (23), whereas what Theseus receives is a token of legitimate love, an unwithered, "blameless" (114) garland that has graced the more than heroic marriage of divinities.[16] Theseus is thus differentiated from Minos as he is given the promise of a lawful union, but the wreath marks him in another way as well for it is (like the necklace of Harmonia) the kind of heirloom that a mother gives her son, that he may give it to his bride, that she may give it to her son, and so on.[17] It is, in other words, the outward sign that Amphitrite has adopted Theseus,[18] and consequently it is a proof that he had even more right than he supposed when he claimed equality with Minos, being in a sense the Cretan's superior. That lustful man was engendered by Zeus upon Europa, yes, but this one whose loves are still potential is not only Poseidon's son by Aithra, but also Amphitrite's child. He is doubly connected with the gods.

All this is implicit in the progression from scratch of lust to wreath of roses; what of that from lightning bolt to purple robe?[19] The proof of paternity that Minos asks and obtains gives him the appearance of being the high priest of a primitive weather-god, and the poet enhances this effect by making him utter his prayer in the character of "Helius' son-in-law" (50).[20] He is very much the son of the sky as he raises his hand into the miraculously clear air[21] from which the paternal bolt has come, and when he challenges his opposite, the son of the sea, he names what is finally at issue between them. "I am sure," he says, "that your Cronian father will bring your fame to perfection (that is, bring it to an end in death, *telei . . . kleos*, 79–80) throughout the well-wooded land." His heavy irony means, on a personal level, that he expects Theseus to drown, whoever his father may be, but on another level it contains another sort of taunt. "Fame is *all* you will have on the fertile land," he says in effect, "whereas I shall go ashore and rule!"

Minos and Theseus are a pair of mythic heroes, one of whom presumes to chide the other, but they are also nature's rivals for the rule of earth, and in this larger context the apparently incongruous parallelism of bolt and mantle finds its significance. Had Poseidon simply matched the gesture of Zeus and distinguished *his* son with an earthquake (as the epithet at 58 hints he might) the quarrel between the two would have been redefined so as to split the cosmos and leave the "well-wooded earth" victim of one cataclysm or the other. Had Poseidon made any gesture at all, in fact, we would have been left with an uncomfortable sense of a split among the male Olympians, and this of course is unthinkable. Consequently the poet arranges that Theseus shall return to the ship fully validated as Poseidon's son,[22] yet in no way associated with natural or supernatural disasters; as far as the poem goes, he has not even come in contact with his father. By removing Poseidon from the scene of the undersea reception Bacchylides thus avoids any sense of rivalry between that god and Zeus, and at the same time he rejects the dangerous fairy-tale motif of the three wishes that were Poseidon's traditional gift to his son. Theseus is equipped instead with a miraculous gift that is entirely humane and benign in its meaning; it is brought up from the sea yet derives from earth; in no way does it challenge, yet it is in every way the opposite of the lightning bolt. A mantle is made by the hands of women inspired by Zeus' daughter, Athena; it brings comfort; it means civilization; and passing from father to son it acknowledges and welcomes the adult. It also confers honor, since it marks the magistrate or the priest or the leader of a chorus, and when it is purple it suggests superior power. This particular mantle is by responsion equated with heroic self-control (23), with the inevitable force of the future (46), and with Moira (89). Obviously it wraps Theseus not only in Poseidon's recognition but also in his own potential as a civilizing ruler.

Structure and image thus take care of the story that the singers choose to leave untold, for by these non-narrative means the listener is convinced that the wreath and robe of Theseus are a more than adequate response to the lust and thunderbolt of Minos. In final confirmation, Minos' lost ring provides imagistic proof that the Cretan is the loser in this present contest, despite his continued command and his undiminished ability to send Athenians into the labyrinth. Meanwhile, what the chorus chooses to tell is an abrupt sequence of affront, quarrel, dive and

return, their evident goal being the great maritime cantata that celebrates Theseus' reappearance. This huge burst of music is what they
have been singing towards, but it is inseparable from the deed that it
applauds and so the essential question about this ode, when it is re-
garded as a choral performance, is why, during an altar-centered solid-
ground festival on Delos, an audience should be asked to listen to a
hymn sung on the water and why, in this moment that commemorates
Theseus' secure foundation of an island cult, spectators should be made
to watch his rash jump into the sea.

Mechanically speaking the paean is the product of Theseus' dive, and
this truth is expressed structurally. The musical outbreak in the second
epode (125 ff.) responds to Minos' initial command in the first (60 ff.),
and the words "young men sang the lovely song" (129) are accompanied by the same melody as "cast your body boldly down" (63). The
dive is the only preeminent action[23] that the song depicts, and in spite of
the pace and economy of the performance it is given a special dimension
by four separate representations. Its potential is doubly depicted in
Minos' two commands, his first (57 ff.) making it a heroic test, his second (76 ff.) suggesting that it is a form of suicide, but also a possible
source of power. After these prefaces, the deed itself is realized twice (at
81–85 and at 94), so that as we watch it we can also observe its effects,
first upon Minos and then upon the Athenians. The technique is something like that of certain vase-painters or illustrators of codices (like that
of modern animators) who duplicate a scene with minimal changes and
so achieve an effect of motion. In addition, this action and this one alone
is located in a specific physical setting. Minos does not stand on the deck
or clasp the rail, and Amphitrite does not even have a throne to sit upon,
but Theseus, with his unflinching heart, climbs upon an explicitly solid
bench (*eupaktōn ep' ikriōn*, 82–3), pauses, and then jumps into the sea.
This the dancers mime, and they imitate first the astonishment of Minos
(86), then the desolation of the abandoned adolescents (92 ff.), so that
the event is no longer merely visual but is invested now with passion.

No subsequent deed is allowed to take on anything like the poetic actuality of Theseus' dive. A narrative intended for pleasure or even simple instruction would have offered a better view of Amphitrite's
gesture—if not with words or dress at least it would have provided her
with a hand for the giving of her gifts. Such a narrative would also have
let us watch the hero in his final encounter with Minos, so that we could
observe some evident reversal in their situations. Here, however, the
only visualized actions to follow the dive are those that bring it to its
completion, as the man who leapt first sinks and then rises. What is
more, the song is so organized that this single deed seems to transform
the world that it reflects, and with that world its own style.[24] The dive at

the end of strophe two shifts the song from the wind-inspired world of
Zeus—a place of men and lust and words—to the submerged realm of
Amphitrite where there are female creatures and dancing but no voice is
heard. Simultaneously, the dive puts an end to the rhetorical, epic-style
realism of the opening, and inaugurates the imagistic, lyric and fantasti-
cal movement that will bring the performance to its close.

The dive has a powerful effect upon the poem, no effect whatsoever
upon its fiction, and in consequence we are persuaded that it operates in
some realm that is not the world. It belongs to no reasonable causal
chain within the story since jumping will not protect Eriboea any more
than it will change the nature of the waiting Minotaur. Nor can the dive
be said to be ethically illustrative, for Theseus moves into it without a
word, as soon as Minos' command has been given, and we are instructed
to see his bravery as a marvel, not as a mundane example of human virtue. In fact, the fear of his companions reminds us that Theseus, when
he dives, actually abandons his wordly responsibility since by any ordinary rule he should, as their leader, stay to see them through the coming
"dread necessity." All of these fictional negatives work to persuade the
listener that when Theseus abandons the field of morality and goes
overboard he exceeds even his royal function. His dive amounts to a de-
fiance of all that is normal in creation and it is also, in a world where
only physical laws prevail, tantamount to suicide, which of course is exactly why Minos made the challenge. Theseus in a sense acts on a dare
when he dives, but the dive constitutes his own dare, thrown out to the
elements: "Save me if you can!" His deed thus asks that the laws that
govern nature shall be broken for him and consequently, while Minos
stands back in astonishment, the spectator feels a terror that is metaphysical. His pang of fear comes not because Theseus is in danger, and
not because the Athenians are left without their prince, but because this
act for an instant puts the whole system of the ordinary into jeopardy.
Chaos may ensue, when a breathing prince leaves his duties and the region of air to enter the sea.

The Greeks were not a swimming people,[25] and for them a dive was
both a fabulous and a significant act. In myth, a dive could change a
mortal into an immortal, as Glaucus proved when he made himself
deathless by jumping into the sea (Paus. 9.22.6; Strabo 9.2.13 p. 405).[26]
Ino plunged to immortality with her son in her arms (P.O. 2.32 ff.)[27]
and when the mother of Cycnus did the same, Apollo turned mother
and son into swans. Eumolpus, thrown into the sea at Eleusis, was saved
by Poseidon, married an Oceanid, and returned to earth to become the
founder of the mysteries (Apollod. 3.15.4; cf. E. fr. 349N).[28] At Rhodes,
Halia leapt into the sea and became a goddess, though she was the sister
of the magician-craftsman of the place (Diod. 5.55.7); Britomartis leapt

into the waves to become Dictynna (Call. *h. Art.* 189; Paus. 2.30.3; Diod. 5.76; Strabo 10.474; Ant. Lib. 40), and Boline was also immortalized after jumping into the sea (Paus. 7.23.4).[29] One could dive to salvation, too; in the Chersonese the daughters of Staphylus jumped into the sea but were saved by Apollo (Diod. 5.62),[30] and Homer reported that Dionysus, when he was pursued by Lycurgus, threw himself into the sea and found refuge with Thetis and the Nereids (*Il.* 6.130 ff., esp. 136). A mythic dive might also vindicate an innocent; Cephalus jumped into the sea at Thoricus to clear himself of a murder charge (Apollod. 3.15.8; Paus. 1.37.6; 10.29.6), but when the sailors from Dionysus' ship threw themselves into the water they, being guilty of blasphemy, remained there in dolphin form (*h. Bacch.* 52). A dive into a river, however, often succeeded in cleansing a criminal, especially if, like Telchinus (Diod. 5.55.7), Tanais (Plut. *De fluv.* 14), or Alpheius (ibid., 19), he was guilty of a sexual or a kin crime.

The rare plunges of the non-mythic world were likewise acts of extraordinary meaning,[31] since the sea was not only dangerous, but magical and occupied by monsters who could change their forms (cf. e.g. *Od.* 5.419; 12.96). It was ancient, changeless, and beyond pollution; it was unforgetting and incapable of lies, as Hesiod said of Nereus (*Theog.* 233–6), and so it could both prophesy and judge.[32] There is some evidence of actual Hellenic practices of *ordalie*, corresponding to the mythic ordeals of Danaë or the daughter of Sciron, when an accused person was thrown into the sea to survive if he were innocent, drown if he were not.[33] The sea could also cleanse and confer some of its own changelessness, and this power was illustrated in the periodic immersion of certain cult statues in sea-water,[34] for the result was purification and a renewal of their quality of sacredness. Even a living man could enjoy a version of this same cleansing experience;[35] in addition sinking and rising again simulated death and rebirth,[36] and since water separated one continent from another it also figured the passing from one phase of life into another.[37]

A dive could convey the idea of a passage from blight to blessedness, or from youth to maturity, but whether this means that initiatory diving rites actually existed is not certain. There was at Athens in the late fifth century a not very reputable sect called the Baptai[38] whose members apparently made a ritual descent into the sea, but there is no explicit suggestion that they dove. Probably the most famous Greek plunges were made at Leucadia,[39] where Sappho was said to have jumped, and it is generally agreed that the Leucadian leap was a ritualized activity, but there is no proof that it was a form of initiation. Certainly the place was associated with notions of afterlife, for Homer has the souls of the dead depart from the Leucadian rock and follow Ocean's course to the gates of the sun, the people of dreams, and the meadow of asphodel (*Od.* 24.11–12). Certainly also Sappho's leap was used as a mystic emblem by the much later Roman sect that frequented the underground basilica at the Porta Maggiore.[40] None of this, however, can produce more than a strong suspicion that the Leucadian dive was actually a form of initiation. The best piece of evidence for a dive as a mystic rite is probably the early fifth-century painting on the sarcophagus lid of the Tomba dello Tuffatore at Paestum.[41] That scene obviously has a special significance since it is placed immediately over the dead man's head, and the tower from which the figure dives proves that his was no casual athletic pastime. Probably the dead man who lay beneath the diving scene was meant to be reminded that he had undergone some initiatory rite, but of course the painted dive may be only a visual metaphor for that rite, and not its literal representation. There are, however, a few facts that strengthen the presumption that there had been in some places primitive Greek coming-of-age ceremonies that included diving into the sea. To begin with, Hesiod notes (*Theog.* 347) that the Oceanid nymphs have the duty of bringing males to puberty, and there were, in later times, contests of swimming and diving at Hermione, dedicated to a Dionysus Melanaigis whose dark epithet suggests the blackness of the ephebe (Paus. 2.35.1).[42] At Miletus the gymnastic agones of the ephebes were undertaken in the names of Cycnus or Palaimon, both of whom had been changed by a plunge (Conon. 33), and at the Isthmus the young men's games were dedicated to Melicertes, Leucothea's son in his alternate form.[43]

Immortality, salvation, judgment, and initiation were thus the ideas that Greeks associated with the act of plunging into the water, and all these invest the dive that Bacchylides makes central to his Delian song. Its judicial significance is most obvious, for Theseus' plunge serves almost literally as an ordeal which the challenged party undergoes to prove his own truth, and it is notable that in this case Theseus dives only when Zeus, as judge, has ratified the trial with his thunderbolt. The dive and the safe return then justify Theseus' right to chide Minos as an equal. Nevertheless, Bacchylides' song works to minimize this significance, since it refuses to show any alteration in the relationship of its two parties after the judgment is made, and we are certainly licensed to recognize other meanings as well. In that Theseus enters the water as a hero who claims one divine parent but emerges with two parental divinities, and so almost as a god, this dive is reminiscent of the dive to immortality. Plainer than this, though it does not work on the surface of the present fiction, is the related meaning of salvation, for Theseus' successful dive prefigures the future successful actions that will rescue him and his companions and all future young Athenians from a threat of death. In that it is a descent to an underworld and an enriched return from it, it is the emblem not only of the dark trek in and out of the labyrinth but also of the whole journey to Crete that liberated Athens and brought back the statue of Aphrodite, to be deposited at Delos.[44] And finally, on the level of metaphor, the significance of initiation makes itself strongly felt,[45] particularly because the poet has so strongly emphasized the extreme youth of Theseus and all the Athenian victims. (It is because of their youth, for example, that the eyelids of the weeping companions are likened to flowers at 95; because of his youth that Theseus' hair is thick and curly at 113.) Like a boy who withdraws into lawless liminality, Theseus dives and separates himself from his community at the command of an older man.[46] He goes in obedience, but he returns in disobedience, without the ring that would have denoted subordination and slavery. His refusal to bring back the king's property marks his liberation from childish dependence, while the robe and the wreath confirm his new equality with adult authority, for a change of clothing almost always accompanied the ritual passage from youth into manhood. The robe readies him, at the very least, for the agora, while the wreath of pleasure serves as a sign that its bearer may now enter the company of men at the banquet and of women at his own hearth. Theseus left the ship a boy but he returns a man, prepared for a form of marriage with Ariadne, and prepared also to assume his father's duties when he gets back to Athens.[47] The whole city will come of age through him when he returns from his larger labyrinthine initiation to become its king and the founder of its reborn power.

In the course of his plunge Theseus is vindicated, adopted by a gracious goddess, and brought to manhood. His happy return to the air is a portent of his coming escape from the Minotaur and a promise that Athens will be liberated from the Cretan levy. All this means that the dive was a brilliant choice as the principal device in a Theseus poem, and it also suggests that, when it was recreated by the Ceans in their performance at Delos, it brought some of Theseus' contact with divinity, some of his success-magic, and some of the initiate's ritually enhanced newness of strength to every spectator there. Perhaps that is all anyone should try to say about the dive of Theseus, but even when it is expounded in these ways, this mythic gesture does not seem quite large enough to balance the cosmic grandeur of the paean it provokes in Bacchylides' song. Why should nature itself join in, as the Athenians celebrate the coming-of-age of their prince and (unknowingly) their own imminent release? A conjectural answer to this question can be found, but only if we abandon the territory of mythic orthodoxy and enter the unknowable realm of archaic folk belief.

There is a widespread fairy-tale type described by Mircea Eliade[48] in which a sorcerer or creator plunges into the sea to bring up from its depths the ur-substance from which all things are made. The tale of the cosmic dive sometimes concerns, not the original creation but its completion or recreation, and it has innumerable variants, since it has been told for centuries and in places as disparate as Aryan India, Southeastern Europe, Siberia, Iceland, the Pacific, and North America.[49] There are, however, two principal models, since the dominant cosmic creature may plunge into the inchoate waters himself, or he may command a subordinate (who often has an animal shape) to do it in his stead. In this second, more complex case, the motif of the challenge may appear, as for example when Christ says to Brother Satan, "You boast that you are more powerful than I—bring up some sand from the bottom of the sea!"[50] The secondary creature will then, after one or more attempts, succeed in obtaining some of the magic substance that is in the depths, and here again the fictional possibilities are dual. Either he hands it over or he refuses, and in the latter case the second, upstart power becomes the maker of the world.

The episode of Minos and Theseus does not belong to a story that deals explicitly with creation, and yet its challenge, its dive, and its bringing of power-tokens up from the sea all function just as they would if this were a version of the primordial plunge. Is the similarity accidental, or could Bacchylides have found Theseus' dive in a story that derived from some tale in which the beginnings of things were in question? One's first impulse is to deny the possibility of any connection, on the grounds that the creation dive is not a part of the Hellenic tradition. Second thoughts, however, suggest that, since the likeness is so compelling and the popularity of the dive-tale so extensive, the question deserves further investigation.

The tale of the creation dive reflects the general human belief that water was the first fruitful element and so, where other theories of the world's creation had become canonical, it could only survive in vulgar and surreptitious forms. In Greece, Hesiod's sex-and-dismemberment version of the beginnings very early imposed itself as the received Hellenic cosmogony, and once this had happened there could be no official place for a creative plunge. There had, however, been alternatives, and one of them was a philosophical myth that described the sea-goddess Thetis as she created day and night, earth and heaven, sun and stars, with the aid of two daimonic helpers called Poros and Tekmor.[51] This Hellenic water-based cosmogony was apparently abandoned by respectable poets after the end of the seventh century—we know it only through a papyrus commentary on a song of Alcman's (5 fr. 2 *PMG*)— but nevertheless it expressed a conviction that could not be wholly forgotten.[52] Folktales continued to treat Thetis as a form-changer and poets knew her as a potential rival to the greatest of the Olympians, Zeus and Poseidon, and one who might destroy the order of heaven (P. *I.* 8, 26 ff.; Aesch. *PV* 907 ff., 922–25).[53] It is not surprising, then, to find that the most reputable Hellenic version of the tale of the primordial dive was told in connection with her. Paradoxically, it is Homer, the champion of the Olympians, who preserves this bit of primitivism; he does not present it as the plunge of the creator, but what else is Hephaestus' dive down into Thetis' realm to bring up the science of making things from metal?[54]

Another example of a Greek "creation dive" appears in a Lesbian foundation myth.[55] When the seven original kings were about to establish their community, they were told that a daughter of one of them had to be given to the sea. A girl was chosen and on the appointed day she was thrown into the water as a sacrifice, but then an anomalous event occurred: her lover, Enalus, dove in after her. Some time later he reappeared to report that the girl was living with Poseidon and the Nereids, having been saved by dolphins; with him he brought back an object— either a cup that made mortal gold look like copper, or else a magic stone, borne along by cuttlefish that followed him in a chorus. The gift from the sea was dedicated in a local shrine and the kings went on with the creation of their new settlement.

A third story is at best a dubious example of the primordial dive, but it puts a god into the water, and it also provides the motif we began by looking for—music in which gods and men join. Engaged in the creation of his Delphic shrine, Apollo came to the phase in which men should appear; he entered the sea, leapt out in dolphin form (*h. Ap.* 400), and commandeered a ship with its Cretan crew. Then, when he and his new population stepped ashore at Delphi, he joined with them in the performance of the world's first paean (*h. Ap.* 515–16). In this case nothing was carried up from the bottom of the sea, the men were merely taken from its surface, but the tale nevertheless shows a god who immerses himself as part of the process of creation. Apollo, in his two forms, suggests both the cosmic lord and his animal assistant, as is proper since his work at Delphi was only an imitation of Zeus' in establishing the Olympian order. Most important for Dithyramb 17, however, is the fact that this story, with its musical aetiology, is one that any maker of paeans would know.

At Delos, too, there were stories of how the place was created, and one of these involved a dive. As at Lesbos, the plunge is given a fictional disguise—this time as a dive to escape pursuit—but the result here is no mere establishment of a constitution. It is the making of earth itself, for when Asteria leapt into the sea to save herself from Zeus, the island of Delos rose up in her place (Call. *h. Del.* 36 ff.; Apollod. 1. 4. 4. 1). And

in one telling the girl was transformed into a bird, like the animal apprentice, before she made her dive (Hyg. *fab.* 53, 140).

These various stories take on a primordial quality because their
plunges are associated with acts of creation—with the working of metal
and the founding of city, cult, or island. They suggest that the notion of
the creator's dive did exist, half-forgotten, in Hellenic minds, and so it is
legitimate to ask how the Bacchylidean episode would strike an audience
unconsciously aware of such a model. Minos, the Cretan law-giver and
city builder,[56] would become the original lord of all, while Theseus,
commanded to jump into the sea and bring something back—Theseus
who is closely identified with the dolphin[57]—would conform exactly to
the type of the creator's often bestial apprentice. When he returned, not
with Minos' ring but with the more powerful tokens of his own, he
would become the doublet of the secondary daimon who rebels and
himself becomes a creator. He would be observed to bring plants (rose
wreath) and animals (woolen robe)[58] up out of the waters, as a creator
should, and he would be about to have (according to the old lord's own
words) a fame that would spread across the well-wooded land (80). He
would be the successor of the first lord because Minos belonged to a
phase of inachieved order when men and beasts still mixed (as witness
the Minotaur), whereas Theseus, the final author of order, would be
about to kill that hybrid monster and so complete the discrimination of
the species. This diver would then go back to Greece to become, himself, another Minos—a city-builder and law-giver. And on his way he
would stop at Delos and there perform his first act of positive creation
by establishing Aphrodite's cult.

Every association fits both the myth and the ceremonial occasion.
Theseus was the official creator of a part of the festival that the present
audience enjoyed, and the festival was a part of the human order that
was the ultimate achievement of all creation. Every part of that order
had to be periodically reaffirmed, and this meant that the Delian cult,
like all others, had to be regularly reinvested with the force of its original
act of foundation. Such a reinvestment could have been wrought by a
chorus that sang of the first dancing of the crane dance, but Bacchylides
did not choose to let them do that. It looks as if he wanted to bring a
more awesome and fundamental force into the present day, and it looks
also as if he wanted to salute Theseus as if he were the creator of the entire Delian cult, in spite of the fact that mythically he was only a late-
comer.[59] Other parts of the Theseus saga had already likened him to the
dragon-killing creator, making him kill the Minotaur and the bull of
Marathon, but Bacchylides saw that this character was not appropriate
to the creative role that the hero had played at Delos. There, where
Theseus arrived by sea bringing a gracious Aphrodite, he could better

appear as a creator of another sort, one who commenced with water and one whose power began with a dive.

Perhaps these suggestions are too fanciful, but the fact is that whether or not Bacchylides wished us to sense something primordial in Theseus' plunge, he gave an explicitly cosmic scope to the argument that preceded it and likewise to the paean that saluted its completion. The fulfillment of the dive is greeted by nonhuman creatures who invent a song never before heard, and they are joined not only by the Athenians but also by the Sea itself. This elemental music is of the sort that properly celebrates the coming of a god or the beginning of a new age,[60] and a subtle poetic trick brings three notes from it directly into the dancing place at Delos, where they throb with perceivable sound. When the chorus sang these words—

> ... bright-robed[61] Nereids
> with festive newmade melody
> cried out in praise; the Sea
> sang too, and close by the god-like
> sweet voiced youths intoned Apollo's song—

they had come to the end of the story of Theseus, but the listening audience had no way of knowing this. (It knew that the chorus had almost reached the end of a triad, but it did not know how many such were yet to come.) Consequently, when Bacchylides' singers continued with their cry of "*Dalie!*" the listeners' natural supposition was that this was the beginning of the mythic paean that was sung as Theseus rose up from the waves. The three syllables were heard as if they sounded from shipboard and sea, as if they were formed by the throats of beautiful Ionians and sparkling ocean spirits and also by the ancient and truth-telling mouth of Pontus.[62]

As the chorus continued, the audience had to revise its attribution, because the next words to be sung were, "let dancing Cean men rejoice your heart" (130 f.). The last three lines announced that the chorus had returned to itself and was finally going to work on its second task of mythifying the present occasion. Nevertheless, there had already been an instant of bewitching ambiguity in which the present paean-singing Ceans were indistinguishable from the Athenians of old, and in that instant the actual, mortal festival performers had been joined, just as their mythic doubles were, by caroling nymphs and the bass voice of the Sea. The two groups had been confounded in the listener's experience, and by way of that confusion the paean of the past had been able to invade the present song, bringing the overt daimonism of the exploit of Theseus into the actual Delian ceremony. Twentieth-century rationalists will call this a clever manipulation of artistic illusion, and so it is, but the fifth-century holiday-makers who gathered on Delos had in many ways a richer life than ours. They too will have known that Bacchylides had made a fine song, but in addition they will have been touched, thanks to that ode, by the inaugurating force of Theseus' dive and they will have found themselves and their rite renewed and transformed.

3. THE EPINICIAN BURDEN

No one knows exactly how and when the chorus that danced heavenly power into earthly events became associated with athletic victory.[1] The only thing that is certain is that the victory songs of the early classical age did use the magical unison of choral gesture and voice, in spite of their ostensibly secular occasion, and that an epinician ode in consequence put pressure on the supernatural world, just as a dithyramb or a paean did. The strength of a man was hymned with tones and postures associated with the immanence of the divine, and this meant that the composer of such an ode was conscious of great power, but also of a strong tension between the matter and the manner of his song. He had to stretch a single web of praise between earth and heaven—as Pindar put it, between a mortal who is nothing and gods who live forever in the bronze houses of the sky (N. 6.3)—and the tissue sometimes showed the marks of strain.

The earliest poet from whom epinician odes were preserved was Simonides,[2] but the ancients liked to credit Archilochus with the first performance of this sort, for victory song in some form or other was as old as athletic competition. Like a triumph in battle, a triumph in contest was gained only with divine favor, and consequently the victor's first act, once his crowning was over, was to give thanks for that favor in the shape of offerings, banquet, and song. The model for his celebrations was provided by the ceremonies that followed upon a military victory,[3] and that is one reason why the athletic victor's song was sung by many voices instead of just one. The parallel of war suggested that at this moment not only the victor but the whole community owed a thankful return to the gods, best made with dance and with many-voiced song.[4]

The fact that the victory song had always been a multiple affair is proved by its name, which (until Hellenistic critics made the word *epinikion* fashionable) was *enkōmion:* song sung by a group of masculine revellers. Such a group can be seen on black-figured pots from the mid-sixth century, where the victor with his prize is surrounded by dancing elders with cups, or by young men of his own age, led by a flute player.[5] By the time of Pindar and Bacchylides these joyful relatives and friends had been replaced by a picked chorus rehearsed by a hired poet, but the memory of simpler, wilder times was still honored, for the performing group was often called a *kōmos*, its activity referred to as *kōmazein*.[6] The games had become panhellenic, athletes left home to compete, and formal victory celebrations waited upon their return, but the need for an immediate response to success was still answered by improvised singing and dancing on the triumphal evening.[7] "His friends kindle a great commotion," says Pindar (*O.* 10.72 ff.), "and in the evening the full moon shows her lovely light and the whole sanctuary sings with the pleasures of the banquet—songs in the encomiastic mode." One of Bacchylides' odes is or appears to be just such a song, one meant to be performed on the spot, which is Isthmia, by the Cean athletes who were the victor's friends (2.1 ff.):[8]

> Ἄ[ϊξον, ὦ] σεμνοδότειρα Φήμα,
> ἐς Κ[έον ἱ]εράν, χαριτώ-
>   νυμ[ον] φέρουσ' ἀγγελίαν,
>   ὅτι μ[ά]χας θρασύχειρ⟨ος⟩ Ἀρ-
> 5 γεῖο[ς ἄ]ρατο νίκαν,
> καλῶν δ' ἀνέμνασεν, ὅσ' ἐν κλε[εν]νῶι
> 7 αὐχένι Ἰσθμοῦ ζαθέαν
>   λιπόντες Εὐξαντίδα νᾶ-
>   σον ἐπεδείξαμεν ἑβδομή-
> 10 κοντα [σὺ]ν στεφάνοισιν.
> καλεῖ δὲ Μοῦσ' αὐθιγενὴς
>   γλυκεῖαν αὐλῶν καναχάν,
>   γεραίρουσ' ἐπινικίοις
> 14 Πανθείδα φίλον υἱόν.

Rush away, Rumor, sacred and generous,
carry this message with its rewarding name
   to Ceos: say that the battle-bold
   hand of Argeios
   captured the prize,

recalling to us those other fair deeds
done in the far-famed neck of the Isthmus
   where, come from our holy Euxantid
   isle, we seventy times
   paraded with crowns.

Now the Muse of our native place
calls for sweet chatter of flutes,
giving the gift of victory songs
to Pantheides' much-loved son.

The hymns that were performed some weeks later, however orderly
and magnificent they might be, were in a sense only a reflection of this
initial celebration, and as a link between the immediate and the postponed, the improvised and the composed (the old and the new), there
were sometimes light-hearted serenades by revellers as soon as the victor
came home. Bacchylides, for example, made a short greeting for a boy
runner in which a prominent early pun[9] strikes a note of frolic that is
held throughout the song (Ode 6):

Α'   Λάχων Διὸς μεγίστου
        λάχε φέρτατον πόδεσσι
     3 κῦδος ἐπ' Ἀλφεοῦ προχοαῖσ[ι νικῶν,
        δι' ὅσσα πάροιθεν
     5 ἀμπελοτ|ρόφον Κέον
     6 ἄεισάν ποτ' Ὀλυμπίᾳ
        πύξ τε καὶ στάδιον κρατεῦ[σαν
        στεφάνοις ἐθείρας
Β'   )—
        νεανίαι βρύοντες.
    10 σὲ δὲ νῦν ἀναξιμόλπου
     3 Οὐρανίας ὕμνος ἕκατι Νίκ[ας,
        Ἀριστομένειον
    13 ὦ ποδάνεμον τέκος,
     6 γεραίρει προδόμοις ἀοι-
    15   δαῖς, ὅτι στάδιον κρατήσας
        Κέον εὐκλέϊξας.

Lachon now takes on
best fame from Zeus
for using his feet at Alpheus' mouth!
Often before
has vine-nursing Ceos been
sung at Olympia,
    hymned as the best in ring or race
by youths who sport clustering

crowns in their curls. So now
Ourania, mistress of melody,
gives you a song thanks to your victory,

o Aristomenid boy,
wind-fleet of foot,
to sound at your doorstep
    here, where your stadium prize
makes Ceos more famous!

The immediate rejoicings of the contest night hailed and thanked the
gods, and the first revels of the return expressed the city's thanks to its
fame-giving son—what then was left for the formal epinician ode? With
religious and secular debts technically paid, it was quite plainly a luxury
and not a necessity, and this its physical surroundings proudly proclaimed. The performance took place at a large party where noble young
men met with fathers, uncles, cousins, grandfathers and relatives by
marriage, along with foreign guest-friends, to eat and celebrate. The
group was exclusive, since the festivity belonged essentially to one family, and the host was rich because only the rich could afford to patronize
a poet, not to mention compete in the greater contests. The ode was thus
sung in an atmosphere warmed not only by success but also by wine,
food, a show of wealth and the pride of blood, but nevertheless it did not
descend to the level of mere entertainment.[10] Emanating as it did from
the author of the victorious deed, this final song could hardly pretend to
repay the victor for his effort,[11] and what it did instead was reconstitute
the act that had put the community into his debt. Through musical performance the foreign exploit was revived, brought back, made to bloom
again, and offered to the gathered guests, that they might have the pleasure of participating in it (P. N. 9.48–9). The victor's glory (*kudos*) had
been the gift of god; song now fixed it in an enduring earthly form and
caused it to radiate upon city and friends as fame (*kleos*).[12]

All this Bacchylides makes one of his choruses explain, as they sing to
the Athenian friends of a youth who has taken the running prize at
Isthmia (10.9–14):

> 9 Ἀ[γ'λ]άῳ καὶ νῦν κασιγ'νήτας ἀκοίτας
> 10 ‿ναςιῶτιν̄ ἐκίνησεν λιγύφθογγον μέλισσαν,
> 1 ἕ[γ]χειρὲς ἵν' ἀθάνατον Μουσᾶν ἄγαλμα
>   ξυνὸν ἀνθρώποισιν εἴη
> 3 χάρμα, τεὰν ἀρετὰν
>   μανῦον ἐπιχθονίοισιν,

For Aglaios now his sister's husband has
aroused the sweet-voiced island bee
so that the deathless tribute of the Muses
might become for men

a common happy property—
announcement made of your fair deed
to those who live on earth . . .

Apparently heaven already celebrates Aglaios' crown with an immortal victory song—the Muses' deathless composition. Now, thanks to patron and poet, an earthly chorus dances out the same message about the virtue of the victor, making it the possession of all (compare the *agathon xunon* of P. *I.* 1.46). Translated into an epinician ode, the fame that the single runner has earned can be recognized and appropriated by the whole aristocratic group, and meanwhile the "island bee" (Bacchylides) gives that fame a kind of immortality by attaching today's song to the eternal one that is heard above.

All of which means that though we do not know when epinician began, we do know why it took and kept a choral form. The numbers of the chorus generalized the singular success of the victor so that it could be set before his numerous contemporaries—his one crown, multiplied in the crowns of the *kōmos* (Ba. 6.8–9), became the many wreaths of his banqueting friends.[13] In a more theoretical sense, contact with god, experienced elsewhere, was to be felt here and now,[14] and it took a multiplicity of dancers to recreate the daimonic aspect of the moment in which the prize had been won. The victor's temporally isolated act had not only to be danced into the present, however; it had to be danced on into the timelessness of eternal reputation and given an air of mythic permanence, and for this all the powers of replicated gesture and tongue were required. The choral form was thus both mechanically and magically appropriated to the double purpose of bringing victory home and giving it eternal fame, but nevertheless a number of dangers lay ambushed in this practice of dedicating a danced celebration to an episode of athletic success. The more frivolous practitioners of the art may not have been troubled by them, but the two great epinician poets were constantly aware of these risks and in their awareness they created the strangely defensive, almost apotropaic magnificence of ripe epinician poetry.

To begin with, there was an obvious religious risk in this sort of performance, for how could it be safe to set a procession of costumed men in motion, not in the service of god, but in praise of one who was like themselves? The spread tapestries of Clytemnestra's victory celebration are a relevant reminder that greetings such as these skirt the borders of prideful blasphemy. Indeed, the victor was traditionally greeted as "blessed," almost as if he were a god, so that the potential offense came close to being actual.[15] The choral form suggested praise proper to a divinity and so did words like *olbios* and *makarios*, and consequently the dance that glorified a man hinted at a culpable deification of mortality.

Such was the religious risk. It was clear and fundamental, but it was not the worst of the problems that inhered in the genre, for in the early fifth century epinician praise could easily offend society as well as the gods. Group performances had originally served the whole community as it sought a common advantage from supernatural powers, and the chorus in consequence was associated with ideas of general social use-fulness.[16] Here, however, was a multiple performance that quite bla-tantly did not work in the interest of all, but instead borrowed the magical means that rightfully belonged to the community and used them for the advantage of only a few. The danced victory ode did not strive to make the common earth more fruitful or the general rains more frequent; instead it strove to make the rich and the physically strong even prouder and more fortunate. In theory, of course, the nobles were proxies for their communities and the cities were expected to shine in the reflected light of their aristocrats' victories. In fact, however, the magical communion that the chorus offered—its gift of participation in the bliss of the victory crown—was received only by the guests who had been called to the performance, not by all of society. For this reason a choral song of victory threatened to arouse not only a jealous anger among the gods, but also the just resentment of the mortal com-munity.

This double danger was inherent in the victory ode as soon as it re-placed the informal *kōmos* with a trained chorus like that of a public festival,[17] and it was exacerbated by a pretentious rationale that had been inherited from earlier, nonathletic praise. In the deep past, public praise had been kept for courageous fighting men, and it was a reward that properly came to them after they had died.[18] Spartan generals hop-ing for such a recompense made offerings to the Muses before they went into battle (Plut. *Lyc.* 21.7; *Apo. lacon.* 221A), and Tyrtaeus reminded the whole fighting force of the reputation that followed upon bravery, the ill-fame that came with cowardice (9.27 ff.; 6.3 ff., and 8.15 ff.). Such praise could be given individually in *skolia*, or by a chorus in victory celebration or funeral dirge,[19] but since its burden was always death—death escaped or death splendidly met—these songs ran no risk of ou-traging heaven by seeming to make gods of their subjects. And on the other hand, their communal function was obvious to all, since lauding bravery and reviving the spirit of victory were actions necessary to a city's survival. Fine deeds set forth in song aroused the spirit of emula-tion and the chivalrous rivalry that were indispensable in an archaic army, and so praise of this sort could never offend. In consequence, the primitive praise-giver had no need either to curb his words or to give them any particularly bewitching power. In his way he was as important to his city as a priest or a military commander, but he only gave tongue to matter that was known and believed by all.[20]

Primitive praise was thus a practical affair, but as time went on it was influenced and finally altered by a theory of poetry that seems to have been widespread, though it had never been precisely enunciated. According to this theory, all poets were servants or companions of the Muses (Bacchylides once calls himself the "god-like prophet of the Muses," 9.3), and all had been granted a vision not confined to the present and the actual. They knew the mythic past and through it could glimpse the future,[21] for they had a sense of the songs that were sung in the courts of Olympus. To the bard, the Muses granted the ability to get the details right when he told of legendary matters, and to the poet who sang about men of his own time these goddesses gave a more extended power, for they allowed him to transform ephemeral events into the legend whose truth they protected. In the ordinary course of things, time would hide today's deeds in silence and darkness, but the singer could work against time by keeping certain creatures and their actions bright. Pindar explained it this way in the *Seventh Isthmian:*

> The splendor of the past sleeps
> and men are without memory
> unless the bloom of what the poet knows
> be joined with words
> in glorious streams.

Because the notion of poetic preservation had an eschatalogical quality, it was often expressed in geographical terms which placed men's deeds either in a hidden place of dim forgottenness (like the Hades of Sappho's rival, 55V) or else in a landscape of luminous openness much like the meadow of the blessed dead.[22] In this second spot all that would be remembered wandered at ease, thanks to the poets who gave (and forbade) entrance to the realm of Aletheia.

Praise gave the kind of conspicuousness that kept a thing from being hidden; praise showed that a deed was unforgotten and belonged to the company of unforgotten events that filled the memory of man, and so it proved that a thing was "true" where truth meant consecration by memory.[23] Any least word of laudation rescued an action from *lethe* for the moment, but the words of the poets were the most perfect embodiment of this kind of truth because they were themselves most apt to be unforgotten: music conferred *aletheia* upon praise, just as praise conferred it upon the deed to be remembered. Poets' minds, moreover, were the archives of mythic deeds, and consequently poets were, of all men, the best equipped to discover which fresh actions matched the old ones and should be given over to Mnemosyne. In earlier times the poet of praise had been the guardian of communal virtue and communal history, but now he was also a priest of memory and a hierophant whose rites meant immortality for deeds and reputations. Like a lawgiver, he molded the ordinary man's distinction between what was admirable and what was base with his choice of what to commemorate, and in addition he decided questions ordinarily left to the gods, for when he sang of a fine action he gave it an eternal life of truth, and when he judged a thing shameful, he could obliterate it simply by holding his tongue.[24]

This is the "pretentious rationale" mentioned a moment ago. Ostensibly it meant that an epinician singer could impose the values of the agonistic aristocracy upon men in general, while he elevated a particular athlete and made him an equal of the heroes. Not surprisingly, this view of the function of praise-poetry appears most clearly in the work of poets and there is no way of knowing whether it was ever widely accepted. What we do know, however, is that by the end of the sixth century it was out of harmony with the way that most men thought and lived. Cities had begun to replace smaller social units, money was in general use, and aristocratic governments lost vitality as commerce created new bases of power and currency made large fortunes possible. Tyrants appeared in many places, and mercenaries changed the aspect of the battlefield, so that it ceased to be the scene of conspicuous acts of noble bravery.[25] Virtue was no longer the same thing as courage, deeds worth remembering were not so easily recognized, and victory in the games was no longer easily assimilable to martial victory, no longer necessary to the health of all. In consequence the chorus that hailed an athlete had a hard time pretending that it represented the whole community in its grant of Unforgetting, and for the most part it withdrew into courtyards and palace dining-halls. In these private surroundings the developed epinician ode began to reflect the increasing elitism of athletic victory by growing longer and more elaborate—more than ever like Agamemnon's tapestries—just at the moment when it was for the first time open to a charge of frivolity. At the end of the sixth century, choral praise of a victor's strength might have to compete for a tyrant's attention with choral praise of a favorite boy's beauty,[26] and meanwhile a very different sense of what was truly praiseworthy was spreading through other parts of Hellenic society.

In the lost (and perhaps only imaginary) world of simple praise and genuine aristocratic values, it had been excess that counted, for only with an extreme of ferocity or liberality or strength could a noble stand out among his noble peers. Extremes were in themselves glorious to that old way of thinking: riddles and sayings were always looking for the superlative in any category, and when the arms of Achilles were to be awarded, it was natural to ask who of all the Greeks had been most fearsome in the eyes of the enemy. In the same way, it had once been thought a good thing to arouse envy among one's companions. The envied man was certain that no one smirched him with pity (*phthonou mallon ē oiktirou* was one of Thales' sayings),[27] but there was more to it than that, for *phthonos* came from the ordinary man as praise did from the poet, in positive recognition of one's excellence. "The fairest thing to be is noble and much envied by a multitude of men," says Bacchylides anachronistically (10.47–8; cf. P. *P.* 1–85).

An archaic man who was not the object of envy was nothing (*dēlon hōs anēr par' ouden esth', ho mē phthonoumenos*, Epicharmus B 34),[28] and if he felt no envy of others he might forget to try to match his exploits to theirs.[29] In the late sixth century, however, when values no longer pretended to derive always from the battlefield and extremes of pride or gluttony or luxury were to be seen, excess was no longer intrinsically admirable and envy might mean that a man's fellow citizens would try to confiscate the means of his distinction.[30] Even when it was valued, excess had been considered insecure because of the possible envy of the gods, and now it became politically dangerous as well.[31] Sumptuary laws gave an economic turn to the Delphic adage, *mēden agan*, and the thinkers who followed in Solon's wake more and more came to admire the mean.[32] Moderation, not extreme preeminence, was the way, and safe tranquility, not glory, the goal. Even superlative excellence was to be avoided, and public praise was positively unwanted, since an encomium would destroy the inconspicuous mediocrity that the truly moderate man desired.

These changes in society, in the style of praise, and in men's views about what was admirable were accompanied by an important change in the praise-poet's status, for sometime during the sixth century this creature who was in theory part hierophant and part lawgiver began to hire himself out for pay.[33] In the ancient world this new practice was said to be the invention of Simonides' greed,[34] but in fact it was the new importance of private wealth that made professionals of the choral poets. An Alcman or a Stesichorus had been associated with the city to which he supplied public music and where he got in return honor and traditional prizes—perhaps an ox for himself and a tripod for his chorus. Now, however, there were rich men and tyrants who could tempt a poet to leave his own community, and in answer to the widespread demand for *mnemosyne* a poet could become a traveling impresario like the urbane Arion. In these changed circumstances, local honors, gifts, and hospitality could hardly serve as an adequate recompense, for the poet needed something that could be stowed on a ship (a temptation to pirates!) and taken along to the place of his next commission. When offered gratitude by a client, Simonides is supposed to have answered, "Sir, I have two chests: a full one where I keep gratitude and an empty one where I keep pieces of silver."[35]

As a commodity in what was more and more a money economy, choral poetry came to be bought and sold.[36] This was perfectly natural, but unfortunately the new determinant in its distribution was at odds with the product itself, since praise had claimed to respond only to the truly memorable, conferring a glory that was different from mere notoriety precisely because it could not be bought. Tyrtaeus had said explicitly that it was only the bold virtue of a man of action that he would sing, not wealth and not even strength (9D), but now the poet went where he was hired, sang as much or as little as his pay would cover, and made his rich client as praiseworthy as he could. He was open to popular charges of prostituting *aletheia* to the rich in the interest of his own stomach and, perhaps more important, he was himself forced to reassess his product. Like an artisan,[37] he considered the market, asked his price, and confected a product that would please his immediate client and advertise himself for further commissions. At the same time, if he still felt himself to be a poet of praise in the ancient sense, he considered his song and asked himself whether the inner value of his work could survive the touch of the money it had earned.[38]

By the time that Pindar and Bacchylides began to compose for choral performances the victory hymn had thus become a highly retrograde and difficult form of song. Its mere multiple performance made it suspect in the eyes both of heaven and earth, and meanwhile its overweening ancient pretensions to truth served to emphasize the present possibility of sordid corruption. Its patrons were at best anachronistic, at worst, rich ruffians or overbearing tyrants who were not themselves even victors but only patrons who had paid the cost of a contestant.[39] Worse still, in order to please such clients, the fifth-century poets had to make the old brief song of praise longer and heavier than it once had been. They had wider scope for their own talents now, but with the new style that was more ceremonious and more highly decorated two new risks joined the old ones of blasphemy and elitism, since an ode might now either anger a patron by scanting his praise or offend his guests by carrying it too far and falling into unctuous flattery. This disheartening complex of religious, ethical, social, and aesthetic problems is what I have termed the epinician burden: it was very real, and its weight had much to do with the shape and the mood of the classic victory ode.

4. BEARING THE BURDEN

The chorus that praised an athlete in the early fifth century had only a short step to take before it found itself singing a hymn to riches and reaction, but neither of the surviving practitioners of the victory ode was a sycophant, and neither Pindar nor Bacchylides took that step. They accepted epinician commissions wholeheartedly—*peithomai eumareōs* says Bacchylides (5.195)—because they believed in the games and in the old order that had established them. To their way of thinking there was a beauty and a deep necessity in the fierce training of fine bodies, in the testing of tempers formed by a ceremonious use of wealth, and in the proud certification of triumph when it came. Bacchylides figured the splendor of future actions as rising from the deeds of the present, duly praised, just as a growing stem rises from a bulb or a root (5.197–8), and Pindar held that song could nourish and augment noble endeavor just as wind fed sails and rain encouraged fields (*O.* 11.1 ff.).[1] In addition, both poets saw victory itself as a religious experience: the great contests were dedicated to the gods, and in the moment of his coronation the victor was in communication with the powers that had helped him win. At Olympia it was "Zeus who set the grey crown of Aetolian olive upon his head" (Ba. 8.28), but wherever he was when the wreath touched his brow, the winner knew a blessedness like that of heroes or gods. And it was finally this victorious contact with power and bliss that Pindar and Bacchylides tried to fix in the measures of their songs, even as they distributed it among the wealthy guests, for both believed that the qualities displayed by athletes and the daimonism that lodged in their victories were crucial to the maintenance of Hellenic society.[2]

Precisely because they idealized victory, these two urbane and eminent poets were conscious always, not only of the potential blasphemy, but also of the possible injustice that inhered in the practice of their profession. They had to laud men who were exclusively aristocratic and rich, and so they created for this purpose a complex form that was meant to neutralize the risks. The oldest dangers were the easiest to check, and both poets blocked the possible jealousy of the gods with seemingly spontaneous glorification. Occasionally an ode was offered directly to a god with an invocation like that of a hymn in its opening lines.[3] The victory was formally subordinated to the will of heaven when the song began, like the one Bacchylides made for a noble Thessalian horseman: "Gold-garmented Hestia, it is you who foster the high fortunes of this rich and famous family . . !" (14B 1 ff.). However, a chorus that began in this fashion might strike the victor as positively bending over backwards in its piety, and the practice of direct sacred invocation was evidently not much desired by the patrons of song. As an alternative, the poet could work retroactively, using his final lines to recognize and placate the heavenly powers. Bacchylides, for example, at the close of Ode 5, collects past victory, future deeds, and the songs that will link them together and puts them all under divine protection: "May the great paternal Zeus guard them all and keep them untroubled in peace" (5.199–200; cf. the final prayer to Zeus at O. 13.110, or to Apollo at P. I. 7.49). Time and again the singers name a divinity as the source of the victory that they celebrate (Ba. 1.148; 4.1; 11.37; 13.79 and 195),[4] time and again they pray that this heavenly favor may continue (Ba. 5.36; 9.97; 11.115), and a short ode for a Cean athlete closes like a formal hymn of gratitude: "Oh Zeus, master of the thunderbolt, you have fulfilled his prayers for god-given glory." (8.26 ff.). By means such as these the epinician singers offered mortal victory back to the gods, using the danced performance as if it were a way of spilling first-fruits or setting up an ex-voto.[5]

More characteristic, perhaps, of the ripe epinician style was the practice of passing from occasion to myth (and back again) by way of a sudden prayer, or a brief aside in which the chorus recognized the decisive role of divinity in every form of success. One group of Bacchylidean singers pulls itself up short at the richest point of its myth, crying: "Muse, stop your chariot here and sing instead of Zeus, the leader of the gods!" (5.176 ff.). Another chorus breaks off its description of the man-made beauties of Delphi with a similar exhortation addressed this time not just to itself but to all of the audience—to all Hellas, in fact: "but it is god, god who must be magnified!" (3.21–2). This transitional technique was in fact just as formal as the formal opening or closing prayers, but it had a charming air of ingenuousness about it, as if the chorus had almost forgotten itself. There is wit here, as well as conscious art, for when the singers pretend that they have almost been tempted into an improper praise of humanity, the mortal patron is reminded that he has been lauded to the very limits of safety, even as the divine listeners are assured that no poetic élan is beyond arrest at the call of reverence.

The envy of the excluded was dealt with in ways rather more various, the simplest of which was a poetic identification of the victor with his city. The athlete's crown enhanced his birthplace as well as his family, as a Bacchylidean chorus assured a winning runner (10.16 ff.): "Binding your fair head with flowers, because of victory, you built up glory for Athens and reputation for the Oenidae."[6] In theory the victory ode "decorated" the city as well as the winning athlete (12.6–7), and it could do so in practice by choosing a myth that enhanced the locality. The whole island of Ceos is flattered, in Ode 1, by the tale of Minos and the daughter of the Telchines, and Aegina, in Ode 13, is praised first in nymph form (13.77 ff.; 182 ff.) and then as a polity as the victor's *aretē* brings honor to an island already rich in glory (182 ff.). The fame of a city was made by the fame of its victors, and a present victory had the power not just of recalling but of revivifying past victories, thus causing the whole history of the place to shine with fresh lustre. The crowns of today's chorus mingle with those of other years when Bacchylides sings of Lachon (6.8–9), for a deed is like a song in its power to bring other deeds out of obscurity (cf. 2.6) and also in its ability to confer *eukleia* (6.16). When the victor was a tyrant, his relation to his city was all too evident, and Bacchylides made grander claims to cover the special case of Hieron. His winning horses brought the "flower of happiness" to Syracuse (5.184), his Pythian triumphs were evidence that "Apollo still loves Syracuse" (4.1), but the Sicily that shared in his victories was prudently said to belong finally to Demeter and her daughter (3.1).

Praise of the city may have been an element inherited from the much more ancient songs of military praise, since it identified victory with the life of the community. With such praise, the poet pretended that every citizen had his share in the victor's achievement, even though the song that revived and apportioned the victorious deed was sung only to a few. It was as if a second, plainer table had been set up outside for those who were not among the chosen banquet guests, and partly in deference to that second board the epinician poets continued also in another ancient practice, the use of gnomic speech. The generalities of folk wisdom had always been appropriate, since they allowed the poet to assure the gods that the victor, in spite of appearances, was in truth no rival of theirs. Gnomes could also, however, be used at the other end of the scale, to lessen the distance between the wealthy aristocrat and an envious populace. The storehouse of proverbial wit was filled with observations on the blindness of man, the brevity of life and pleasure, the emptiness of hope, and the truancy of luck, and by the end of the sixth century these old saws had been disciplined by meter and made subtle by manifold contexts. One or two such denigrating maxims, employed like drops of vinegar, could correct the excessively sumptuous flavor of a rich man's success. The gnome was by nature leveling, since it was true for all mankind, and consequently not only the gods but also all less fortunate men felt appeased and contented when the victor was marked in this fashion as belonging after all to the commonality of those who must die.[7]

Both Pindar and Bacchylides deployed mottos and sententiae for this double audience of gods and men, but each had a wise-man's manner all his own. Pindar liked to move on from genuine proverbs or sayings into pseudo-gnomes of his own invention, using the mask of folk-wisdom to cover thoughts that were peculiar to himself. Favorite concepts like the power of inborn nature, or the radiance lent by victory, were slipped in among the old phrases to pass themselves off as if they were familiar.[8] Bacchylides' gnomes, by contrast, were more limited in subject, giving the impression of being closer to what wise old men really did mutter to one another.[9] When he speaks of mortal success, his emphasis is more strongly on its god-given aspect, less strongly upon the necessity for kin and song, and when he talks of man's ordinary life his tone is even more popular. *Brachys estin aiwn*, he says—"a lifetime is short" (3.74),[10] just as an old man anywhere will sing out, "Man born of woman has a short time to live!" Hope deceives high and low alike (3.74; 9.18 cf. 13.157); it is hard, that is, impossible, for a mortal to turn aside the intention of god (5.94–5); even Heracles joins the miserable population of the world in saying, "The best fate for a man would be never to see the light of day" (5.160). Nevertheless, phrases like these do not mean that Bacchylides' poems propose life as a dreary affair. Conventional pessimism of this sort has in fact a practical and positive effect, for it works like a child's crossing his fingers against bad luck, protecting the victor's exotic and expensive achievement from the envy of both gods and men.

Bacchylides' deeply sophisticated, though apparently simple, way with gnomes can be recognized in an ode (Ode 14) that devotes its initial and only surviving triad entirely to sonorous generalities. It was made for a Thessalian charioteer who seems to have come from an old-fashioned knightly family, for there is no mention of city here. The song opens with a pithy announcement of the essential aristocratic claim that rank is god-ordained. When a man has a fine portion of what the gods give—when his birth and hereditary position are high—he has what is best (cf. 4.18). This, however, is only an ideal best, for in the real world such a one is subject to chance like any other, a chance that can bring pain, can even reverse his relation to those who are less favored by the gods (14.1–7):[11]

A'　　　Εὖ μὲν εἱμάρθαι παρὰ δαίμ[ονος ἀν-
　　　　θρώποις ἄριστον·
　　3 σ]υμφορὰ δ᾽ ἐσθλόν ⟨τ᾽⟩ ἀμαλδύ-
　　　　νει β]αρύτ᾽λ[α]τος μολοῦσα
　5 5 καὶ τ]ὸν κακ[ὸν] ὑψιφανῆ τεύ-
　　　　χει κ]ατορθωθεῖσα· τιμὰν
　　__　δ᾽ ἄλ]λος ἀλλοίαν ἔχει·

　　　For men, to be well-portioned of the gods
　　　　is finest, but
　　　experience that comes as suffering
　　　　subdues the noble man
　　　while upward-lifting fortune gives the base
　　　　preeminence. Honor varies as it comes
　　　now to one, now to another man.

The nobleman can be reduced (softened or made weak, *amaldunei*
11.3–4) by chance-brought suffering,[12] the base-born can be propped
up into a kind of eminence by a favoring gesture of fortune, and the
world may respond by shifting its honors to such chance-made men.
At this point in the demonstration (the end of the first strophe) this
original proposition might still feed the pride of an aristocrat, for it
only repeats many of Theognis' proud and bitter observations. That
pride, however, has been shown to hold no practical threat to the man
who does not have a splendid portion to start with. Because of the per-
versity of chance, the noble may lose his power in the polis and consequently this present chorus that dances his present victory need not
give rise to envy.

All this, however, is only a prelude to what the poet really has to say,
and he continues (8–18):

　　　1 μυρί]αι δ᾽ ἀνδρῶν ἀρε[ταί,] μία δ᾽ ἐ[κ
　　　　πασᾶ]ν πρόκειται,
　10 3 ὃς τὰ] πὰρ χειρὸς κυβέρνα-
　　　　σεν δι]καίαισι φ᾽ρένεσσιν.
　　　5 οὔτ᾽ ἐ]ν βαρυπενθέσιν ἁρμό-
　　　　ζει μ]άχαις φόρμιγγος ὀμφὰ
　　　__　καὶ λι]γυκ᾽λαγγεῖς χοροί,
　15 1 οὔτ᾽ ἐ]ν θαλίαις καναχά
　　　　χαλκ]όκτυπος· ἀλλ᾽ ἐφ᾽ ἑκάστωι
　　　3 καιρός] ἀνδρῶν ἔργματι κάλ-
　　　　λιστος· [ε]ὖ ἔρδοντα δὲ καὶ θεὸς ὀ[ρθοῖ.

> Many kinds of mortal excellence there are, but one
>   takes precedence, found
> where man controls the task in hand with justice
>   in his heart and mind.
> In grievous battle-skirmish neither lyre
>   nor poignant choral cry
>   can sound with harmony,
>
> nor is the clang of bronze in tune
>   with festive joy. There is
> a best response each deed can offer to its hour.
> God rights him, when a man works well.

Of course entrance to the games is restricted to the rich and well-born—that goes without saying—but access to the true essence of victory is open to men of every station because that essence is simply excellence. In this shifting world of chance the one fairest pursuit is the pursuit of *aretē* (this abstract good is played against the pragmatic *timē* that comes and goes with prosperity just above) and this superlative quality can be found in every form of activity. What is more, the best excellence does not belong to a single class or profession, but may be discovered in all modes of life, whatever the calling of him who seeks it out.

"Man's life can take many forms" is a conventional Greek trope,[13] but usually it leads to the making of a hierarchy, whether explicit or only implied. Pindar, for example, has a similar passage in which he implicitly ranks the kinds of human endeavor and places the making of prophetic poetry at the top of his list (*O.* 9.107, taking *sophiai* in its usual Pindaric sense of wisdom skillfully cast into song; cf. *I.* 1, 47 ff.). This conclusion is anything but consoling for the ordinary man since only a kind of vocation, in addition to blood and breeding, can justify anyone in making a bid for glory, and glory is found only in the realms of contest and song. Bacchylides' effect is just the opposite, for instead of making a hierarchy[14] he counteracts the elitism of the victory ode with a familiar lesson about *kairos*—the opportunity to which one must immediately respond if anything worthwhile is to be done. Instead of looking for the most valuable kind of human activity, he looks for a strain of "most valuable" that is common to them all, and what he discovers is that true excellence depends, not on wealth or birth or calling, but simply on that just sense of timing that is as significant among farmers, sailors, and artisans as it is among horse-trainers, runners, and singers of songs.[15] Seen in this way, the noble Thessalian victor is only one more example of a man who has given an appropriate response to his moment and so has been "set right" by god. His triumph has for this brief space been demystified and he is seen, not as one of the blessed, but as one who is like a drum in battle, like a lyre among banqueters, but also like any man with a piece of work in hand.[16]

If the aristocratic athlete was subject to the same gods and the same laws of mortality and chance as were all men, then his experience was not wholly disengaged from that of the less fortunate. His victory, however, was most immediately to be shared with his peers, men who were simply a little less strong, perhaps a little less rich, than he. For these listeners the poets strove to make the act of winning as immaterial—as little a matter of training, technique, equipment, and exertion—as was possible.[17] Their songs are not about men's muscle or the flesh of horses or the make of chariots, and they do not even record wonderful displays of skill, though these are exactly the details that would have been noted by an epic reporter. Instead, the poets of victory make use of generalized concepts and an abstract vocabulary as they try to transcribe the peculiar electricity of a triumphant race or javelin cast. Bacchylides, for example, takes from the nerve and sweat of an actual horse only a negative sense of the purity of speed, which he captures in this phrase (5.43-6):

> 3 οὔπω νιν ὑπὸ π'ροτέ[ρω]ν
> ἵππων ἐν ἀγῶνι κατέχ'ρανεν κόνις
> 45 5 πρὸς τέλος ὀρνύμενον·
> ῥιπᾶι γὰρ ἴσος βορέα

> not once in the race was he stained
> by dust of horses that stole his lead,
> for he fled to the finish-line
> swift as a north wind blast . . .

Pindar, about the same horse, is equally oblivious of any physical race-track, for he refers to another of his performances simply as the time when (O. 1.20-2)

> he ran beside the Alpheus
> holding himself to the course
> unwhipped, joining his master to victory.

This kind of dematerialization was of course not merely a defensive ploy. Rather, it expressed a positive conviction (shared by both poets) that a moment of victory held a beauty that nourished society (a *charis zōthalmios*, P. O. 7.11). It was this beauty which song could offer as a "common happy property" (B. 10.12-13), sometimes dissembled be-

hind the beauty of a myth, sometimes directly evoked, as it is in an ode
that Bacchylides made for a Nemean victor from Phlius (9.27–36):[18]

B′   )—
   1 πενταέθ'λοισιν γὰρ ἐνέπ'ρεπεν ὡς
     ἄστρων διακ'ρίνει φάη
   3 νυκτὸς διχομηνίδο[ς] εὐφεγγὴς σελάνα·
 30 τοῖος Ἑλλάνων δι' ἀπ[εί]ρονα κύκ'λον
     φαῖνε θαυμαστὸν δέμας
   6 δίσκον τροχοειδέα ῥίπτων,
     καὶ μελαμφύλλου κλάδον
   8 ἀκτέας ἐς αἰπεινὰν προπέμπων
 35 αἰθέρ' ἐκ χειρὸς βοὰν ὤτρυνε λαῶν
 36 1 ἢ τε[λε]υτάσας ἀμάρυγ'μα πάλας·

    In the pentathlon he was preeminent
      like the surpassing light
    of a mid-month moon among stars;
    so he appeared when he passed through the circle
    of Greeks, his marvelous limbs revealed,
    to cast the discus-wheel; so he appeared
    when he made the dark-leaved elder branch
    leap from his hand towards the steep air
    and roused a shout from the crowd; so again

    in his last lithe twist in the wrestling ring.

This is the poet's closest approach to a report of athletic events, and it
is a perfect example of how, for him, victory was one of beauty's forms.
The actual athlete is transmuted as the moon simile makes his preeminence cool and inevitable, a kind of epiphany (*phaine*, 31), though the
Sapphic echo at the same time lends a hint of eroticism to this body that
is glimpsed only in motion. Even the implements of sport are divested of
the specific and made more ancient and general, the discus assimilated to
the wheel, the lance to the tree, and what the athlete does with them,
according to this "record," is elicit from other men an intangible, immaterial cry of admiration. His exertion is translated into sound, for it will
end as reputation, and meanwhile the present banqueting song gives its
version of the shout that recognized success. Its specially chosen language, however, asks that the present listeners should respond to the
victory of Automedes with the same awestruck wonder that a splendid
natural event might inspire.

Pindar, like Bacchylides, believed that victory contained virtue as the
moon contained light, and that its virtue had to be remembered if Hel-

lenic culture was to remain true to itself. In this fundamental faith the two poets were similar, but they took to their common work of praise in two very different moods, for Pindar was confessedly uneasy as he composed his songs, while Bacchylides was unperturbed. Pindar wanted to maintain the ancient claims of the poet at their fullest, or rather he wished to expand them. He was the equal of kings (O. 1.115; cf. fr. 137 T), he had a holy vocation (N. 4.43; O. 11.10), but he was also charged with a public mission (O. 13.49), and his odes had an awesome power since they controlled memory. However, because he was conscious that he worked for hire (e.g., I. 2) and that saleable power might be misused, Pindar balanced his tremendous claims with an equally tremendous show of anxiety. He saw that praise might diverge from veracity and recognized the possibility of a song that lied (O. 1.28; O. 4.21; O. 13.52; P. 1.86), even of a song that deserved blame (P. 1.81). His praise might be scant or be excessive (O. 13.93; P. 1.43; I. 1.20–21), and any errors would be errors against Aletheia, the gods, and an ideally virtuous community. The making of an ode thus became for him an occasion heavy with responsibility; the epinician, like its subject, was a contest in which one could fail, and consequently Pindar's chorus often sang of the risk and the struggle of song.[19]

Bacchylides, by comparison, seems to be almost without a scruple,[20] and his ease and insouciance have caused some who equate art with agony to doubt the value of his poetry. Nevertheless, in spite of his seeming light-heartedness, it is easy to see that he had his own sense of the moral challenge of his genre and his own way of meeting it. To begin with, he did not have to doubt himself as a practitioner because he had a superb faith in the purity as well as the plain necessity of his art. Virtue becomes bright in the form of fair deeds and the Muse nourishes that brightness (3.90 ff.). What is fine among men is attuned to the will of heaven; it is manifest and cannot be mistaken by the observer, so that one may sing it without fear that one's praise is misapplied (13.175–81):

175   οὐ γὰρ ἀλαμπέι νυκ[τός
   11 πασιφανὴς Ἀρετ[ὰ
     κρυφθεῖσ᾿ ἀμαυρο[ῦται ◡__
   1 ἀλλ᾿ ἔμπεδον ἀκ[αμάτᾱι
    βρύουσα δόξᾱι
180   3 στρωφᾶται κατὰ γᾶν [τε
   καὶ πολύπ᾿λαγκτον θ[άλασσαν.

   Conspicuous aretē
   is never bedimmed
   or hidden in lightless obscurity;

it roams abroad
   teeming with restless fame—[21]
it moves across the dry land
and over the roaring sea.

The rendering of this ideal fame into words was the plain and grateful duty of all, especially of poets. It was an uncomplicated task, however, like making a translation from a lucid original, and the Muses stood ready to help.[22] Ideally, when he composed, a Muse dripped song into Bacchylides' mind like honey, filling his words with pleasure and dictating an announcement that was to be made to all people (13.228–231). Naturally, then, he was not afraid of his own *charis*,[23] and the nearest he seems to come to worrying about a failure of veracity is when he speaks of "touching earth," as a guarantee of the truth of his words (5.42; 8.19–20; the fact that he uses the phrase twice suggests that it was conventional). He is the Muses' prophet (9.3), and through him the Charites can grant a persuasive earthly glory (*doxa*) to deeds that are celebrated in heaven. As he brings a deed's eternal reputation into time, he has the power to mark that action as superlative, raising it from fine to finest (9.85 ff.):

> τό γέ τοι καλὸν ἔργον
> γνησίων ὕμνων τυχόν
> 6 ὑψοῦ παρὰ δαίμοσι κεῖται·
> 85 σὺν δ' ἀλαθείαι βροτῶν
> 8 κάλλιστον, εἴπ[ερ καὶ θάνηι τις,
> λε[ί]πεται Μουσ[ᾶν ◡--- ἄθ]υρμα.

Surely the fine deed
that meets with noble song
is stored away among the gods above.
Thanks to unforgetting praise
it is a thing most fine, and if a man should die
it lives, a pleasure that the Muses have.

The relation between achievement and praise was one of justice, fixed by the law of equal recompense. Because it was just, praise was a part of the order of nature and it was balanced by its ancient companion, public blame, or the silence that could damn. "When a thing is well done, it is not Silence that should be its decoration," says Bacchylides (3.94), which is tantamount to announcing (appropriately by aposiopesis) that when, by contrast, a thing has been basely done, Silence should strip it of all decoration.[24] In another song he says (13.202 ff.):

βροτῶν δὲ μῶμος
(170)   πάντεσσι μέν ἐστιν ἐπ᾽ ἔργοι[ς·
6 ᾷ δ᾽ ἀλαθεία φιλεῖ
205   νικᾶν, ὅ τε πανδ[α]μάτω[ρ
χρόνος τὸ κᾱλῶς
9 ἐ]ργμένον αἰὲν ἀ[έξει·

> Blame
> hangs over every human act[25]
> but Unforgetfulness
> loves victory
> and Master Time abets her,
> ever giving augment to fair deeds.

Here he uses the old word for praise, *aletheia*, that remembering repetition that marks a thing as True,[26] and he seems to imagine two almost allegorical figures, Momos and Aletheia, who sit sorting through men's various needs, each claiming his own. Bacchylides says elsewhere, again with an air of allegory, that this remembering praise that is called Aletheia "shares a city with the gods, and she alone" (of worldly creatures) "is asked to dine with them" (fr. 57S).

Because Praise and Blame are the just and natural projections of noble and ignoble deeds, the force that can distort them is not the poet's equally natural talent and will. It must be something unnatural, and Bacchylides finds this disorderly power in the post-aristocratic Envy (*Phthonos*) that had grown up in the early-classical world.[27] This sentiment was not a source of fruitful emulation among peers; it had become a grasping, grudging feeling that kept men from recognizing divine will and mortal virtue in the successes of others. The old Envy had worked to increase excellence, but this new sort tried to destroy it wherever it was found. It was expressed now in words instead of deeds (it was *thersiepēs*, with an echo of envious Thersites' name, 13.199–200), and it was a threat to the natural act of praise because it violated a man's inborn sense of justice (13.199–202):

Ζ'   )ˉˉ1 ε]ὶ μή τινα θερσι[ε]πὴς
200   φθόνος βιᾶται,
3 αἰνείτω σοφὸν ἄνδρα
ϙὺν δίκᾱι.

A man must (unless hot-worded Envy
  does him violence)
give praise in accurate recompense . . .

In a word, envy is the enemy of the rule of repayment of fair things with
fair, and the epinician poet, acting for all, must repel it with just words
of praise (5.187–89):

> χρή] δ' ἀλαθείας χάριν
> 13 αἰνεῖν, φθόνον ἀμφ[οτέραισιν
> χερσὶν ἀπωσάμενο͞,

One must for Aletheia's sake
give praise, thrusting Envy back ·
with both hands.[28]

Because he was in this sense a champion of archaic justice, Bacchylides felt comfortable in his calling. He knew the ethical and political
traps of his genre as well as any man, but as a second-generation artist he
faced them with tried poetic techniques instead of introspection. He
could maintain his old-fashioned view of the epinician function because
he was a man of simple convictions; he did really see abstract excellence
and the touch of god even in second-hand victories, and he did really
believe that choral song perpetuated and increased such excellence. Because of this faith, when there were actions of real grandeur to sing
about, he felt a kind of ecstasy in his own answering deed of praise.
Here is his picture, not of the victor and not of himself, but of the act of
praise. It is his portrait of the abstract artist in the act of lauding the abstract splendor of a victorious deed, and it comes from his Fifth Ode
(16 ff.):[29]

> βαθὺν
> δ' αἰθέρα ξουθαῖσι τάμνων
> 3 ὑψοῦ πτερύγεσσι ταχεί-
> αις αἰετὸς εὐρυάνακτος ἄγγελος
> 20 5 Ζηνὸς ἐρισφαράγου
> θαρσεῖ κρατερᾶι πίσυνος
> 7 ἰσχύϊ, πτάσσοντι δ' ὄρνι-
> χες λιγύφθογγοι φόβωι ·
> 9 οὔ νιν κορυφαὶ μεγάλας ἴσχουσι γαίας,
> 25   οὐδ' ἁλὸς ἀκαμάτας

26 11 δυσπαίπαλα κύματα· νω-
      μαῖ δ' ἐν ἀτ|ρύτωι χάει
   13 λεπτότ|ριχα σὺν ζεφύρου πνοι-
      αῖσιν ἔθειραν ἀρίγ|νω-
30 __ τος {μετ'} ἀνθρώποις ἰδεῖν·

                Steep air
    the eagle cuts
with swift and tawny wing,
    high messenger
of great-voiced Zeus, the king,
    and bold in knowledge of
his overbearing might, as small
    shrill birds sink down in fright.
Not fenced by broad earth's peaks
    nor by the untiring sea,
though tall waves boom,
    he navigates the changeless void
lifted high on slender plume
    and wheeling with the wind,
    bright sight for eyes of men.

5. HIERON AND CROESUS

Bacchylides took on the epinician burden gladly, and he bore it with a combination of simple faith and elaborate poetic science that is to be found in all of his songs of victory. One work in particular, however, displays most clearly the complexity of the genre's problems and the geniality of the poet's solutions, and that is Ode 3. It was commissioned by Hieron of Syracuse to celebrate the Olympic victory of his chariot team, won in the year 468. This was in fact Hieron's third victory at Olympia, though his first with the chariot, and added to his three Pythian crowns it made him unique as a multiple victor.[1] Two years earlier he had missed the distinction of being the only mortal with four Delphic and two Olympic wreaths (see *O.* 4.15 ff.) but now the tyrant's extremest ambition was met.

A' Ἀριστο[κ]άρπου Σικελίας κρέουσαν
      Δ[ά]ματρα ἰοστέφανόν τε Κούραν
      ὕμνει, γλυκύδωρε Κλεοῖ, θοάς τ᾽ Ὀ-
      λυμ]πιοδ'ρόμους Ἱέρωνος ἵππ[ο]υς.
   5 σεύον]το γὰρ σὺν ὑπερόχωι τε Νίκαι
      σὺν Ἀγ']λαΐαι τε παρ᾽ εὐρυδίναν
      Ἀλφεόν, τόθι] Δεινομένεος ἔθηκαν
      ὄλβιον τ[έκος στεφάνω]ν κυρῆσαι·
      θρόησε δὲ λ[αὸς ◡__.
  10 ἇ τρισευδαίμ[ων ἀνήρ,
      ὃς παρὰ Ζηνὸς λαχὼν
      πλείσταρχον Ἑλλάνων γέρας
      οἶδε πυργωθέντα πλοῦτον μὴ μελαμ-
)__ φαρέϊ κ'ρύπτειν σκότωι.

B′   15 βρύει μὲν ἱερὰ βουθύτοις ἑορταῖς,
βρύουσι φιλοξενίας ἀγυιαί·
λάμπει δ᾽ ὑπὸ μαρμαρυγαῖς ὁ χρυσός,
____ ὑψιδαιδάλτων τριπόδων σταθέντων
πάροιθε ναοῦ, τόθι μέγι[στ]ον ἄλσος
20 Φοίβου παρὰ Κασταλίας [ῥ]εέθ᾽ροις
Δελφοὶ διέπουσι. θεὸν θ[εό]ν τις
____ ἀγ᾽λαϊζέθὼ γὰρ ἄριστος [ὄ]λβων·
ἐπεί ποτε καὶ δαμασίπ[π]ου
Λυδίας ἀρχαγέταν,
25 εὖτε τὰν πεπ᾽[ρωμέναν
26   Ζηνὸς τελέ[σσαντος κρί]σιν
Σάρδιες Περσᾶ[ν ἁλίσκοντο στρ]ατῶι,
)____ Κροῖσον ὁ χ᾽ρυσά[ορος
Γ′   φύλαξ᾽ Ἀπόλλων. [ὁ δ᾽ ἐς] ἄελπτον ἆμαρ
30 μ[ο]λὼν πολυδ[άκ᾽ρυο]ν οὐκ ἔμελλε
μίμνειν ἔτι δ[ουλοσύ]ι αν, πυρὰν δὲ
____ χαλκ[ο]τειχέος π[ροπάροι]θεν αὐ[λᾶς
ναήσατ᾽, ἔνθα σὺ[ν ἀλόχωι] τε κεδ᾽[νᾶι
σὺν εὐπλοκάμοι[ς τ᾽] ἐπέβαιν᾽ ἄλα[στον
35 θ]υ[γ]ατ᾽ράσι δυρομέναις· χέρας δ᾽ [ἐς
αἰ]πὺν αἰθέρα σ[φ]ετέρας ἀείρας
γέ]γ[ω]νεν· „ὑπέρ[βι]ε δαῖμον,
πο]ῦ θεῶν ἐστι[ν] χάρις;
πο]ῦ δὲ Λατοίδ[ας] ἄναξ;
40   ἔρρουσ]ιν Ἀλυά[τ]τα δόμοι
_◡_×_◡_×] μυρίων
)____ _◡_×_◡_]ν.
Δ′   ×_͜ω×͜ω◡_◡]ν ἄστυ,
ἐρεύθεται αἵματι χρυσο]δίνας
45 Πακτωλός, ἀ[ε]ικελίως γυνα[ῖ]κες
ἐξ ἐϋκτίτων μεγάρων ἄγονται·
____ τὰ πρόσθεν [ἐχ]θρὰ φίλα· θανεῖν γλύκιστον.‟
48 τόσ᾽ εἶπε, καὶ ἁβ᾽[ρο]βάταν κ[έλε]υσεν
ἅπτειν ξύλινον δόμον. ἔκ᾽[λα]γον δὲ
50   παρθένοι, φίλας τ᾽ ἀνὰ ματρὶ χεῖρας
ἔβαλλον· ὁ γὰρ προφανὴς θνα-
τοῖσιν ἔχθιστος φόνων·
ἀλλ᾽ ἐπεὶ δεινο[ῦ π]υρὸς
λαμπρὸν διάϊ[σσεν μέ]ιος,
55 Ζεὺς ἐπιστάσας [μελαγκευ]θὲς νέφος
)____ σβέννυεν ξανθὰ[ν φλόγα.

E′   ἄπιστον οὐδέν, ὅ τι ϑ[εῶν μέ]ριμνα
      τεύχει· τότε Δαλογενὴ[ς Ἀπό]λλων
      φέρων ἐς Ὑπερβορέο[υς γ]έροντα
60   σὺν τανισφύροις κατ[έν]ασσε κούραις
      δι᾽ εὐσέβειαν, ὅτι μέ[γιστα] ϑνατῶν
      ἐς ἀγαϑέαν ⟨ἀν⟩έπεμψε Π[υϑ]ώ.
      ὅσο[ι] ⟨γε⟩ μὲν Ἑλλάδ᾽ ἔχουσιν, [ο]ὔτι[ς,
      ὦ μεγαίνητε̄ Ἱέρων, ϑελήσει
65 φάμ]εν σέο πλείονα χρυσὸν
      Λοξί]ᾱι πέμψαι βροτῶν.
      εὖ λέₗγειν πάρεστιν, ὅσ-
      τις μ]ὴ φϑόνωι πιαίνεται,
      . . . . .]λη φίλιππον ἄνδρ᾽ ἀ[ρ]ήϊον
)70 . . . .]ίου σκᾱπτρ[ο]ν Διό[ς]

F′   ἰοπ|λό]κων τε μέρο[ς ἔχοντ]α Μουσᾶν·
72 . . . .]μαλέαι ποτ[ὲ . . . . . .].᾽ιων
  . . . .]νος ἐφάμερον α[. . . . . .]·
      . . . .]ᾳ σκοπεῖς· βραχ[ύς ἐστιν αἰών·
75 πτεₗρ]όεσσα δ᾽ ἐλπὶς ὑπ[◡◡_ν]όημαₗ
      ἐφαμ]ερίων· ὁ δ᾽ ἄναξ [Ἀπόλλων
      . . . . .].᾽λος εἶπε Φέρη[τος υἷι·
      „ϑνατὸν εὖντα χρὴ διδύμους ἀέξειν
      γνώμας, ὅτι τ᾽ αὔριον ὄψεαι
80   μοῦνον ἁλίου φάος,
      χὤτι πεντήκοντ᾽ ἔτεα
      ζωὰν βαϑύπ|λουτον τελεῖς.
      ὅσια δρῶν εὔφραινε ϑυμόν· τοῦτο γὰρ
) κερδέων ὑπέρτατον."

Z′ 85 φρονέοντι συνετὰ γαρύω· βαϑὺς μέν
      αἰϑὴρ ἀμίαντος· ὕδωρ δὲ πόντου
      οὐ σάπεται· εὐφροσύνα δ᾽ ὁ χρυσός·
      ἀνδρὶ δ᾽ οὐ θέμις, πολιὸν π[αρ]έντα
      γῆρας, ϑάλ[εια]ν αὖτις ἀγκομίσσαι
90 ἥβαν. ἀρετᾱ[ς γε μ]ὲν οὐ μινύϑει
      βροτῶν ἅμα σ[ώμ]ατι φέγγος, ἀλλὰ
      Μοῦσά νιν τρ[έφει.] Ἱέρων, σὺ δ᾽ ὄλβον
      κάλλιστ᾽ ἐπεδ[είξ]αο ϑνατοῖς
      ἄνθεα· π|ράξα[ντι] δ᾽ εὖ
95 οὐ φέρει κόσμ[ον σι]ω-
      πά· σὺν δ᾽ ἀλαϑ[είᾱι] καλῶν
      καὶ μελιγ|λώσσου τις ὑμνήσει χάριν
      Κηΐας ἀηδόνος.

1 str.   Sing the mistress of fruitful Sicily, sing
           Demeter and Kore, violet-crowned,
           and, sweet patroness Klio, sing too
               of Hieron's swift Olympic team!

ant.   They ran, and Aglaia and glorious Victory
           paced beside them; there by the broad-swirling
           Alpheus they fixed for Deinomenes' son
               bliss and the right to wear a crown.

ep.   Voices cried from the gathered crowd:
               "Ah, thrice-bless'd the man
           who holds as his portion from Zeus
               the prize of broadest rule among Greeks
           and knows not to hide his towered wealth
               in black-veiling shadow!"

2 str.   Altars bloom with the blood of beasts;
           streets that love strangers bloom with men;
           gleams of glistening gold escape
               from tripods supremely wrought and set

ant.   facing a temple where, in Phoebus' grove
           close by the rippling Castalian spring,
           Delphians celebrate. It is god,
               god one must praise, for that is the best of wealth!

ep.   So it was long ago with the lord
               of Lydia's horse: when,
           because of the fated and finished
               judgment of Zeus, the city of Sardis fell
           to Persia's attacking horde, then
               Croesus was saved by the gold-armed

3 str.   god, Apollo. Entered upon the day
           no one expects, he chose not to wait
           for tearful slavery but ordered that
               before his bronze-walled court

ant.   a pyre be built. There, with his worthy wife
           and his long-tressed girls who didn't forget
           to weep, he went up, lifted
               his hands to the steep air

ep.   and cried out, "O proud Spirit, where
           now are the gracious thanks of god?
        Where is Leto's lordly son now?
           The house of Alyattes has crumbled

4 str.   ... city,
        Pactolus' once-golden streams flow red
        and women of race are roughly pulled
           from magnificent halls, enslaved.

ant.   Detested, but now desired, death is most sweet."
        He spoke, and he ordered a slippered slave
        to kindle the wooden tower. Wails
           came from the girls; they cast their arms

ep.   round their mother (the worst death
           is immediate death) but then,
        just as the luminous force
           of fearsome flame leapt up, Zeus
        covered it over with black cloud
           and the gold-red fire was suppress'd.

5 str.   Nothing defies belief if care of the gods
        has contrived it: next Apollo, Delian-born,
        carried the old man off to Hyperborean lands,
           there to live with his light-limbed girls

ant.   because of actions of piety! He of all had made
        gifts the most splendid at Pythia's precinct.
        And no one of all who live in Greece, o
           laudable Hieron, now could boast

ep.   of sending more plentiful gold
           than you have sent to Loxias.
        Praise is at hand (unless a man
           has fattened himself upon envy)
        for here is a warlike equestrian lord,
           the rod of ruler Zeus,

6 str.   favored too by the purple-wreath'd Muse.
        Times past, you [raised a terrible fist]
        but now you seek a sufficient joy
           according to each day. Life is short;

ant.   hope enters on wings into the minds
              of ephemeral men. Lord Apollo himself
              in bucolic mood, spoke once to Pheres' son:
                 "Man, being subject to death, must

ep.   ever be of two minds: count tomorrow
                 the last day of your life,
              believe as well in fifty long years
                 of unplumbed wealth to come!
              Rejoice your heart with reverent deeds
                 for they bring the highest gain."

7 str.   Sung to the wise my song is plain.
              Deep air knows no taint; sea's
              brine cannot rot, yet gold is happiness.
                 No man, when grey old age

ant.   has come, may gather the flowers of youth
              again. The gleam of splendid deeds alone
              remains when the flesh grows dim, for
                 they are the Muse's care. Hieron, your

ep.   wealth you display among mortals in
                 its fairest bloom. Silence is no
              fit decoration for best success. Not for-
                 getting your deeds, men will sing this
              recompense offered you by the Cean
                 honey-tongued nightingale.

   Hieron was happy, but the occasion bristled with elements that might
seem to baffle the poet's faith in excellence of deed and justice of praise,
for Bacchylides had to hymn one of the richest and most unpopular men
of his time. Indeed, if Plutarch can be believed, Themistocles had tried
to get the other Greeks to burn down his tent when he came to Olympia
(*Them.* 25). Hieron was a great soldier, but he was also a cruel ruler
known for his greed, his luxury, and his sophisticated use of domestic
spies. Worse, perhaps, for the man who composed his Olympian ode,
was the fact that the victor did not drive his own team or even train his
own horses, but simply paid the bills. It was a flagrantly bought triumph that the poet had to praise, but Bacchylides produced for Hieron
an ode in which there is no bitterness, no hypocrisy, no cynicism, and
no reproach. With an idealism apparently undaunted, he searched as
usual for virtue and the answering touch of god, and gracefully managed
to find them, even in this somewhat tarnished victory.

The crown in a sense didn't really belong to Hieron, but the money that had bought it did, and instead of avoiding or disguising this plain truth, Bacchylides embraced it with audacious aplomb by making the victor's riches the open subject of his song. Hieron's wealth is treated exactly as another victor's athletic success might have been, for it is evoked as actuality, generalized with gnomes, probed for inner excellence, rendered dynamic by means of myth, and displayed in its finest outward form, which of course is gold. For the man of gold the poet sang a golden song, saying in language that is charmingly easy that though mortals may possess or give away golden objects (65; cf. 17), gold is a part of nature (a river may run with it, 44), one of the enduring elements of creation (along with air and water, 87), and an attribute of god (28). In its glancing fashion the song addresses more difficult matters as well—the relation between gold and two sorts of wealth, material (*ploutos*, 13; cf. 82) and spiritual (*olbos, -ios*, 8, 22, 92), and also the connection between gold and happiness (83, 87). Still on this level of wise banality the ode asserts that gold at its best is gold that is brilliantly used; it must be made to shine (as it does in line 17; cf. the negative statement at 13–14), and the song itself becomes a demonstration by placing its metallic subject in a verbal setting that is full of light and sparkling surfaces. A great fire is kindled, and three swirling streams (Alpheus, Castalia, and Pactolus) seem to increase the general glitter of the images so that at the poem's end only brightness remains. Its gold has been transformed by a kind of reverse alchemy, and what entered the song in a solid state—piled up (8) or cast into tangible items of sacred furniture (18)—emerges from it as a light (91) that flowers from the bliss of fair deeds (94).[2]

This act of transubstantiation is the peculiar achievement of Ode 3, but the poet also meets all of the traditional epinician demands with a fine economy. The song opens with a dedication to Demeter and Kore, so that its hymning of Hieron shall not be misunderstood in heaven. Next, it picks out the daimonic quality of the contest with a phrase that sets the goddesses Nike and Aglaia running beside Hieron's winning team (5–6), and then it completes the disembodiment of the actual victory with a reference to the crown that is its emblem (8). The immortal instant is now ready for translation to the present, and this is done with a bit of open drama as the chorus suddenly breaks out of its own narrative, takes a role, and makes its voice the voices of the spectators at Olympia. The shout that went up there is reshouted now in the banquet hall at Syracuse and so, already at line 10, the guests are given direct participation in Hieron's victory. Nevertheless, this is all mere prelude to what Bacchylides means to do, and it is exactly at this point that he introduces the real matter of his song, for he makes the chorus prolong the triumphal shout with words that were never heard in the dust and sweat of Olympia. "Thrice-blessed," yes, but the men on the bleachers never went on with, "the man . . . who knows that no black veil should shadow his towering wealth"!

Bacchylides means to show that there is a vital form of virtue at work within Hieron's wealth, and he wisely makes his claim early, in the sacred context of this extended victory cry. Hieron is thrice-blessed because he is victor, because his excessive power comes from Zeus, and because he knows the best way to treat his equally excessive wealth; he knows how to burnish his gold with pious good fortune. Before there is time for the listener to resist this suggestion in any way, the song rushes on to make this active virtue of wealth-unveiled one more part of the spectator's direct experience, just as in the previous lines it has made the victory present to him. The choral imitation of the Olympic cry ends at a stanza break (14), and when the singers launch into their next phrases there is a moment of ambiguity, like the one we observed in the Delian paean when the spectator did not know whether he was on Delos or out in the Cretan Sea. Here, at line 15 of Ode 3, we might still be at Olympia in the stadium, or we might have returned to Syracuse, as the new triad begins, and so we hold ourselves tentatively in both places during the brief strophe, only to discover from the antistrophe that the scene in fact has shifted to an unexpected, phantasmagorical Delphi. Not until the chorus sings the words "Phoebus" (20), "Castalia" (20), and "Delphi" (21) does the poetic location become clear—not until then does the gold that is so bright localize itself and begin to decorate Apollo's far-away Pythian shrine.[3] The effect is like that of montage in film, for it makes the three places momentarily one, while it wraps them all in the teeming[4] splendor of the victor's wealth.

But why Delphi? Why does this Olympian ode sing Apollo more extensively than it does Zeus, just as it sings wealth more extensively than it does victory? Apollo, of course, is a golden god, and Apollo has been particularly friendly to Hieron. "Still does he love the city of Syracuse, our golden-haired Apollo! Still does he cherish its founder, Hieron!"—so Bacchylides had sung in Ode 4 when a Pythian victory followed upon an Olympian defeat. These are contributing causes, but the real reason for this curious swerve in divine emphasis seems to lie in Bacchylides' single-minded attention to his one true subject, for it was at Delphi that Hieron's wealth could be seen, indeed counted up, by all. There it stood, in the form of dedications, two tripods to Gelo's one, a perfect example of *ploutos* transformed into *chrysos*[5] so that its heaped-up substance should not remain in shadow (13; cf. 17). The pair were conspicuously placed on the Syracusan terrace at Delphi, outshining every other dedication as they magnified Apollo with their brilliance. In them inert metallic wealth had become active, and since, in theory at least, all Syracusans shared in this use of gold to worship god,[6] Hieron's wealthy deed was shared by all. It even became something that ordinary people could emulate on a less magnificent scale, and to drive this point home Bacchylides makes the Delphian passage end with a general exhortation directed to every mortal man (21–22): "It is god, god one must praise, for that is best wealth."

In this first short section of his song Bacchylides has done all he can to lend nonsubstantiality to the substantial wealth of Hieron, while he simultaneously fixes gold as a part of nature. The metallic tripods are apprehended as burning, glittering light (17) in a Delphi identified by water (20), and they seem almost to flower forth in the grove where finite ritual actions are said to "teem" or "bloom" (15, 17). Nevertheless, once these bright images have flashed by, the spectator is still in possession of a leaden truth, for he knows that Hieron did not raise the cattle of his sacrifices or work the gold of his offerings, any more than he trained or drove his winning team of horses. With all his light effects and his cinematic élan, the poet has only progressed from praise of a bought victory to praise of bought devotions, as he moves into his second triad. In the stanzas that follow, however, he makes use of a chorally revived fiction in order to reconstitute the true excellence of his present case. Choosing Hieron's greatest rival in the glorification of the Delphian shrine, and taking advantage of an illuminating pun,[7] he presents the figure of Creosus (a man whose name sounds like the word for gold, *chrysos*) and uses him as a commentary upon the wealth and the present good fortune of Hieron.

Croesus and Hieron occupy the eastern and western extremities of the Hellenic world, as if to prove the universality of the truth they embody. Both are preeminent in wealth and power, both are soldiers, both are rulers of horse-loving peoples, and both are great religious donors, known for their gifts to Apollo. And Bacchylides extends the parallel, for the first thing the song says about the Lydian king is that he stands at a moment of Zeusian judgment, just as one does at the Olympic games; with a bit of secondary word-play this moment is called a *krisis* (26). Zeus is judge, as he is also at Olympia, but the contest over Sardis is unlike Hieron's Olympic contest, because Croesus has just been defeated. Nevertheless, it is announced at the outset of this "mythic" example[8] that what we are to see is how Apollo protected this loser, and so we know that a reversal is to come. Indeed, the poet's skill shapes this programmatic statement so that Croesus' seemingly golden name and Apollo's truly golden sword shall stand side by side in playful proof of their relationship: *Kroison ho chrysaoros phylax' Apollōn* (28–29).

Croesus builds himself a high funeral pyre and as he mounts upon it with his wife and his lachrymose daughters[9] the chorus for a second time takes up a dramatic role, using its voice this time to imitate that of the Lydian king as he speaks his final words. A few moments ago they cried out, as the throng at Olympia, addressing a victorious mortal almost as if he were a god, but now they balance those dangerous phrases by taking on the persona of a defeated man and calling out to a daimonic force with a full admission of mortal weakness and incapacity (37). As a result of this echoing structure, the proud invocation to Hieron—*triseudaimōn anēr!*—is now replaced and reversed by a helpless call from Croesus—*hyperbie daimōn!* Where the earlier bit of direct speech described the vast, Zeus-given power of Hieron (11 ff.), this one depicts the dissolution of a similar worldly power (40 ff.) and the apparent withdrawal of divine favor. "Where is Apollo?" Croesus asks,[10] for his city has fallen, his palace is in ruins, the gold-swirling waters of Pactolus are red with blood, and freeborn Lydian women are led away as slaves. Disorder has reached such a pitch that the most hated event of all, death, seems sweet[11] and so, asking nothing of the god whom he has indirectly called to witness, Croesus commands a handsome page to light the funeral fire. The girls recognize this move with louder cries, finding this conspicuous death the worst of all,[12] but the force of the flame begins to rush up through the wooden structure. Then comes a double miracle. Zeus squelches the flame with a dark raincloud, after which—and here a swift gnomic interruption like an indrawn breath marks the wonder of it (57; cf. the parallel labeling of a miraculous moment at 17.117)—Apollo simply lifts the whole group from their smoldering pyre in a multiple assumption.[13] When he sets them down again in a heavenly land of quasi-immortality,[14] though the old man is still old, the girls have stopped crying and are remarkable now for the fineness of their ankles (60). And an urgent phrase in enjambement insists that the whole wonderful event has come about "through piety" (61), because Croesus had given more grandly at Delphi than any other man.

There the "mythic" section ends, and one naturally asks just how the poem's praise of wealth and power has been clarified by this substitution of a Croesus for a Hieron. Initially the fiction has said (with a picture instead of a gnome) that fortune's overturn strikes all alike, that a great army may know defeat, a great king may submit to capture, and a great city suffer total destruction. These are standard sage observations and essential, if the poem's praise of high success is to avoid offending gods and men. Nevertheless, the climax of the Lydian story as Bacchylides tells it reverses this negative reminder with an overturn of the opposite, happiest kind. (This overturn is verbally promised by the word *phylax* in 1.29 and it also appears emblematically in the figure of the elegant page, for he belongs to a mask, not to a tragedy.)[15] At the end of the tale Bacchylides' Croesus gains a blissful version of immortality, but it is not his reward that is here the subject of full poetic emphasis, any more than his earlier errors were. What the poet *has* chosen for full depiction is instead a single hybrid action of the king's: the moment he reconstructs is the one in which Croesus fixes his own death and calls upon Apollo to watch his brilliant demise. This deed of mingled pride and resignation must be the one that is meant to illuminate Hieron's deed of victory, and on the human level it places its emphasis upon the king's decision. At the same time, however, the man on the pyre is displayed like an emblem, which means that the design of the scene is as important for this song as its psychic quality is.

The king whose name sounds like gold steps into fire; Zeus applies water; Apollo carries him off to a place where no one dies. The event is mysteriously suggestive, for a pair of divine smiths have made an eternally happy golden man, as they might have done on Lemnos. It is morally instructive, as well, since a man has brought the rough gold of his virtue to the purifying fire[16] of action and that virtue, with the water of god's help, has been changed into permanent fame. Considered ethically, the episode shows a Croesus who has submitted to a divine decision made manifest in contest and, having lost his wealth, has taken his life and his kingliness—all he has left—and made of them a final conspicuous offering to the powers that rule him. His action recapitulates others that have been characteristic of his life, and it provokes an instantaneous reversal from disfavor to miraculous benefaction on the part of heaven. Translated into the language of the games, Croesus would seem to figure the contestant in the moment that he enters the field, deciding to offer himself conspicuously to gods who may already have arranged for his defeat, but glorifying them nonetheless with the expense of his whole spirit. Victory, won with such consciousness of god, is like being whisked away to the Hyperboreans, but it comes only when a man has put his entire substance—his "gold"—into the agonistic fire. Above all, the Croesus stanzas show a man who knows, even in defeat, how to keep shadow from his possessions. Croesus substitutes the brightness of fire for that of his lost gold and uses it as a means of communicating (though in bitterness) with god. The gods then do what men must not do, darkening the temporary flame of his offering[17] and substituting for it the lasting brilliance of their miracle.

These and many other glosses can be made upon the tableau of Croesus on his pyre, for an image, as Ezra Pound once said, is a "luminous node of meaning." This one, in fact, is so protean and so filled with power that it might easily have made of Ode 3 a Croesus poem instead of a victory song for Hieron. The scene of the miracle has been given a sensual reality that nothing else in the poem has; the bronze court, the

pretty page, the wooden structure, and the weeping girls have been revived and brought into the present performance by a poetic miracle that
rivals that of Apollo in carrying them off again. Now, however, this
mythic energy from the past must be used to further the largest purpose
of the song, and its exploitation is no easy affair, for Bacchylides has to
find and fix the power of his wonderful cipher without destroying either
its vitality or its mysterious complexity. Having described Croesus' almost defiant self-immolation, he cannot say, "and this is exactly what
Hieron has done," because of course it is not. Nor can he spell out a general everyday moral of the "so should we all do" sort, for it is extremely
hard to apply the gold-flowing Pactolus, the crumbling palaces, and the
flaming pyre to any crisis in ordinary life. Furthermore, if the poet
should suggest that his tale is allegory, he would betray all the bizarre
and fabulous effects that he himself has created, all the magic reality that
he has given to this moment. Any banalization of his scene will break its
spell and cause his song to end in anticlimax, and yet the king and his
pyre must somehow be applied to the present situation. These were the
problems that faced Bacchylides as soon as he abandoned his fire-lit
Sardis, and he solved them neatly by bringing on a god.

The formal link between the "mythic" and the present moments is
characteristically made of gold—gold used in gestures of worship and
specifically in gifts made at Delphi—for it is in their golden dedications
that Croesus and Hieron are ostensibly alike (61 ff.).[18] This, however,
only brings about a return to the golden tripods that have already spar-
kled out from the second strophe. Gold in a hard metallic form is precisely what the poem would leave behind and so, after a swift and gnomic sketch of Hieron's triple nature (he is warrior, ruler, and one who
knows the arts),[19] the chorus suddenly delivers the speech that Apollo
once made to Admetus, in long-ago, faraway Thessaly.

For a third time the poet makes use of direct discourse, so that Apollo
now speaks with the immediacy of the Olympic victory cry and the last
earthly words of Croesus. The god's voice comes from a scene that has
nothing to do with either Hieron or Lydia and yet, following as it does
upon the Lydian king's superb question, it gains a kind of formal relevance. "Where is Apollo?" Croesus asked, and within that story the god
responded with a saving epiphany; now, however, the same god answers
vocally, speaking from another place, another time, and another story altogether. The shout of the crowd at Olympia had addressed a victorious
man as if he were a god, calling him *triseudaimōn*, then the prayer of
Croesus had transferred this reverential address to a god who was *hyperbie daimōn*, and now Apollo completes this thorough neutralization
of the victor's *makarismos* by describing man as subject to death—
thnaton eunta, "being mortal," is how he begins (78).

Apollo is speaking across the intervening stanzas to Croesus, and speaking as well to Hieron, but within his own fiction he is addressing his mortal friend Admetus, and so the figure of this Thessalian hero now enters the song to add a third aspect to its composite victor-king. When Apollo knew him, Admetus was not an old man like the other two, nor was he yet a tremendously wealthy one, and his prime virtue was in no way restricted to the rich, for instead of offering gold at Delphi he offered hospitality at home. His reward too was one that the commonest man could understand, for it was not a metaphysical trip to Never Never Land but a splendidly practical multiplication of flocks and fields, a princess for a bride, an addition to his lifespan, and a god for his good friend. Admetus' recompense is not directly referred to in this song, but it lives in the "fifty years of richly blessed life"[20] that Apollo mentions, and so it becomes a mundane alternative to the unimaginable bliss of Hyperborean lands or the unique exaltation of wearing a second Olympic crown.

Admetus is a thoroughly mythic figure as, of course, Croesus is not, and what is more he is quite invisible here, but he nevertheless serves to secularize and almost democratize the poem's vision of wealth turned into piety. Admetus is to Croesus and Hieron as nobleman is to king or tyrant, and for the nobles who listen to this song he is one of themselves—a man who loved the banquet's good cheer. In consequence, Apollo's advice to him seems to be offered to every present guest, and through it Hieron's success is made available to all.[21] The Croesus story has proved that a single extraordinary moment could be one of simultaneous defeat and victory, and now Apollo transposes this statement into another mode by insisting that every ordinary moment is simultaneously one of life and death. Every action must be made confidently, as if it were the prelude to good things to come, and magnificently, as if it were one's last, and from this it follows that every action, by recognizing death, will recognize the power of god both as benefactor and as witness. Such is the general tenor of Apollo's teaching, but we notice that this elevation of every moment of life to the status of high drama is accompanied by the unobtrusive introduction of a new notion, that of pleasure.[22] For the first time a sung phrase suggests the possibility of mortal joy (*euphraine thymon*, 83) and it is this humane and Hellenic notion that finally allows Bacchylides' song to move on strongly past its evocation of the suffering Lydian king.

The example of Admetus makes the whole song more available, and the Thessalian is also instrumental in the shift that Bacchylides now engineers from concepts of literal, material riches to the idea of a psychic wealth that is a richness of contentment. It is obvious that the life of "unplumbed wealth" (82) is a life of healthy children, good harvests, and fair fame—a life rich in delights of the kind that Apollo gave to Admetus—and this sense is confirmed when Apollo turns to his final point. Admetus will know pleasure, and it is important that he should know it in its highest form. The pleasure of reverent deeds, says the god, is wealth of a supreme sort, "of all profits the highest" (84). In the same triadic position, the chorus has already produced its first direct reference to wealth ("he knows . . . no veil . . . should shadow wealth," end of first epode); in antistrophe 2 it has also announced (with a superlative like the one that Apollo now uses) the conclusion to be drawn from the glitter of Delphic tripods: "It is god, god one must praise for that is best wealth." When those two passages are heard simultaneously with the present one, the full message of the three wealth statements is clear: "Best wealth equals best reverence equals best pleasure, and this three-in-one superlative is to be found where a man makes a fair show of the riches that he has, in confident tomorrowless rejoicings that are a praise of god." Those who dine with Hieron today are thus commanded by a divinity to do as Admetus did when he dined with Apollo in that other time, or as Hieron did when he entered a chariot team at Olympia—for pleasure (like Croesus' suffering) can be converted into a brilliant gift for god.

Apollo's words suggest the familiar Greek doctrine of living for the day, which was a form of piety open to the very poor and the very rich as well, as Bacchylides reminded us by praising Hieron as one who understood the ephemeral quality of life (73). The pleasures of the day are available to any man who is wise (cf. the *phroneonti* at 1.85),[23] and indeed the leveling of this gnomic way of thinking might seem to have gone too far at this point, since one could argue from Apollo's counsel that a banqueteer's libation, offered in joyous piety, comes to the same thing as one of Hieron's golden offerings. The notion of joy was needed to correct the too Oriental quality of Croesus' fiery self-destruction. In addition, it was an essential element in the piety of the games, since they were festivals in which strong and joyous gods chose favorites among strong and joyous men. For both of these reasons the idea of pleasure has been introduced, but the poet will now have to put even pleasure in its place if Hieron is to be elevated to his proper victorious position above every one of his subjects and his guests. And so, in the last triad of his ode, Bacchylides sorts back through all the concepts that he has proposed and evaluates them according to a standard that is the direct opposite of ephemerality. Where in all of this does anything permanent lie?

The last triad answers this question with what has often been called a tissue of commonplaces. Old sayings, however, are where truth lives, and Bacchylides here manipulates his gnomes like parts of speech, constructing a language that is both popular and elegant as the medium for conclusions that are inarguable precisely because of their familiarity. He begins with a pared-down priamel that looks for the best of all the elements and he produces gold as its final term,[24] giving it extra value by introducing the tangential notion of pleasure. Air and water are immutable but gold alone, in addition to being changeless, can transform a man's life by bringing him joy.[25] This in a sense is what the poem has said about the gold of Croesus and Hieron and whatever similar wealth an ordinary man may have: well used, it has been seen to bring the joy of victory, the joy of escape, and the joy of entertaining gods. There is, however, no pause here; instead, the newly introduced idea is at once put through the same kind of test as the poet glances at a second priamel, one that searches for the best of joys. Using his initial value, permanence, as his continuing measure, he swiftly passes over all mortal pleasures as worthless because they all are subject to decay. Joys bought with gold, youth, even beauty or love (one or the other had a place in the regular versions of this sequence and will have been understood here), disappear or are tainted as men move toward the death that Apollo told us always to remember. Consequently the poet caps his sequence, as wise men before him had done, with another sort of human experience. Virtue alone resists the body's diminishment, virtue as it is distilled in the accomplishment of a splendid action, then collected and cherished in song.

In the Croesus tale it was gold that influenced the two gods to pit heavenly water against mortal fire and then to defy air by carrying human bodies through it. In the Thessalian story, Admetus and Apollo shared the joys of love and youth, but it was Admetus' virtue of hospitality that brought rewards, among them the bit of advice repeated in the present song. All this has been restated in the two priamels which propose two triangles with gold at the apex of one, virtuous deeds at the apex of the other. The schematic form of the priamel has in fact made the two figures congruent, and all that remains is to place Hieron now at the apex of this song, a Hieron who uncovers the joy of metallic gold while he also shows forth the pleasures it can create—horsemanship, hospitality,[26] and the best pleasure of piety. Hieron has left love and youth behind, but in submitting himself to the Olympic judgment of Zeus he has changed gold and pleasure into the virtue of active pious glorification of god. The fire of contest has purified his wealth and turned it into pure light (*pheggos*, 91) and in this very moment the Muse is tending it as if it were a plant that blooms (the sense is contained in *trephei*, 92, in conjunction with the *anthea* of 94, which echo the *bruei* of Delphi in festival at 15–16, the flower of youth at 89, perhaps even the flower crowns of Kore, 2, and the Muse, 79).

The Cean nightingale that sings this virtuous show of wealth into a Hyperborean state of immortality is the agent of the Muse. He is proud to be doing her work, and so he should be,[27] for his unsilent, unforgetting song—a repayment,[28] a gesture of gratitude, and a graceful act all in one (*charis*, 97)[29]—has accompanied the transformation of gold into light through all its mysterious phases. What begins as sordid riches becomes, under the influence of this music, a strange alloy of gold, fire, water, light, and bloom, and it ends as the enduring possession of Hieron.

6. THE CUT OF THE MYTH

The many singers of an epinician ode acted for the victor when they offered his moment of glory to his many guests. They also acted for those guests, however, and for the whole aristocratic community, when they returned an answering gift of unforgetful praise, and it is time now to think more about this second choral function. The idea that song conferred a kind of immortality was a commonplace even in Homer's time (see, for example, *Od.* 2.203), but the fact was that a victory ode could never have the same kind of immortalizing power that the epic poems had. The point about an epic, after all, was that it would be repeated. The bard who recited it would recite it again, elsewhere, and others would take his lines and half-lines and chant them over in their own fashion, in later generations, everywhere in the Greek-speaking world. In this way epic could literally keep a man's deeds alive in the mouth of posterity. A victory ode, on the other hand, was sounded out only in its one costly performance and was never produced again. A written text would be preserved, probably in the victor's family archives (probably too by the poet himself), but since these were compositions meant for many voices they could not live on in the repertoires of traveling bards or after-dinner performers.[1] Consequently it could not be said with accuracy that Pindar and Bacchylides kept a victor's name physically on men's tongues, as Homer had the name of Agamemnon, Mimnermus the name of Nanno, and Theognis that of his friend Kyrnos.

Clearly the *aletheia*—the not-being-forgotten—that was the gift of the epinician ode was something other than epic's straight preservation of noble actions in continuing song. On a mundane level, of course, the ode invited lesser expressions of praise, marking the victory as one to be cited whenever men sat remembering the prowess of famous boxers or runners or charioteers. That, however, was only fitful gossip, whereas the epinician poets promised to confer an almost supernatural fame that could reach even the dead in their graves (P. O. 14.20 ff.; cf. N. 4.85–88). On an opposite, philosophical level the victory song touched eternity by imitating the songs that the Muses sang, and to the degree that it approached abstract perfection the ode itself would partake directly of immortality. That, however, is not the same thing as endowing its victor with lasting repute among men, which was what the poets promised with phrases like Pindar's near the beginning of *Nemea* 4: "Words live longer than deeds when a tongue that the Graces favor draws them from a deep heart."[2] No, it was on a third human but magical level that the single performance achieved a gesture of remembrance that would operate forever.

The many voices, hands, and feet that reinforced each other of a necessity ritualized the epinician performance and liberated it from the confinement of the unique. The performers danced the moment of victory into the present moment of celebration, thus removing that celebration from the pressure of the causal and the chronological. Daimonic success-magic that had passed from god to crown to victor in the past was today applied to enacted praise, and in this way the report of an athletic deed became almost indistinguishable from the sung commentary that accompanied acts of cult, since it stretched, like sacred song, forward and backward in time. Choral praise was in this sense magical, even in a minimal production, and in the grander performances its power was still greater, for there the singers went further and imitated the sacred choruses in their dynamic employment of myth. The religious singers, instead of narrating whole tales, reconstituted isolated scraps of mythic experience to make them bear upon the present, and the epinician chorus often did exactly the same. The poet would choose a particular fabled moment, have it danced into vitality, and then cause it to invade the simpler mixture of victory moment with immediate festival, so that three sorts of time were superimposed. In this way, the acts of victors in contest and the acts of dancers in praise were mingled and confounded with acts of a Pelops or acts of a Heracles, and in consequence all partook of the eternal *aletheia* that attached to the ceaselessly repeated myths.

This process of remembrance by association can be observed by default in Ode 3 of Bacchylides, where the fiction could *not* really bestow unforgetfulness because it was not really mythical. The tale of an actual king had been chosen, in that special instance, not because it could lead the way to *aletheia* but instead because of the king's name and the king's gold. Naturally, the poet did all he could to contrive a sort of myth for Croesus, appealing to a "memory" of him that he pretended lived in the audience's mind. The best he could do, however, was to give the Lydian king a touch of the legendary and as a result Ode 3 is an intellectual, but not a magical success. Croesus succeeds as a cipher because his figure says something about wealth, but he does not succeed as a conductor of immortal fame, for the simple reason that his own is merely historical. His actuality limits him and, paradoxically, he has less vitality and less complexity than a Cadmus or a Peleus would have shown. They, or any of the legion of fully mythic figures like them, could by contrast bring into a victory ode the very substance of Memory because myth, being the property of Mnemosyne, defied envy, forgetfulness, silence, blame, and all the other enemies of praise. It is not hard, then, to see why Croesus remains as a single unrepeated experiment in epinician historicity[3] and why all the other major odes evoke moments from the experience of heroes or divinities.

Obviously when Bacchylides or any other poet decided to lend his victory permanence by giving it a mythic familiar, his success depended first of all upon his choice of a fiction. For aesthetic reasons, the images, the ethical questions, and the deep conceptual suggestions that entered with each fabulous figure had to be both relevant and suitable. On another level, the magical imposition of one moment upon others would proceed most effectively if there were some fundamental kinship between the shape of the mythic event and the shape of the present success or its celebration. Thus the general nature of the mythic material and also the pattern of the particular swatch that was cut had both to be considered, as well as the means for joining it to the whole fabric of the ode, and it is Bacchylides' special manner of choosing, shaping, and attaching that I want to consider next.

To a modern, the battlefield deeds of the epic heroes might seem to provide the best doublets for athletic victories, but the epinician poets, though they did use such materials, did not use them regularly. Homer had rationalized and humanized the sagas, expurgating the miraculous and grotesque wherever possible, dissipating wonder in explanation and dissolving what was strange in a flood of everyday detail. Most of the Trojan fictions had been rendered at least as secular as the tale of Croesus, and for many of their heroes there was a well-established report of death. In consequence the fame of these warriors had become finite and natural; one admired them for their achievements and strength, but not as vessels in which a supernatural force had been conveyed to the surface of the earth. Fortunately, however, while this one branch of Greek art was at work to reduce the daimonic factor in the national legends, others maintained the irrational motifs that had proliferated in folk-tales in spite of the epic austerity.[4] Vase painters, metal workers, and temple sculptors made use of more popular materials and, in the realm of words, the public choral performances made reference to en-

chantments, tokens, monsters, and minor sorceries. Because of their relative brevity and their licensed incoherence, such productions could
lead their spectators to a marvel—a *thauma* like Theseus' appearance
from the sea—and abruptly abandon them there.[5] With no explanation,
the wonder would keep its full impact, and this was the effect that the
epinician needed. Wonders and miracles had their own intrinsic fame,
the notoriety of the impossible, and when a victory was associated with
an event that was both mythic and frankly marvelous, it was doubly assured of the quality of being unforgettable.

An awesome moment that strained rational belief was thus the deepest requirement for an epinician myth; a more superficial but equally
essential one was that the fiction should show some structural or imagistic congruity with the occasion of victory. This element of congruity,
however, has often been misunderstood. Critics have assumed that the
myth was supposed to be literally connected, in its original form, with
the actuality of victory and then, finding that poets chose tales of every
sort, they have complained. In this they have been led astray by the fact
that Pindar and Bacchylides did sometimes choose stories from the legends of the victor's family and city, or from the aetiological myths about
the founding of the festival where he won his crown. They did also
sometimes choose a tale in which a mythic hero simply won a victory,
thus establishing an almost geometric congruency of pattern. Local materials were, however, too frequently tedious and obscure (see Appendix), and imposing one contest upon another was apt to lead to effects
that were tautological and unilluminating, particularly to the eye of a
poet who meant to mystify and idealize the actual athletic event. For
these reasons Pindar and Bacchylides very often moved off into fictions
that had no immediate connection with either victor or victory, and even
when they seemed to retreat to the obvious choice, a complicated purpose usually lurked behind the appearance of arcane mythic simplicity.

Such is the case with Bacchylides' Ode 13, which happens to be his
earliest datable poem and comes from the year 485.[6] Here the selection
of fictions is almost ostentatiously naive, for a present Nemean victory
in wrestling is attached to Heracles' original, aetiological victory over
the Nemean lion, and a visible Aeginetan victor is conflated with two
Aeginetans who battled at Troy. Both stories were exceedingly familiar:
the tale of Heracles was known from Hesiod (*Theog.* 327–332), the lion
had been a favorite with painters for more than a century,[7] and was
shown in a metope of the Athenian treasury at Delphi, while Ajax and
Achilles had been thoroughly sung by Homer. Nevertheless, if this in-
genuous choice of matter led any one of Bacchylides' listeners to expect
a like bluntness of manner, that man was soon astounded, for this is in
fact one of the poet's most sophisticated (and tortuous) exercises in the

art of praise. The opening is lost, so that for us the song begins at the end of its second strophe, at which point the chorus is imitating the voice of an unidentified creature who speaks prophetically (44 ff.):

11 ὔβ'ριος ὑψινόου
45 ____ παύσει δίκας θνατοῖσι κραίνων·
1 οἵαν τινὰ δύσλοφον ὠ-
μηστᾶι λέοντι
3 Περσείδας ἐφίησι
χεῖρα παντοίαισι τέχ'ναις·
50 οὐ γὰρ] δαμασίμβροτος αἴθων
6 χαλ]κὸς ἀπ'λάτου θέλει
χωρε]ῖν διὰ σώματος, ἐ-
(20) γ'νάμ]φθη δ' ὀπίσσω
9 φάσγα]νον· ἦ ποτέ φαμι
55 τᾶιδε] περὶ στεφάνοισι
11 παγκ]ρατίου πόνον Ἑλ-
____ λάνεσσι]ν ἱδρώεντ' ἔσεσθαι."
1 ἐκ τοῦ παρ]ὰ βωμὸν ἀριστάρχου Διός
Νίκας] φ[ε]ρ[ε]κυδέος ἀν-
60 στεφθε]ῖσιν ἄ[ν]θεα
61 4 χρυσέ]αν δόξαν πολύφαντον ἐν αἰ-
ῶνι] τ'ρέφει παύροις βροτῶν
(30) 6 α]ἰεί, καὶ ὅταν θανάτοιο
κῦάνεον νέφος καλύψηι, λείπεται
65 8 ἀθάνατον κλέος εὖ ἐρ-
____)___ χθέντος ἀσφαλεῖ σὺν αἴσαι.
Γ' 1 τῶν κα[ὶ σ]ὺ τυχὼν Νεμέαι,
Λάμπωνος υἱέ,
3 πανθαλέων στεφάνοισιν
70 ἀνθ]έ[ων] χαίταν [ἐρ]εφθείς
. . . . . .]πόλιν ὑψιάγυιαν
6 . . . . τε]ρψιμ[β]ρότων
(40) .[. . . . .] ἀβ[ροπν]όων
κώμ[ων] πατρ[ώια]ν
75 9 νᾶσο[ν], ὑπέρβι[ον] ἰσχύν
παμμαχίαν ἄνα φαίνων.
11 ὦ ποταμοῦ θύγατερ
____ δινᾶντος Αἴγιν' ἠπιόφ'ρον,
1 ἦ τοι μεγάλαν [Κρονίδας
80 ἔδωκε τιμάν
3 ἐν πάντεσσιν [ἀγῶσιν,
πυρσὸν ὡς Ἑλλ[ασι ‿ ⏑

(50) φαίνων· τό γε σὸν [κλέος αἰ]νεῖ
      6 καί τις ὑψαυχὴς κό‹ρα
85   __υυ_υυ‹ραν
86   πόδεσσι ταρφέως
      9 ἠΰτε νεβ'ρὸς ἀπεν[θής
        ἀνθεμόεντας ἐπ[' ὄχθους
      11 κοῦφα σὺν ἀγχιδόμ[οις
90   θρώισκουσ' ἀγακ'λειτα[ῖς ἑταίρα]ις·
      1 ταὶ δὲ στεφανωσάμε[ναι φοιν]ικέων
        ἀνθέων δόνακός τ' ἐ[πιχω-
(60)   ρίαν ἄθυρσιν
      4 παρθένοι μέλπουσι τ[........]ς, ὦ
95   δέσποινα παγξε[ίνου χθονός,
      6 Ἐν]δαῖδα τε ῥοδό[παχυν,
        ἅ το[..].' [..]ων ἔτι[κτε Πηλέα
      8 καὶ Τελαμ[ῶ]ι̯α [κρα]τ̯[α]ι̯[ὸν
)   Αἰακῶι μιχθεῖσ' ἐν εὐ[ναῖ·
Δ' 100 1 τῶν υἶας ἀερσιμάχ[ους,
        ταχύν τ' Ἀχιλλέα
      3 εὐειδέος τ' Ἐριβοίας
(70)   παῖδ' ὑπέρθυμον βοά[σω
        Αἴαντα σακεσφόρον ἥ[ρω,
105   6 ὅστ' ἐπὶ π'ρύμναι σταθ[εὶς
        ἔσχεν θρασυκάρδιον [ὁρ-
        μαίνοντα ν[ᾶας
      9 θεσπεσίωι πυ[ρὶ __
109   Ἕκτορα χαλ[κεομίτ'ρα]ν,
110 11 ὁππότε Πη[λεΐδας
        τρα[χ]εῖα̯ [Ἀτ'ρείδαισι μ]ᾶνιν
      1 ὠρίνατ[ο, Δαρδανίδας
(80)   τ' ἔλυσεν ἄ[τας·
      3 οἳ πρὶν μὲν [πολύπυργο]ν
115   Ἰλίου θαητὸν ἄστυ
        οὐ λεῖπον, ἀτυζόμενοι [δέ
      6 πτᾶσσον ὀξεῖαν μάχα[ν,
        εὖτ' ἐν πεδίωι κλονέω[ν
        μαίνοιτ' Ἀχιλλεύς,
120   9 λαοφόνον δόρυ σείων·
        ἀλλ' ὅτε δὴ πολέμοι[ο
      11 λῆξεν ἰοστεφάνο[υ
(90)   Νηρῆιδος ἀτ'ρόμητο[ς υἱός,
      1 ὥστ' ἐν κυανανθέϊ θ[υμὸν ἀνέρων
125   πόντωι Βορέας ὑπὸ κύ-
        μασιν δαΐζει,

4 νυκτὸς ἀντάσας ἀναπ[‿◡◡‿
    λῆξεν δὲ σὺν φαεσιμ[βρότωι
6 Ἀοῖ, στόρεσεν δέ τε πό[ντον
130   οὐρία· Νότου δὲ κόλπ[ωσαν πνοᾶι
    ἱστίον ἁρπαλέως ⟨τ'⟩ ἄ-
132)— ελπτον ἐξί[κ]οντο χέ[ρσον.

E' (100) 1 ὣς Τρῶες, ἐπ[εὶ] κλύον [αἰ-
    χματὰν Ἀχιλλέα
135 3 μίμνο[ντ'] ἐν κλισίηισιν
    εἵνεκ[ε]ν ξανθᾶς γυναικός,
    Β]ρ[ι]σηΐδος ἱμερογυίου,
6 θεοῖσιν ἄντειναν χέρας,
    φοιβὰν ἐσιδόντες ὑπαὶ
140   χειμῶνος αἴγλαν·
9 πασσυδίᾱι δὲ λιπόντες
    τείχεα Λαομέδοντος
(110) 11 ἒ]ς πεδίον κρατερὰν
    ἄϊξαν ὑ[σ]μίναν φέροντες·
145 1 ὦρσάν τ[ε] φόβον Δαναοῖς·
    ὤτρυνε δ' Ἄρης
3 ἐ]ϋεγχής, Λυκίων τε
    Λοξίας ἄναξ Ἀπόλλων·
    ἷξόν τ' ἐπὶ θῖνα θαλάσσας·
150 6 ν]αυσὶ δ' εὐπρύμνοις παρα⟨ὶ⟩
    μάρναντ', ἐναριζ[ομέν]ων
    δ' ἔρ]ευθε φώτων
(120) 9 αἵμα]τι γαῖα μελα[‿
    Ἑκτορ]έας ὑπὸ χει[ρός,
155 11 ....]εγ' ἡμιθέοις
    .....] ἰσοθέων δι' ὁρμάν.
157 1 .....]ρονες, ἢ μεγάλαισιν ἐλπίσιν
158 ....]οντες ὑπερφ[ία]λον
    ◡‿◡‿‿
160 4 ....]ς ἱππευταὶ κυανώπιδας ἐκ-
    ‿‿◡‿‿‿] νέας
6 ‿‿◡◡ εἰλα]πίνας τ' ἐν
(130) .....]ρεις ἕξειν θ[εόδ']ματον πόλιν.
8 μ]έλλον ἄρα π'ρότε[ρο]ν δι-
165)— ν]ᾶντα φοινίξει[ν Σκ]άμανδρ[ον,
F' 1 θ]νάισκοντες ὑπ' [Αἰα]κίδαις
    ἐρειψ[ιτ]οί[χοις·
3 τῶν εἰ καὶ τ[◡◡‿‿
169 ἢ βαθυξύλω[ι ◡‿‿
    (desunt vv. V)

175 οὐ γὰρ ἀλαμπέϊ νυκ[τός
11 πασιφανὴς Ἀρετ[ὰ
___ κρυφθεῖσ᾿ ἀμαυρο[ῦται ‿__
1 ἀλλ᾿ ἔμπεδον ἀκ[αμάτᾱι
βρύουσα δόξᾱι
180 3 στρωφᾶται κατὰ γᾶν [τε
καὶ πολύπ'λαγκτον θ[άλασσαν.
καὶ μὰν φερεκυδέα ν[ᾶσον
(150) 6 Αἰακοῦ τιμᾶι, σὺν Εὐ-
184   κλείᾱι δὲ φιλοστεφ[άνωι
185   πόλιν κυβερνᾶι,
9 Εὐνομία τε σαόφ'ρων,
ἇ θαλίας τε λέλογχεν
11 ἄστεά τ᾿ εὐσεβέων
___ ἀνδρῶν ἐν εἰ[ρ]ήνᾱι φυλάσσει·
190 1 νίκαν τ᾿ ἐρικυ[δέα] μέλπετ᾿, ὦ νέοι,
Π]υθέα, μελέτα[ν τε] βροτω-
φ[ε]λέα Μενάνδρου,
(160) 4 τὰν ἐπ᾿ Ἀλφειοῦ τε ῥο[αῖς] θαμὰ δὴ
τίμασεν ἁ χρυσάρματος
195 6 σεμνὰ μεγάθυμος Ἀθάνα,
μυρίων τ᾿ ἤδη μίτραισιν ἀνέρων
8 ἐστεφ'άνωσεν ἐθείρας
___ ἐν Πανελλάνων ἀέθ'λοις.
Z'   )
1 ε]ἰ μή τινα θερσι[ε]πὴς
200   φθόνος βιᾶται,
3 αἰνείτω σοφὸν ἄνδρα
σὺν δίκᾱι. βροτῶν δὲ μῶμος
(170) πάντεσσι μέν ἐστιν ἐπ᾿ ἔργοι[ς·
6 ἁ δ᾿ ἀλαθεία φιλεῖ
205   νικᾶν, ὅ τε πανδ[α]μάτω[ρ
χρόνος τὸ κᾱλῶς
9 ἐ]ργμένον αἰὲν ἀ[έξει·
δ'υ'σ'μενέ'ω'ν δὲ μα[ταία
209 11 γλῶσσ᾿] 'ἀϊδ'ὴς μιν[ύθει
(desunt vv. X)
220   ἐλπίδι θυμὸν ἰαίν[-
221 11 τᾶι καὶ ἐγὼ πίσυνο[ς
___ φοινικοκραδέμνοις [τε Μούσαις
(190) 1 ὕμνων τινὰ τάνδε ν[εόπ'λοκον δόσιν
φαίνω, ξενίαν τε [φιλά-
225   γ'λαον γεραίρω,
4 τὰν ἐμοὶ Λάμπων [‿‿__‿‿_
βληχρὰν ἐπαθ'ρησαιστ[‿_

6 τὰν εἰκ ἐτύμως ἄρα Κλειώ
   πανθαλὴς ἐμαῖς ἐνέσταξ[εν φρασίν,
230 τερψιεπεῖς νιν ἀ[ο]ιδαὶ
8   παντὶ καρύξοντι λα[ῶ]ι.

"... arrogant outrage
   he will stop, bringing justice to men.

2 ant.   How heavy the hand this Perseïd
             will place on the hungry lion's neck
          and with what science
          it will do its work!
          The alien gleaming bronze
          that masters men
             dislikes to cut that flesh:
             it bends back, even the blade
          of his sword! So do I decree for this place
          pancratists' crowns
          and the sweat-dripping labor
             of wrestling Greeks."

ep.   For such cause, near to the altar of Ruler Zeus,
          flowers of fame-bearing Nike
             nurse for the few who win crowns
          a murmuring golden repute
             ever, during their lives;
          further, when death's purple mist
             covers them over, their deeds'
          immortal fame stays on
             with permanence as its fate.

3 str.   All this has been yours at Nemea,
             o son of Lampon,
          where, shading your head with
          crowns of blossoming flowers,
          you [honored] your high-built city
          [and sent a chorus of] pleasureful
             ..... sweet-breathing
             revellers to your paternal
          island because you displayed
          your mighty, all-challenging strength.
          O daughter of eddying river,
             Aegina, gentle-hearted,

ant.　　　surely the son of Kronos has
　　　　　given great honor to you
　　　in all of the contests, making you show
　　　among Greeks like a torch-fire.
　　　Your fame is sung
　　　by the proud-throated girl
　　　　　[who dances]
　　　　　on [delicate] feet, swift
　　　as the careless fawn
　　　up the flowery slopes,
　　　running lightly along
　　　　　with familiar fair-famed friends.

ep.　　　Crowned with red blossoms
　　　and reeds these maids,
　　　　　following local ways,
　　　sing your rule, o
　　　　　queen of a guest-loving land,
　　　and sing, too, of fair-armed Endaïs,
　　　　　mother of Peleas and
　　　bold Telamon, both
　　　　　conceived in Aeacus' bed.

4 str.　　Their two bellicose sons,
　　　　　Achilles the swift
　　　and lovely Eriboea's
　　　valiant shield-bearing child,
　　　hero Ajax, I'll sing!
　　　He, planted beside the ships' prows,
　　　　　resisted the bold-hearted
　　　　　onrushing foe who would
　　　burn the ships with a fateful fire,
　　　bronze-girdled Hector,
　　　when Peleas' son
　　　　　had urged up his own harsh anger

ant.　　　against the Atreids, releasing
　　　　　the Trojans from their fate.
　　　They until then had not left
　　　the turreted, visible
　　　city of Troy but had huddled there
　　　in fear of sharp war
　　　　　as long as howling Achilles
　　　　　raged in the field

swinging his murderous sword, but
when he abandoned the battle,
unwounded, the son of the Nereid
   violet-crowned,

ep.   then—just as it is on the purple sea
when Boreas breaks the courage of men
   under the waves,
attacking by night, only to
   fall back with the brightness
of dawn, letting a fair wind
   smooth out the waves while
southerly breezes fill up the sail
   and against all hope sailors reach land—

5 str.   so it was with the Trojans when
   they heard that Achilles' spear
rested inside his tent
because of a fair-haired girl,
Briseïs, made for love.
They stretched out hands to the gods
   for they glimpsed a ruddy brilliance
   just beyond the storm.
All in a throng they left
the walls Laomedon built
and rushed upon the plain
   carrying havoc with them.

ant.   Then they thrust fear upon the Danaans
   and Ares, skilled with the spear,
urged them on, and Loxias, too,
lord of the Lycians—Apollo.
Arrived at the shore of the sea,
where the splendid ships were beached,
   they fought a fierce battle
   and blood of the fallen
reddened the darkness of earth—
blood spilled by Hector's hand
   . . . . . for the demigods
     . . . . . attack of the godlike ones.

ep.   Wretched men, buoyed up
beyond measure by hopes
   . . . . .

... horsemen [expecting to take]
the dark-prowed Achaean ships
. . . . .
and to hold their godbuilt city—
they were doomed, before they should succeed,
to dye the swift Scamander red

6 str.   destroyed by Aeacid
        sackers of cities ...
[whose fame, though they have lain on their funeral
pyres, lives on ... *five lines are missing*]
Not within lampless dark
does all-discovering Virtue
    obscure them and hide them away!

ant.   Instead, constant and teeming
        with restless fame she
roams everywhere through the earth
and over the travelled sea.
Now, I may swear, she honors the glory-filled
island of Aeacus, she
    who with garlanded Eukleia
    governs the city;
Eunomia too, maker of sound opinion
(festival is her portion
and cities of pious men)
    guards this place in peace.

ep.   Sing then, o youths, of Pytheas' victory
spreading its fame, and sing too
    of Menandros whose nourishing care
has often been honored when Alpheus flows
    by one who drives in a golden car—
awesome courageous Athena,
    she who has wreathed the heads
of thousands of men
    in pan-Hellenic games.

7 str.   A man must (unless hot-worded Envy
        does him violence)
give praise to one who knows his work
as accurate recompense. Blame
hangs over all the deeds of men

but remembering Praise loves
   victory, even as Time
   All-conquering ever augments
the deed that is fairly done,
while speech of envious men
uselessly disappears.

   . . . . .

[*nine lines missing*]
heart warmed with hope
and I, putting my trust
   in the red-wreathed Muses,

ep.   show forth this new-plaited
gift of song, my return for
   brightness of hospitality
offered to me by Lampon. [Do not
   resent this grant for your son]
for if in truth bloom-tending Clio
   has dripped them into my mind,
then sweet-worded songs will announce him
   to all, everywhere in the world.

The long ode twists sinuously through its changing mythic landscape and the poet has spent great skill in maintaining its single movement. For the moment, however, we must stop its flow and consider it part by part. The Nemean foundation myth appears in the remains of the second triad (44–66), and it will have been preceded only by invocation and some allusion to the victory occasion, uttered in the chorus' own voice. Then the singers will have shifted to the voice of the prophetic figure for the telling of this first myth, and it proves to be a telling not like any other. We of course are accidentally confounded because we do not know who is speaking,[8] but the audience who had heard this speaker introduced will have been likewise troubled, and intentionally so, for the narration deprives all listeners of their temporal footing. The poet has decreed that anyone who listens to these stanzas shall experience four levels of time simultaneously, and as if that were not enough, he has also forced the auditor to perceive separate events as if they had no temporal confinement—as if they expanded like vapors into what would normally be defined as future and past. All this is achieved with a bit of story-telling machinery that is something like the "over-voice" of modern cinema.

    The singers could have narrated the famous wrestling match as if the

Muse had granted them direct access to it; they could have brought the contest before the spectator as a plain past event about which they knew the truth, but this the Bacchylidean chorus does not do. Instead it summons up an ancient nymph or divinity and reports the whole affair from the standpoint of a narrator who speaks from a time *before* Heracles. What the poem actually imitates is thus an impressive neutral figure who has the bloodless tranquility of a monument, but it gives us this figure in the act of describing another figure, one who is paradoxically engaged in a past contest that has not yet occurred. The effect of this trick is a calculated confusion, for the listener is not presented with a verbal picture of Heracles' past deed in which he is invited to participate retrospectively, as he would in an event from an ordinary tale. Instead, he is given a picture of someone making a picture, and he has the dizzy experience of looking into a future that holds a Heracles. Though it is a mythic struggle that took place in the time before the Trojan War, he sees the scene as if it were a vision in a crystal ball, and what is more, his attention is not directed so much toward the scene as beyond it, to what lies in its future but his own past. From the prophetic speaker's point of view the physical contest between hero and beast is of no interest in and of itself; its significance lies only in its consequences. And in fact, the one dramatic deed that the choral mimesis offers directly to our experience is this speaker's decision (or recognition, *phami*, 54) that the future (past) contest of Heracles shall be commemorated with an even more future (repeatedly past) athletic festival. It is thus not Heracles' muscular conquest of the lion[9] that the song offers to its listeners' perceptions; what it asks us to recognize and almost see and feel is instead the fame of that conquest—a fame so strong that it could be felt before the deed had occurred, so strong that it could persist into the present in the reified form of the Nemean games.

The song thus teaches it spectator to ignore time, as the divine speaker does, while he apprehends as a single experience the moment of the prophecy, the moment of the lion-combat, the repeated moments of all the Nemean contests ever held including the victor's own, and the moment of the present performance. The all-knowing prophet in this way enforces the spell of unforgetfulness that Bacchylides' song casts upon the victor's deed, but this oracular speaker serves the poet in other ways as well. Through her Bacchylides is able to purge his mythic event of all that was childish or grotesque in the old Orientalizing tale while he extracts the essential quality from the quantity of strength that the scene necessarily contains. If his combat is to be transformed into a show of virtue that lasts forever at Nemea, this heavy hero must be made weightless, and so in the prophetic vision the brute power of Heracles is not measured directly; rather it is described indirectly through a description of the power of his brutish adversary. And even with the lion, it is not the physical aspect of his strength but instead its magical aspect that the speaker asks us to observe. This is no ordinary beast, she says, which means that his opponent (who is not directly named) is no ordinary strong man, and what is extraordinary in the situation is made plain with an emblematic marvel that attaches characteristically not to Heracles but to the animal. The mythic wrestling match, and so all of the Nemean matches to follow, will be determined by a fairy-tale wonder, for when Heracles tries to use his sword it will bend away and refuse to touch the beast.[10]

Like the pagan weapons that were similarly useless against Christian saints,[11] this bent sword is the measure of a daimonic power that resides in the unwoundable victim. The motif, however, is here employed in a very different way, for in this tale the victim's power of invulnerability is merely magical, whereas the aggressive power of the sword-wielder derives from the Olympians. Consequently the useless sword of Bacchylides' song actually redounds to its owner's credit[12] by making way for an alternative weapon, which turns out to be the hero's naked but knowing hand. The sword, after all, is often an instrument of hubris and injustice, and by using it Heracles might have made himself the ethical replica of his adversary, whereas the hand denotes what Pindar liked to call *phya*. A god-given ability resides in it, one that comes through breeding and acts as a kind of vocation. Of course, a hand as well as a sword could also be associated with the wrong kind of violence, and it is illuminating to watch the poet as he parries this possibility. He wants to capture for his poem the justice-potential of extraordinary strength and he wants to take this force at its fullest, before it has been spent in physical consummation. And so he fixes this ominous peloric hand, not as it seizes the beast in a stranglehold, not as it rests satisfied on the monster's corpse,[13] but just as it first touches the lion in a quiet preliminary move that promises mastery. Indeed, though it is easy to speak of this passage as a description of Heracles as he wrestled with the lion (as Jebb does, *ad loc.*), there is no syllable of struggle here. Instead of a specific, grunting, blood-stained contest there is only the single astonished phrase that marks the hand of Heracles as an object that can make even a prophet marvel: "How prodigious the hand ...!" Here is a wonder greater even than that of the unwilling weapon.

The Heracles of fable has been denuded of all his Farnesian flesh, his whole force being rendered by two images, the bent sword and the huge hand. We see also the lion's pelt and the matching metal of the blade (its epithet, *aithon*, was often used of the skins of animals), but that is all that the poet has offered sensually to our vision, and it is notable that he has made an equally narrow choice among the ethical connotations that his tale conveys. According to the speaker, Heracles is here engaged in putting a stop to the monstrous violence that kept men from living in order and security, but his action is not merely negative, for it is also described as "bringing justice into being for men" (45).[14] It is as if Bacchylides had added an inscribed motto to the blason of Heracles and the lion, and the phrase plainly says that this hero is not the boisterous companion of the satyrs, nor yet the picaresque adventurer of folk tale and Stesichorus' western songs. This is instead the son that Zeus prepared through generations as the agent of his kinder will. This Heracles is a part of the Olympian process by which civil society was established on earth, and his battle with the lion, like Apollo's with Pytho or Zeus' with Typhon, is a version of the fundamental Near-Eastern myth about the beginnings of the cosmos.[15] The conquest of the Nemean beast is seen by Bacchylides as a continuation of the initial creation of order, and by association, the contest that Pytheas has won at Nemea partakes of the same spirit. With this first myth, then, the poet creates a conviction that the present winning action is an exploit that nourishes justice and keeps society secure. This view stays with us and is reinforced later, in another kind of discourse, when in a passage of straight praise the chorus announces that Pytheas' glory joins with the personified figures of Reputation and Order to rule the city of Aegina and keep it in safety and peace.

Such is Bacchylides' city-minded, wholly ingenious presentation of the simplest epinician myth, an aetiological tale of the contest place. The prophetess was made to stand at Nemea (*taide*, 55) as she delivered her speech, and the singers continue to regard that spot as they sing epode two in their own neutral tones. By way of Nemea, the song can then pass back to its victor, since Pytheas has just come from the games there and has won the "murmuring golden repute" that derives from Heracles' contest. By bringing it home to his city he has caused the present revelries, and so, in lines 73–4, the chorus finds itself singing of itself singing, just like the girls of the *Partheneion*. Indeed, these could be the penultimate phrases of a brief but perfect epinician that ended at line 76, for at this point the spectator's immediate and tangible Here and Now has been ritualized, raised out of the quotidian, and made to mingle with other places and times, just as the victor's fame has been made to mingle with a Heraclean fame that will never end. Everything has come full circle, and yet we know this to be a false *envoi* since it comes in the wrong structural spot, towards the end of a strophe. The poet in fact has another and much more extensive fiction ready, for this is one of his grandest commissions. His ode must move on, but how can it pass from its fulfilled and exalted present back into another and quite unrelated myth without seeming to be either over-contrived or out of control?

Bacchylides with characteristic insouciance makes it follow local nymphs down musical paths that lead, by way of women, to the Trojan War.

Aegina is called upon to receive the fame-fire that her victor has brought home, but she is invoked as a figure with no outline, part idealized city and part hazy river nymph.[16] Her god-given glory is then translated into audible praise as a generalized but flesh-and-blood girl hymns Aegina in some local ceremony. There is an instant, in the course of the third epode, when we ourselves almost hear her song, for at that point the visible *kōmos* of boys briefly represents an invisible troupe of girls who sing of a nymph who is part of the fame of the island. Through the boys' mouths the girls sing her name—Endaïs—and with this name we arrive. The song is now in position for its next myth, for this is the mother of Peleas and Telamon, the grandmother of Achilles and Ajax.

Such is the stitching together. The movement from a realized present back into a world of timeless potentiality has been given the simplicity of dancing and wreath-weaving, but the poet's difficulties are just beginning. Those who are paying for the ode have evidently insisted that Ajax and Achilles must appear,[17] and this means that Bacchylides has some intractable material to cut, for this second story is egregiously ill-suited to his song. The exploits to be recounted derive from that rationalized epic tradition that does not lend itself easily to the best epinician use and, what is worse, the deeds of the two heroes are awkwardly separated, since Ajax moves precisely at a time when Achilles is still.[18] The two men really belong to two stories, not one (unless that one be the whole *Iliad*), and their two sets of battlefield successes would thus seem to defy the compression and intensity of choral song. And yet Bacchylides finds a way of joining the disparate Aeacids; what is more, it is a way that brings them into a conceptual relationship with his just-told Nemean myth, a way that allows his ode to finish and be whole.

In the earlier stanzas the poet gauged the strength of Heracles by the strength of the beast that he mastered; now, following the same method, Bacchylides measures and unites his two epic figures with a description of their common foe. Instead of splitting his stanzas between the divided Aeacids he uses his song to consider the Trojans to whom both did such harm, and the boldness of his solution is apparent when we note that neither hero takes part in the scenes that are realized.[19] The enemy's dread ferocity is the overt subject of the passage: the Trojan rush across the plain and the battle at the ships are what we actually observe. The true subject, however, is the ferocity of Achilles, and this we recognize as we look at what his absence has created.[20] And in case we need help in drawing this inference, the poet offers a great Homeric simile that occupies all of the fourth epode and applies, ostensibly, to Hector and the

Trojans. They are like sailors released from storm, a favorite Greek cipher for salvation, but in effect the figure is neither so banal nor so smiling as it seems since its explicit equation of Achilles' absence with fair wind and the brightness of dawn implies another in which his presence equals night and the northwind. He is variable weather to Trojans who are sailors with no power over their own destinies, and so the long simile acts to credit the wild Trojan assault, not to Hector but to the Achilles who is not here. And what is more, it marks the assault as temporary and literally ephemeral. It belongs only to the brief brightness that the Trojans glimpse (1.139–40), and, as night follows day, Achilles will certainly return.

The singers bring the Trojans to the ships and make us see the blood of the battle that is fought there (1.153), but as far as we can tell from the damaged text Ajax is not mentioned at this point. He had been set in position, ready to receive the assault, at line 105, and consequently the mad force of the enemy has been made, by the structure of the song, to begin and end with him, even as it has been shown by the simile to be controlled by his cousin Achilles. Ajax cannot be given realized deeds because that would break the balance between the two heroes, but the fact that he checked the fire the Trojans would have carried to the ships is announced at the start (1.106–8), so that it will sound like a held chord throughout the passage. Then, once the moment of highest Trojan success has been evoked, the chorus lets the sound of battle die away into prophecy—their own backward-looking prophecy this time. Neither hero could be given credit for Troy's ultimate fall, while mention of the slaying of Hector would lend too much importance to Achilles, and so the whole Hellenic victory is ingeniously depicted in reverse, as the frustration of Trojan hope. *This* was the common work of the Aeacids (166).

Troy and Hector have been made to serve the grandsons of Aeacus as the lion did the great-grandson of Perseus, and by means of the Trojans the primitive social promise of the first myth is somewhat modernized. It is a little like the citation of a single motif in its Old and New Testament forms, for the poem has presented the mastery of brutality and injustice, first as the miraculous conquest of a folk-tale beast, then as the magnificent but completely secular defeat of a fiery enemy from legendary history. Ode 13 thus produces two myths of victory in which strength wins immortal fame by checking violence, but to say this and no more would be to give a false impression of the temper of the song, for it is not, in its entirety, a song given over to contest and strife. It also proposes a series of softer images which represent the rewards that are won for all society by such victories.

There are mild and joyous female figures placed at intervals throughout Ode 13, supporting its structure as a series of caryatids might. First (to our knowledge) is the prophetess or female divinity who appears at the beginning, applauding the gift of justice and decreeing the establishment of the Nemean contests. And last is the Muse to whom the poet's final words are given, the Clio who encourages the flowering of all song, and who drips honey into particular epinician odes as if they were blossoms ready for bees (228–9).[21] Between these Aegina stands as a central feminine presence, evoked by a prayer that calls her "gentle-souled" and placed in a neutral zone between the meadow where Heracles met the lion and the battlefield where the two Aeacids fought. Around her the poet has gathered a troupe of proud-throated girls who sing of local heroines, but Aegina also receives and transforms the renown of her hero sons. The fame of Aeacid virtue is proclaimed and brought home to her (182–3), just as the fame of the victor Pytheas is (74–6), but where the victor's renown is subsumed into the torch-like glory of the island, the excellence of the two heroes of Troy becomes, when it joins Aegina, yet another female power, Areta. What is more, this island Areta joins with two more allegorical ladies, Euclea and Eunomia, in the rule of the city, and this trio is in a sense in view throughout the present performance, for Areta and Euclea are its cause and its result, while Eunomia holds the present dance and banquet as her allotted portion (187). Her name spells out Fair Order, she has feasting as her province, and above all she and her victory celebrations keep pious men in peace (188–9).

The many feminine creatures of Ode 13 are thus explicitly civilizing forces and with them Bacchylides softens and transforms the effects of his two tales of mythic and legendary violence. He has figured Disorder as beast or Trojan, but because the ladies are here, Order is not finally imaged as a heavy-fisted Heracles or a battle-mad Achilles. It is represented instead by a river nymph who is lovingly called temperate and by the dancing, flower-crowned girls who belong to her, and then it is represented once more by a personified Eunomia and by the dancing, crowned young men who are performing the song we are even now hearing. The chorus cries out to itself, as it enters the final phase of its song (ō neoi, 190), returning to the exact level of exalted self-portrayal that it had reached earlier (with the reference to kōmoi at 74), but having its present activity now more fully identified than it was at strophe three. Today's performance is the reification of Order in its fair and nourishing form,[22] part of the justice that Heracles made when he put a stop to bestial violence, part of the triumph gained by Greeks when they halted the Trojan attack, part of the glory won by Pytheas when he bested his opponent in the Nemean wrestling match. That glory, meanwhile, has been made part of the illumination of Aegina and part of the ancestral virtue that rules her and protects her peace.

7. INAUSPICIOUS TALES

Because the myths of the victory odes were conveyors of force and links with fame, not mere embellishment, they did not have to be happy or even auspicious. Stories of crime, disaster, grief, or suffering could give a richer and more serious tone to praise, as long as the poet provided some positive ballast, and this both Pindar and Bacchylides knew very well how to do. The negative myth could be made to produce some joyous detail; it could be moralized and used as a warning; it could be paired with a second, happy story, or another sort of compensation might be offered in the form of smiling allegorical figures. All this is well illustrated by Bacchylides in his (badly damaged) Ninth Ode which, like Ode 13, was of magnificent proportions and made for a Nemean victor. Once again the poet has chosen an aetiological myth, but this time he has decided to explain the Nemean contest with a tale about the Argive Seven on their way to Thebes.[1] The story is blatantly inauspicious, since all but one of its heroes are about to perish, and even in the section that the poet has cut for his present song the subject is violent death. With such a tale, the funereal significance of the athletic contest[2] is openly revived, and the victor Automedes is shown to have won the pentathlon on a spot marked by portentous human blood.

A'   1 Δόξαν, ὦ χρυσαλάκατοι Χάρι[τ]ες,
         πεισίμβροτον δοίητ᾽, ἐπεί
      3 Μουσᾶν γε ἰοβ'λεφάρων θεῖος προφ[άτ]ας
         εὔτυκος Φλειοῦντά τε καὶ Νεμεαίου
      5 Ζηνὸς εὐθαλὲς πέδον
      6 ὑμνεῖν, ὅθι μηλοδαΐκταν
         θρέψεν ἁ λευκώλε[νο]ς
      8 Ἥρα περι[κ'λει]τῶν ἀέθ'λων
         πρῶτον [Ἡ]ρ[α]κ'λεῖ βαρύφθογγον λέοντα.

10 1 κε[ῖθι φοι]νικάσπιδες ἡμίθεοι
πρ[ώτιστ]ον Ἀργείων κριτοί
12 3 ἄθλησαν ἐπ᾽ Ἀρχεμόρωι, τὸν ξανθοδερκής
πέφ᾽ν᾽ ἀωτεύοντα δράκων ὑπέροπ᾽λος,
σᾶμα μέλλοντος φόνου.
15 6 ὦ μοῖρα πολυκ᾽ρατές· οὔ νιν
πεῖθ᾽ Ὀϊκ᾽λείδας πάλιν
8 στείχειν ἐς εὐάνδρους ἀγ[υιάς.
ἐλπὶς ἀνθρώπων ὑφαιρ[εῖται νόημ]α·
1 ἃ καὶ τότ᾽ Ἄδ᾽ραστον Ταλ[αϊονίδαν
20 πέμπεν ἐς Θήβας Πολυνείκεϊ πλα. ι[‗‿‗
3 κείνων ἀπ᾽ εὐδόξων ἀγώνων
ἐν Νεμέᾱι κλεινο[ὶ β]ροτῶν
5 οἳ τριετεῖ στεφάνωι
ξανθὰν ἐρέψωνται κόμαν.
25 7 Αὐτομήδει νῦν γε νικά-
)__ σαντί νιν δαίμων ἔ[δ]ωκεν.
B′   1 πενταέθ᾽λοισιν γὰρ ἐνέπ᾽ρεπεν ὡς
ἄστρων διακ᾽ρίνει φάη
3 νυκτὸς διχομηνίδο[ς] εὐφεγγὴς σελάνα·
30 τοῖος Ἑλλάνων δι᾽ ἀπ[εί]ρονα κύκ᾽λον
φαῖνε θαυμαστὸν δέμας
6 δίσκον τροχοειδέα ῥίπτων,
καὶ μελαμφύλλου κλάδον
8 ἀκτέας ἐς αἰπεινὰν προπέμπων
35 αἰθέρ᾽ ἐκ χειρὸς βοὰν ὤτρυνε λαῶν
36 1 ἢ τε[λε]υτάσας ἀμάρυγ᾽μα πάλας·
τοιῶ[ιδ᾽ ὑπερθ]ύμωι σ[θένε]ι
3 γυια[λκέα σώ]ματα [πρὸς γ]αίᾱι πελάσσα[ς
ἵκετ᾽ [Ἀσωπὸ]ν πάρα πορφυροδίναι,
40 τοῦ κ[λέος π]ᾶσαν χθόνα
6 ἦλθε[ν καὶ] ἐπ᾽ ἔσχατα Νείλου·
ταί τ᾽ ἐπ᾽ εὐγαεῖ πόρωι
8 οἰκεῦσι Θερμώδον[τος, ἐ]γχέων
ἵστορες κοῦραι διωξίπποι᾽ Ἄρηος,
45 1 σῶν, ὦ πολυζήλωτε ἄναξ ποταμῶν,
ἐγγόνων γεύσαντο, καὶ ὑψιπύλου Τροίας ἕδος.
3 στείχει δι᾽ εὐρείας κελε[ύ]θου
μυρία πάντᾱι φάτις
5 σᾶς γενεᾶς λιπαρο-
50 ζώνων θυγατ᾽ρῶν, ἃς θε[ο]ί
7 σὺν τύχαις ὤικισσαν ἀρχα-
)__ γοὺς ἀπορθήτων ἀγυιᾶν.

Γ′   1 τίς γὰρ οὐκ οἶδεν κυανοπ'λοκάμου
            Θήβας εὔδ'μα[τον πόλι]ν,
    55 3 ἢ τὰν μεγαλώνυ]μον Αἴγιναν, μεγ[ίστ]ον
            Ζην]ὸς [ᾇ πλαθεῖσα λ]έχει τέκεν ἥρω

1 str.   Grant fair repute, o gold-spindled Graces,
                    a fame that persuades all men,
            for the blue-lidded Muses' godly prophet
            is ready now to hymn Phlius and the flowering plain
            that belongs to Nemean Zeus, ground
            where white-armed Hera nurtured
            for the all-famous games
            Heracles' first opponent—
            a sheep-killing deep-roaring lion.

ant.   There did the finest of Argives,
                    heroes half god who carried dark shields,
            first contest in honor of Archemorus
            whom the huge gold-glancing snake had
            killed as he slept: a sign of coming gore.
            O Moira, mistress of all, the son
            of Oecleas could not persuade them
            back towards the populous streets!
            Hope steals the best will of man,

ep.   and hope sent Adrastus the Talionid
            towards Thebes [as ally of Polyneices]
            but from those same well-known
            Nemean games a man returns famous,
            once he has put the three-year crown
                    upon his own fair head.
            And now it is Automedes to whom
            in victory the gods present that crown.

2 str.   In the pentathlon he was preeminent
                    like the surpassing light
            of a mid-month moon among stars;
            so he appeared when he passed through the circle
            of Greeks, his marvelous limbs revealed,
            to cast the discus-wheel; so he appeared
            when he made the dark-leaved elder branch
            leap from his hand towards the steep air
            and roused a shout from the crowd; so again

ant.   in his last lithe twist in the wrestling ring.
            Once his vehement strength
            had brought strong bodies close to the earth,
            he returned to dark-swirling Asopus,
            that stream whose fame covers the world,
            reaching even to furthest Nile.
            Surely those who dwell by the fair-flowing
            mouth of the Thermodon, those daughters of Ares
            skilled with the spear, fond of the spur,

ep.   have tasted of waters sprung from yours, o much-envied
            lord of the rivers, as has the high seat of Troy.
            Broad paths lead ten-thousand tales
            that tell of your rich-girdled daughters
                to every part of the earth, telling how gods
            have set them up with fair fates
                as patrons of cities safe from siege.

3 str.   Who has not heard of the splendid town
                protected by dark-tressed Thebē,
            or Aigina of the proud name, she who
            lay with Zeus and gave birth
            to the hero . . . .

            [*this triad is completed and a fourth finishes the ode*]

   The *thauma* of the opening mythic section, the marvel that lends notorious fame to a present victory, is the gigantic snake, but the portent
was the baby's blood, and its meaning, according to the poet, was perfectly plain. It stood for bloodshed to come, if the Argives attacked
Thebes with Polyneices. Warriors who honored the sign would have refused to continue; they would have let their newly founded athletic
contest replace the war they had intended, and they would have gone
back, as victors should, carrying their agonistic *kleos* to their own cities
and families. This is what Amphiaraeus urged them to do, but the story
of the Seven is not about pious wisdom. It concerns stubborn error and
its punishment, and this the poet makes clear with one of his characteristic apostrophes: "O Moira!" the chorus cries, breaking out of its narrative voice, "the son of Oecleas could not persuade them to turn back!"
(15–16). Led astray by hope (19–20),[3] the Argives leave the splendid
games and move off in a false direction, making for Thebes instead of for
home, and having started them on this wrong road the poet abandons
them (20).

In the first triad of this song a monstrous snake and the blood of an infant have signaled doom for the Argives while they have also brought into being the first Nemean Games. Obviously the poet must now differentiate his victor from the mythic men who refused to listen to Amphiaraeus; he must show him as one who has revived the solemn supernatural force, but not the mortal error, of this original occasion. Such is the epinician necessity, and under its pressure Bacchylides' first tactic is to turn directly to his victor in a passage that is unparalleled in its extent and its poetic detail.[4] Automedes' performance at Nemea is set to music in the second strophe, and he himself is almost deified, as his "marvelous" (*thaumaston*, 31) flesh is made to shine forth (*phaine*, 31) with a splendor like that of the moon. The luminous youth eclipses all his opponents, and as he does so he also obscures the never very strong image of the other naked body, that of the infant Archemorus. Then, in the antistrophe, Automedes (in contrast to the mythic Argives) gives that child's death a proper celebration by inflicting only a mock death upon his adversaries (38),[5] though he does this with a serpentine movement (*amarugma*, 36) that borrows some of the magic of the murderous snake.[6] And finally, when the contest is over, he corrects the error of the Seven by turning back, as they should have done, to his own river Asopus and taking his glory home (39).

Without a pompous syllable the poet in this way manages both to moralize and to reverse a myth of death and doom, but he is not finished. Unfortunately, most of the rest of his song is badly damaged, but there is enough left to show its continuing plan, which was based on the refreshing idea of replacing the baneful water snake of the myth with a rush of lovely rivers. Taking the name Asopus as its sparkling excuse, the song suddenly changes its course (between lines 39 and 40), and the victor disappears in a shining throng as the daughters of this river are named.[7] Their journeying fame (*kleos*, 40; taken up by *phatis*, 48) seems to include that of Automedes and it spreads as far as the city where the Seven fell, making it now a place of good fame, the well-built (54) and impregnable (52) possession of "dark-tressed Thebe" (53–4). The daughters of Asopus apparently take up more than a triad, and they appear not only as rivers but as the brides of various gods (55 ff; 63–65) and the mothers of infant heroes (56). The dead Archemorus, "a sign of coming gore," is in this way subsumed into a system of images that moves from the small mythic body of the snake's victim to the fully formed actual splendor of the victor's limbs, then on to the multiple, once more mythic, bodies of children conceived by river-mothers in the couches of the gods.

In another, much better preserved ode, a myth of overt impiety and its punishment is so extensively related that it takes up more than half of the total singing time. The poem is Ode 11, composed for a Metapontine victor, and the myth concerns the daughters of an Argive king named Proetus, girls who were driven mad because they insulted Hera. The tale is certainly not promising, and what is worse, it is apparently wholly inapplicable. It is not attached to the contest place, which was Delphi; it has no connection with Apollo, but concerns itself with goddesses, and its unpropitious content offers nothing that has any obvious congruity with the experience of victory. As a matter of fact it seems to be the mythic reflection of a Peloponnesian girls' initiation rite, and anything less suitable to the celebration, in South Italy, of a boy's wrestling prize, could hardly be imagined. Nevertheless Bacchylides decided to give it an epinician cut, and he justified himself by attaching the story loosely to the cult of Artemis that was celebrated outside Metapontum at the spring of San Biagio.[8]

A′   1 Νίκα γ‚λυκύδωρε·[◡_ γὰρ
            σοὶ πατ[ὴρ __◡__
        3 ὑψίζυ[γος _◡◡_
     4   ἐν πολ‚υχ'ρύσωι ⟨τ'⟩ Ὀλύμ‚πωι
        5 5 Ζηνὶ ‚παρισταμένα‚
            κρίνε‚ις τέ‚λ‚ο‚ς ἀθανάτοι-
            σίν τε ‚καὶ θ‚νατοῖς ἀρετᾶς·
        8 ἔλλαθι, [βαθυ]π'λοκάμου
            κούρα Σ[τυγὸς ὀρ]θοδίκου· σέθεν δ' ὅκατι
     10 10 καὶ νῦ[ν Μετ]απόντιον εὐ-
            γυίων κ[ατέ]χουσι νέων
        12 κῶμοί τε καὶ εὐφροσύναι θεότιμον ἄστυ·
            ὑμνεῦσι δὲ Πυθιόνικον
            παῖδα θαητ[ὸ]ν Φαῖσκον.
        15 1 ἵλεώι [ν]ιν ὁ Δα[λ]ογενὴς υἱ-
            ὸς βαθυζώνο[ιο] Λατοῦς
        3 δέκτ[ο] β'λεφ[άρω]‚· πολέες
            δ' ἀμφ' Ἀλεξ[ίδα]μον ἀνθέων
        5 ἐν πεδίωι στέφανοι
     20   Κίρρας ἔπεσον κρατερᾶς
            ἧρα παννίκοι⟨ο⟩ πάλας·
        8 οὐκ ε[ἶ]δέ νιν ἀέλιος
            κείνωι γε σὺν ἄματι πρὸς γαίαι πεσόντα.
        10 φάσω δὲ καὶ ἐν ζαθέοις
     25   ἁγ'νοῦ Πέλοπος δαπέδοις
        12 Ἀλφεὸν πάρα καλλιρόαν, δίκας κέλευθον
            εἰ μή τις ἀπέτ'ραπεν ὀρθᾶς,
            παγξένωι χαίταν ἐλαίαι

1 γλαυκᾶι στεφανωσάμενον
30 πορτιτ'ρόφον [. . . .].'[. . . . .]ραν ϑ' ἱκέσϑαι.
31 3 _υυ_υυ_]
    παῖδ' ἐν χϑονὶ καλλιχόρωι
    ποικίλαις τέχ'ναις πέλασσεν·
  6 ἀ]λλ' ἢ θεὸς αἴτιος, ἢ
35   γ]νῶμαι πολύπ'λαγκτοι βροτῶν
    ἄ]μερσαν ὑπέρτατον ἐκ χειρῶν γέρας.
  9 νῦν δ' Ἄρτεμις ἀγ'ροτέρα
    χρυσαλάκατος λιπαράν
    Ἡμ]έρα τοξόκ'λυτος νίκαν ἔδωκε.
40 12 τ]ᾶι ποτ' Ἀβαντιάδας
    β]ωμὸν κατένασσε πολύλ-
)__ λ[ι]στον εὔπεπ'λοί τε κοῦραι·
B'   1 τὰς ἐξ ἐρατῶν ἐφόβησε⟨ν⟩
    παγκρατὴς Ἥρα μελάϑ'ρων
45 3 Προίτου, παραπλῆγι φρένας
    καρτερᾶι ζεύξασ' ἀνάγκᾶι·
  5 παρϑενίᾱι γὰρ ἔτι
    ψυχᾶι κίον ἐς τέμενος
    πορφυροζώνοιο θεᾶς·
50 8 φάσκον δὲ πολὺ σφέτερον
    πλούτωι προφέρειν πατέρα ξανθᾶς παρέδ'ρου
  10 σεμνοῦ Διὸς εὐρυβίᾱ.
    ταῖσιν δὲ χολωσαμένα
  12 στήϑεσσι παλίντροπον ἔμβαλεν νόημα·
55 φεῦγον δ' ὄρος ἐς τανίφυλλον
    σμερδαλέαν φωνὰν ἱεῖσαι,
57 1 Τιρύνθιον ἄστυ λιποῦσαι
58   καὶ θεοδ'μάτους ἀγυιάς.
  3 ἤδη γὰρ ἔτος δέκατον
60   θεοφιλὲς λιπόντες Ἄργος
  5 ναῖον ἀδεισιβόαι
    χαλκάσπιδες ἡμίϑεοι
    σὺν πολυζήλωι βασιλεῖ.
  8 νεῖκος γὰρ ἀμαιμάκετον
65 βληχρᾶς ἀνέπαλτο κασιγ'νητοῖς ἀπ' ἀρχᾶς
  10 Προίτωι τε καὶ Ἀκ'ρισίωι·
    λαούς τε διχοστασίαις
  12 ἤρειπον ἀμετ'ροδίκοις μάχαις τε λυγ'ραῖς.
    λίσσοντο δὲ παῖδας Ἄβαντος
70 __ γᾶν πολύκ'ριϑον λαχόντας
  1 Τίρυνθα τὸν ὁπ'λότερον
    κτίζειν, πρὶν ἐς ἀργαλέαν πεσεῖν ἀνάγκαν·

3 Ζεύς τ᾽ ἔθελεν Κρονίδας
  τιμῶν Δαναοῦ γενεὰν
75   καὶ διωξίπποιο Λυγκέος
6 παῦσαι στυγερῶν ἀχέων.
  τεῖχος δὲ Κύκ|λωπες κάμον
  ἐλθόντες ὑπερφίαλοι κλεινᾶι π[όλ]ει
9 κάλλιστον, ἵν᾽ ἀντίθεοι
80   ναῖον κλυτὸν ἱππόβοτον
  Ἄργος ἥρωες περικ|λειτοὶ λιπόντ[ες.
12 ἔνθεν ἀπεσσύμεναι
  Προίτου κυανοπ|λόκαμοι
)__ φεῦγον ἄδ|ματοι θύγατ|ρες.

Γ′   85 1 τὸν δ᾽ εἷλεν ἄχος κραδίαν, ξεί-
  να τέ νιν πλᾶξεν μέριμνα·
3 δοίαξε δὲ φάσγανον ἄμ-
  φακες ἐν στέρνοισι πᾶξαι.
89 5 ἀλλά νιν αἰχμοφόροι
90   μύθοισί τε μειλιχίοις
  καὶ βίαι χειρῶν κάτεχον.
8 τρισκαίδεκα μὲν τελέους
  μῆνας κατὰ δάσκιον ἠλύκταζον ὕλαν
10 φεῦγόν τε κατ᾽ Ἀρκαδίαν
95   μηλοτ|ρόφον· ἀλλ᾽ ὅτε δή
12 Λοῦσον ποτὶ καλλιρόαν πατὴρ ἵκανεν,
  ἔνθεν χρόα νιψάμενος φοι-
  __νικοκ[ραδέμνο]ιο Λατοῦς
1 κίκ|λη[ισκε θύγατ|ρ]ᾳ βοῶπιν,
100   χεῖρας ἀντείνων πρὸς αὐγάς
3 ἱππώκεος ἀελίου,
  τέκ|να δυστάνοιο λύσσας
5 πάρφρονος ἐξαγαγεῖν·
  ,,θύσω δέ τοι εἴκοσι βοῦς
105   ἄζυγας φοινικότριχας.``
8 τοῦ δ᾽ ἔκ|λυ᾽ ἀριστοπάτρα
  θηροσκόπος εὐχομένου· πιθοῦσα δ᾽ Ἥραν
10 παῦσεν καλυκοστεφάνους
  κούρας μανιᾶν ἀθέων·
110 12 ταὶ δ᾽ αὐτίκα οἱ τέμενος βωμόν τε τεῦχον,
  χραῖνόν τέ μιν αἵματι μήλων
  __καὶ χοροὺς ἵσταν γυναικῶν.
1 ἔνθεν καὶ ἀρηϊφίλοις
  ἄνδρεσσιν ⟨ἐς⟩ ἱπποτρόφον πόλιν̄ Ἀχαιοῖς
115 3 ἕσπεο· σὺν δὲ τύχᾱι

ναίεις Μεταπόντιον, ὦ
χρυσέα δέσποινα λαῶν·
6 ἄλσος τέ τοι ἱμερόεν
119   Κάσαν παρ᾽ εὔυδ᾽ρον †πρόγο-
120 νοι ἐσσάμενοι† Πριάμοι᾽ ἐπεὶ χρόνωι
9 βουλαῖσι θεῶν μακάρων
πέρσαν πόλιν εὐκτιμέναν
χαλκοθωράκων μετ᾽ Ἀτ᾽ρειδᾶν. δικαίας
12 ὅστις ἔχει φρένας, εὑ-
125   ρήσει σὺν ἅπαντι χρόνωι
μυρίας ἀλκὰς Ἀχαιῶν.

1 str.   Nike, giver of sweets . . .
                    to you the father . . . . .
                high-throned . . . . .
                In gilded Olympus . . .
                standing at Zeus' side
                    you judge the fulfillment
                of excellence, mortal and divine.
                Come to us, daughter of long-tress'd
                    right-judging Styx! Thanks to you
                at last Metapontum is taken
                    by fine-limbed boys in troupes,
                by feasting—this god-honored town.
                All sing the Pythian victor,
                    Phaescus' son, followed by every eye.

ant.   With kindly glance the Delos-born
                    son of the slender Leto
                welcomed him, and flowery crowns
                    in plenty fell upon Alexidamus
                there on Cirra's plain where
                    his powerful wrestling style
                    was triumphant over all,
                nor did the sun that day
                    see him sink to the ground.
                I say that also in holy Pelops'
                    sacred glade beside
                Alpheus' swirling streams, had someone not
                turned from the straight path of justice,
                    he would have wreathed his head with

ep.   welcoming grayness of olive,
      he would have come crowned
      back to his fathers' bucolic land!
      . . . . .
      to earth where dancers dance lovely steps
        he pinned the boy with knowing skill
      but then—unless the cause was god—
        the wandering wits of men took back
        the prize, though it lay supreme in his hand.
      That's past. Now Artemis of the wilds,
      renowned for her bow and golden staff, although
      a Gentle Lady, gives him bright victory.
      For her the son of Abas once
        set up a shrine where many pray—
        he and his seemly daughters,

2 str.   girls that a puissant Hera struck with fear
        and drove from Proetus' splendid halls,
      whipping their wits astray, yoking them
        to a dreaded necessity. They,
      though virgins still, had
        entered the area sacred to
        the red-sashed divinity
      and praised the wealth of their father
      as greater by far than the gold owned
      by the fair-haired wife of awesome Zeus!
        She, much angered, assailed their hearts
      with savage unnatural thoughts;
      they fled to the leafy upland glades
        to howl beneath the trees,

ant.   leaving behind them the city of Tiryns,
        quitting the streets the gods had made.
      There, ten years before, a group
        of favored and fearless men
      had settled, leaving the city of Argos,
        coming as bronze-armed heroes
        with their much envied king.
      Turbulent strife had sprung up,
      fraternal and foolish in cause,
      dividing the brothers, Acrisius and Proetus,
        so that the people were ruined
      by violent quarrels and grievous wars.

They begged the sons of Abas
to portion the rich corn land

ep. and to part, letting the younger go out
as founder of Tiryns, lest all should die.
And, because Cronian Zeus
wished to honor Danaus' line
and horse-driving Lynceus' race,
he put an end to the hateful pain.
The monstrous Cyclopes came and toiled
to build a wall for the famous town,
fairest and best, and there the god-like
glorious heroes lived, those who had left
the meadows and horses of Argos behind.
From that same city, when they were mad,
the unwed, dark-haried
daughters of Proetus fled.

3 str. His heart was captive to grief; he felt
the goad of an unfamiliar care
and thought to drive his two-edged sword
into his breast
but the men of his bodyguard
begged him with honeyed words
and held him by force of hands.
Thirteen months were fulfilled
while they roamed the gloomy woods
and ran through the pastures of Arcady
where sheep fed; then,
when they came to Lousos' fair waters
the father stopped, bathed,
and calling on purple-crowned Leto's

ant. ox-eyed daughter he made a prayer,
hands outstretched to the bright
chariot sun, asking that
his wander-wit girls might be led
out of their furious rage.
"For you I promise to kill
twenty red oxen never yet yoked!"
He prayed, and she whose father is best,
she who scouts beasts, heard him; with

Hera's permission she cured the garlanded girls,
   ending their ungodly frenzy,
and at once they made her a precinct,
built her an altar, stained it with sheep's blood and
   set women to dancing around it.

ep.   Thence did you come, my Lady;
you followed the war-loving men of Achaea
   to dwell with fair fortune
in Metapontum,
   golden mistress of arms-bearing men!
You have a lovely grove here
   close by Casa's sweet waters,
founded by men who, when in the end
   the gods willed it so,
sacked Priam's well-built town,
fighting beside the bronze-armed
Atreidae. Any man with a balanced mind
   will ever discover, through all time,
   the Achaeans' myriad deeds.

    The boys who danced this song must have mimed the ravings of the girls who ran howling through Arcadia, and even without being able to watch them we are apt to find the whole song somewhat insane. Why has the poet chosen this story of female lunacy, and why has he let the notion of madness penetrate his entire song, so that it provides the conceit that brings the performance to its close ("Any man with a balanced mind . . ." 123–4)? To answer these questions one must in fairness look first at his own explanation, offered as the myth is introduced. First he makes the singers swerve from their proper happy subject, which is Alexidamus' Delphic triumph, to an opposite one which they announce with an aggressive, "I say and I will go on saying . . ." (*phasō*, 24). An earlier defeat at Olympia is certainly an improper, unhappy subject, but there is method in this madness, for the singers insist that this old evil came about because the Olympic judges were temporarily insane. Considered in this way, the former defeat was a kind of sickness and the present victory in turn becomes a kind of medicament or cure. Furthermore, if the new victory equals a recovery of health, then it must have been the gift of a healing divinity—a Metapontine healing divinity, the Artemis who has a shrine at the springs of Casa (37 ff.; 119).[9] And if anyone should wonder at her interest in a case of madness, let him only remember that she is called Hemera, She Who Tames, and that she once cured the daughters of Proetus.

The illogic of this argument has exasperated certain critics, as has the pile of epithets that makes Artemis a huntress (*agrotera*, 37), a goddess who carries a golden staff (*chrysalakatos*, 38, but is this a rod or a distaff?), she whose work it is to soothe and tame (*Hemera*, 39), one whose fame derives from her bow (*toxuklutos*, 39), all in the space of three lines.[10] The epithets can surely be justified, since they are applied to a power that will tame the girls' wildness and return them to their civilized hearths,[11] but one may still legitimately wonder why the victor and his family were expected to be pleased with the notion that success in wrestling was the gift of the same goddess who had cured the howling Proetids. Bacchylides, however, has chosen this myth and decided to narrate it in the grand manner in a long and splendid ode. Consequently, instead of accusing him of rambling incoherence, as an irritated Farnell did,[12] we must try to discover the fame, the force, and the congruity with victory that he meant to elicit from his inauspicious tale.

The poet's intentions can be most plainly read in the changes that he made in his mythic materials as he adapted them to his epinician purpose. The story of the daughters of Proetus was older than Hesiod and in its more ancient forms it had been a grievous and terrible tale told to explain the division of Argos and the decline of one branch of the house of Danaus.[13] It concerned the race that was finally to produce Heracles, but it used the daughters of Proetus as a reverse definition of their cousin Danaë, for it made them represent all that Zeus did *not* want in an ancestress of his future son. The girls' madness was variously explained—they had offended either Hera (formally, by outraging a cult statue; pridefully, by claiming greater beauty; or morally, by their lewd behavior) or else Dionysus (by refusing initiation).[14] Their symptoms were also variously defined, for sometimes they were stricken with baldness, leprosy, or perhaps some sexual disease, while in the Dionysiac version they went wild with all the women of Argos and, like Bacchants, killed and ate children.[15] They, however, were not at the centre of the old story, for the point of the original tale was that their father had to buy their cure from the seer Melampous at the price of two thirds of his kingdom.[16] The healing was done either with ritual dances or with prayer, but either way the story celebrated the greed and the craft of Melampous, while all of its Argive characters suffered denigration. Proetus lost his daughters, for one died and the other two were claimed by Melampous and his brother,[17] and Tiryns lost more than half of its surrounding lands.

This story, with its great antiquity and its relevance to the birth of Heracles, was a true sample of the Unforgotten, but Bacchylides nevertheless dared to treat it with great freedom. He meant to attach it to Lousoi and to Artemis[18] and so he simply removed what had been its core, the figure of the famous Thessalian seer, and in so doing he erased all of the story's previous political tendencies. With Melampous gone, there is no longer any need to give away territory or to send royal girls into alien homes, and the legend ceases to be one that explains the end of a dynasty. Saved in this new way by Artemis, Proetus can take his daughters back to a Tiryns that has lost none of its power, and with the story cut at the moment of salvation, he seems to continue there as an example of god-favored kingliness. The point is no longer the high price one must pay for mortal craft,[19] but the high reward to be gained by piety, and the emblem of the whole action is the altar that is its physical and its poetic product (110).

The suppression of the seer and the introduction of Artemis allowed Bacchylides to tell a story that enhanced civic power instead of destroying it, and he reinforced this effect with a secondary myth in which a city is miraculously created. The Greeks of the west were especially fond of foundation legends, but Bacchylides was not merely trying to amuse when he gave his Metapontine clients this version of the tale of Tiryns, for once again he has made significant changes in the traditional material. Other versions had dwelt upon the quarrel of the brothers, giving it ugly causes and sometimes making Acrisius accuse Proetus of the rape of his daughter, Danaë. Usually Proetus was driven out of Argos by his brother's army, spent time in exile, and finally took Tiryns with much bloodshed by bringing in foreigners.[20] All of these lurid details Bacchylides has suppressed (note his bland phrase about the quarrel "taking its beginnings from foolish causes," 65), and he has replaced them with a series of happy innovations—the prayers of the people, the kindly response of Zeus, his desire to honor the whole race, and finally the Cyclopean building of the city as a sign of god-favored peace. A gracious Zeus has been made to control this secondary story, just as a gracious Artemis does the primary one, and once again there is a physical emblem, for where the Proetid story produced an altar, this tale produces the awesome walls of Tiryns.[21]

Bacchylides showed a high-handed optimism as he refashioned his mythic materials. He evidently had a clear purpose and a sure confidence in its achievement, and the manner of his narration bears him out, for the artistry of this telling is consummate. The long mythic section (of 71 lines) is presented as a great ring that begins with its own end, the altar and cult of the soothing Artemis of Lousoi (*bōmon*, 41; *bōmon*, 110). Within this Proetid circle, the inner story proposes a second smaller ring, for the foundation legend starts and stops with the settlement of Proetus and his men in their new city (*lipontes . . . naion*, 60–61; *naion . . . lipontes*, 80–81). This notion naturally involves leaving the old city and so it provides the formal link between the two circles as the poet insists that, just as the girls left Tiryns, so did the men leave Argos (*lipousai*, 57; *lipontes*, 60–81). Of course the tale of madness which both precedes and follows the Tiryns legend is chronologically the more recent of the two (just as, in the ode as a whole, the opening and the *envoi* are chronologically most recent of all, since they represent the tangible present), and in the same way within each story the first and last events to be narrated are the most recent ones. The poem's heavily concentric design[22] thus creates a present that surrounds and contains the past, at once shaping it and deriving shape from it in a way that defies any linear sense of causation. In this particular case, the founding of the altar, by defining the whole of the mythic design, seems to demand and justify every other event, and conversely the quarrel of the brothers—the center of a story that is itself a center—seems to send its influence out in all directions: through the building of the walls, the breaking out through those walls, the wanderings, the bath in the river, and the establishment of the new cult. And this means that Zeus and Tiryns seem to stand immediately behind the Proetus of the outer story, so that a civic masculinity radiates from this core even to the perimeter where the altar of Artemis stands.

With his double ring Bacchylides has given his two stories a kind of simultaneity, and yet of course the performance itself imposes its own chronology, since the singers must speak of one thing before another. The material presented to our minds in elaborate circles will continue to cohere in its atemporal oneness, but nevertheless the experiences presented to our senses have occurred in sequence and they consequently arrange themselves in a hierarchy, the more recently felt taking precedence over the earlier ones. This effect is particularly plain when we consider the poem's two miracles—the two *thaumata* with which it courts the fame of the unreasonable. The first of these is the semi-metamorphosis of the girls into something like beasts ("they howled beneath the trees," 56). This marvel is explicitly the work of a divine power, Hera; it is truly strange and outrageous, and it is prolonged by a stanza break, so that whatever imitation the chorus gave of the girls' strange cries will echo in a slight pause. Nevertheless, the wonder of the princesses' transformation is very lightly touched upon and never referred to again in Ode 11. Older poets had hinted at hideous promiscuity and physical disease, and a later one would transform all the girls into imitation cows (Virg. *Ecl.* 6.48 ff.), but Bacchylides changes only the voices of the daughters of Proetus. What is more, as he tells it, the wonder of their behavior lay as much in their leaving their city as it did in their altered tongues. A girl outside the walls was beast enough and marvel enough for him.

The second *thauma* is more sharply delineated and it inevitably crushes the first, as the image of bellowing girls and fluttering trees is replaced by that of giants moving enormous stones. The Cyclopes come, huge and dangerous (*hyperphialoi*, 78), and even they must toil (*kamon*, 77) in order to build the magic wall of Tiryns. These giants satisfy a childish desire for a fairy-tale wonder, just as the beast-girls did, but once again Bacchylides insists that the true wonder lies elsewhere and is connected with the concept of the city. It is the wall, not its makers, that we should marvel at, and in the wall we are to consider, not the size of its stones, but the intangible quality of being superlative. Zeus has commissioned a thing that is *kalliston* (79), of all walls the finest.

According to ordinary rules there ought to be a third marvel, for the story of the madness of the Proetids must necessarily contain the miracle of their cure if it is to come to an end. Bacchylides, however, has decided not to evoke the moment in which this third wonder occurred. He gives us the initial transformation of the girls but not its reversal, and this reticence points up the fact that they are no longer central to his tale as he brings it to its close. The interrupting foundation legend has allowed him to shift the focus of his narration to their father, the king, and it is notable that the third strophe in which the story of the maddened girls is taken up again, begins in this way: "*Him* did grief seize at the heart" (85). And so it is Proetus who bathes at Lousoi (97), instead of the afflicted ones; it is he who makes a prayer, he who promises sacrifice; the song makes his actions the only ones that we can perceive. The healing of the girls is by the poet's contrivance removed from the face of the earth and viewed, not as an experienced human event, but as an indescribable emanation of divine will. Artemis, with Hera's consent, ends the *mania* with a single simple verb (*pausen*, 108) and the only change that we can see is that the girls are suddenly wearing flowery crowns. It is clear that they are cured, but we have not felt their recovery, and this of course is the way the poet meant it to be, for when the final *thauma* is thus smoothly ignored the wonder of the walls the giants built is able to maintain its place as the ruling marvel of the ode.

The lyric narrative, with its circular form and its sequence of wonders, thus subtly gives primacy to what is ostensibly secondary, the apparent digression[23] about the founding of Tiryns. This seemingly perverse emphasis might have been disruptive but in fact the two stories are in no sense alternatives or rivals, nor do they in any way contradict each other. Rather, the poet persuades us that they are two versions of a single essential tale and this he does with a series of verbal and conceptual echoes. The official link between them was made with the repeated notion of departure, as the girls departed from a city built by men who had departed from another city (*lipousai*, 57; *lipontes*, 60; *lipontes*, 81;

apessumenai, 82), but other points of contact are not so artificial. Both stories begin with an unnatural crime, for the sisters quarreled with Hera in a place where they did not belong, while the brothers quarreled with one another in the family palace where no quarrels should occur. In both cases punishment came in the form of further unnatural acts that were perverse and self-damaging (Bacchylides' word for this quality is *palintropos,* 54; contrary, turned back upon itself): bestial unfeminine wanderings for the girls and wasteful unprincely killings for the men. These punishments are in each story called "necesity" (*anangke,* 46 and 72), and in each story a prayer is offered, in the masculine tale by the people of Argos (69) and in the feminine one by the king, Proetus (99). Then the "necessity" of grievous slaughter and the "necessity" of godless ravings are alike simply "stopped" (*ethelen . . . pausai,* 73–6; *pausen,* 108) by the two gods. And finally both stories end with outward and visible signs of the gods' interventions, the walls and the altar (*teichos . . . kamon,* 77; *temenos bōmon te teuchon,* 110). (The fact that one is godmade, and other manmade agrees with the men's generally better relations with god: they were passively afflicted by their *neikos,* whereas the girls went out of their way to pick a fight with Hera.)[24] Such extensive parallelism enforces a kind of conflation, as does the narration in concentric circles, and the result is that when the mythic section of Ode 11 is finished its two monuments seem almost to be one. According to the fictional geography they are separated by many miles of rough country, but the danced song leaves them standing side by side in our minds—an altar of healing and a protective peaceable wall.[25] The characters in the combined tales have offended gods, tribe, and city, but they have found escape from punishment and have returned to the order imposed by the masculine city and the practice of feminine cult.

The myth of the daughters of Proetus thus has, in Bacchylides' telling, an eminently civilized ending. Since madness meant leaving the city, regained sanity implies a return for the princesses, and the natural supposition is that they went back with their father to Tiryns, taking with them the knowledge of the new cult of Artemis. Their flight into the periphery has begun at a temple; it has been supervised by the head of their tribe; it has included a temporary change of personality; it has been contained in a fixed number of months (92); it has ended with women's choruses (112). It has, in other words, resumed the standard schema of an initiation, and the emphasis upon the virginity of the girls (42, 47, 84), the mention of Hera's red sash (49), the ambivalence of Artemis' shaft/spindle (38), the crowns worn at the end (108), and Proetus' plea to the goddess to "lead out" the girls from their madness, as a girl is "led out" in marriage (103), prove that Bacchylides was making conscious use of the initiatory significance of his myth.[26] By implication, then, the city of Tiryns, a place filled with warriors (62), is by this fiction provided with potential brides.

The twice errant mortals and the twice merciful divinities of Ode 11 are reminiscent of the similar, even rosier sequence described in Pindar's Seventh Olympian. Here, however, instead of an island that blooms like a flower, walls raised up by giants appear as the central and enduring image, for this is finally the more secular of the two songs. Tiryns' walls and Artemis' altar prove that men's crimes are sometimes set straight by gods, but even more important, they prove that men and women are meant by heaven to live together in piety and good order. The goddess who tames wildness has been brought into association with the Zeus who ends dissension because the city itself, through its king and its cults, is the answer to impiety, madness, and bestiality.[27] Surely now we can see why men of Metapontum—a city that worshipped Artemis and Zeus, and one that could almost remember its own foundation[28]—might have paid to be told this tale. The fame of Tiryns' magical beginnings will enhance the fame of their own city, and the madness of the Proetids, viewed as a *rite de passage*, completes the poetic representation of what civic strength means. The story of the girls has been transformed so that it can represent the final phases of the organization of a fruitful common life, but the poet has done more, for he has made it into a mythic model for an agonistic contest as well. The boy Alexidamus went out of his city in a kind of sickness of defeat, like the Proetid girls; he travelled to Delphi, as they to Arcadia, and there he was given a healing cure, his victory. He brings that victory back to Metapontum, as they brought back the grace of Artemis to Tiryns, and in this actual moment it is being celebrated, here in Magna Graecia, with dancing choruses of boys (11–12), just as the other healing is celebrated still at Lousoi with women's dancing (112). Today's ephemeral praise of the boy's name is thus attached to a form of cult praise that will go on forever, and in this way the daughters of Proetus assure the permanent glory of the victor Alexidamus. In addition, they reveal a major article of Bacchylides' epinician faith, for the Proetids show that, for him, the great games were a continuation of the primitive rites that defined society and the city and kept them sane and strong.

8. THE TRAGIC MUSE

Bacchylides makes characteristic responses to the generic demands of choral and epinician performance, but his work also displays a quality that seems to be a free gift to the genre and one that is peculiarly his own. On occasion, Bacchylides fills a song with the sense of tragedy, and for proof that such a sense is gratuitous and in no way required by the epinician profession, one has only to look at the work of Pindar. Like Bacchylides, Pindar contrives scenes of action, frequently making his chorus mouth the direct discourse of certain characters, but these scenes are not intended to emphasize the paradoxical coexistence of freedom and destiny that informs the work of the great fifth-century dramatists. There is much that is magnificent and fateful in the Pindaric fictions, and sometimes there are moments of sadness, but never does that poet choose to depict the divided mind, the imponderable choice, and the sightlessness that make a man tragic in the technical sense of that term.[1] Bacchylides, on the other hand, on certain occasions, creates scenes that display the inner condition as well as the outward aspect of their agents. In these cases he depicts the kind of blind but voluntary deed that Aristotle recognized as best for theatre, and once or twice he gives his event the double analysis that is typical of Attic drama, showing it to be no more than a tiny swirl in an enormous pattern of fate, but showing it also to be the largest gesture of a vigorous, separatist, even recalcitrant human will. By these means he gives a choral song the flavor of tragedy.

In Pindar's mythic world, the relation between fate and human will is cordial and natural. The typical Pindaric hero recognizes a pattern of external opportunity that answers a pattern of internal powers existing within himself, and on this sure basis he acts. Consequently, the Pindaric odes are rich in moments of vocation, prediction, and clarification, as man's ambition seizes the best that heaven has to offer. The one who is called cannot feel doubt, for fateful deeds can only be glorious, and so an Iamos listens without a qualm to the bodiless voice of god, a Bellerophon takes the bit that Athena has left him, knowing exactly what he must make of it, and a Pollux chooses in a trice the half-mortal alternative that a present Zeus cleanly outlines for him. These are scenes of luminous ease, for there is no tension in this candid world, though there may of course be error. Even in the negative cases, however, the Pindaric point is that comprehension was possible between earth and heaven; if clarity was temporarily darkened, it was because men foully (like Tantalus) or foolishly (like the early Rhodians) refused to understand. The will of Pindar's heaven is usually radiantly present to the minds of heroes as the gods fill fine men with a longing for fine deeds, just as Hera filled the Greeks with a longing for the Argo.[2] Some creatures refuse to listen, others respond as if bewitched, but the sound of the golden lyre is clearly audible on earth and men can live in accordance with its harmonies.

Bacchylides to a degree shared in this sublime idealism. He too believed that heroes worked to capture heavenly virtue in their deeds, just as poets worked to embrace divine hymns in their songs. Nevertheless, his heroes frequently moved with less assurance than Pindar's, in landscapes where there was more obscurity than Pindar allowed. The Bacchylidean gods were further away, their voices not so audible; fate was not always tailored to its human agent; the call to destined action might be muffled, and the hero sometimes heard as well the conflicting cries of his own passions. Similar human actions could thus have very different ethical qualities, according to whether they were treated by the one poet or the other, and the difference is easy to appreciate if one looks simultaneously at the Pelops of Pindar's First Olympian and the Croesus of Bacchylides' Ode 3.

In spite of differences in age and circumstance, Pelops, when he calls upon Poseidon, is very much like the Lydian king who prays from his pyre. One is about to be carried out on a tide of opportunity, the other has capsized; one wants a divine ally, the other a divine witness, but nevertheless both are in direct contact with supernatural powers who are indebted to them, and each has recognized what is, in his earthly circumstances, the single best thing to do. In neither case do we see a man struggling to make a decision, and in neither case are we shown anything of the hero's inner condition. Each poet has instead spent all his art upon his hero's fate, making that fate as transparent as possible while the creatures themselves—Pelops and Croesus—are purposely left opaque. In all these ways the two scenes are similar, and yet in a deeper sense they are quite unlike, for there is a hint of the tragic in the Lydian king, while there is no touch of tragedy upon Pindar's Tantalid.

The essential distinction between the Pindaric and the Bacchylidean scenes derives not from formal elements in the two situations, not from disparities in the two characters, and not even from variations in the two fates that are so much emphasized. Both heroes will have a kind of final victory, and while Pelops' prize will be a wedding, Croesus will have something even better—endless bliss in the company of the female members of his family. No, the real difference lies in the realm of ignorance and knowledge, and that is exactly where the tragic potential usually resides. Pelops knows the nature of his contest and he knows what he can win by it; he calls upon a god with whom he is carnally acquainted; he races according to an already tested skill and strength, and so he wins in easy complicity with his destiny. Croesus, on the other hand, has wholly misread his condition and acts upon false assumptions, thinking himself deserted by the god of his special cult. He faces, not the known dangers of a chariot course but the wholly unknown experience of death by fire, and meanwhile he is ignorant of his prize. He knows only that his performance will bring a kind of fame.

Pelops, with his justified certitude, is a neat mythic cipher for the nontragic collaboration of real with ideal, and his poet presents him with an almost allegorical objectivity.[3] His coming contest will not be his own, it will be won with Poseidon's team, and even his act of prayer seems hardly to belong to him because it is made in simple obedience to his status as one whom the god has loved. As a result, Pelops' depicted act remains essentially static and nonindividualized. His speech is a decoration, a didactic example, and a portent, but it does not add the speaker's raw experience to our own. By contrast, Croesus' prayer is endowed by Bacchylides with a vivid subjectivity. It is not an orderly proposal that a benefaction should be returned, but instead a disorderly gesture of pride, and it is made—or so Croesus thinks—not with god's help but in spite of god. Consequently it speaks *as action* to that part of the spectator's soul in which his own actions are decided.

In effect, the Bacchylidean Apollo will show himself to be as good a friend to Croesus as the Pindaric Poseidon is to Pelops, but Croesus does not know this, and his ignorance tempts him to judge god like a hero of tragedy. There is a lurid light around him but his two actions (addressing god and climbing upon the pyre) are not dictated by a general clarity in the universe. Quite the opposite: they are the products of the war's dark expression of Zeus' will, and also of Croesus' own blindness, and this makes them the king's own. Later, of course, Croesus too will become a cipher, a mere sign to prove that gods reward human generosity, but while he stretches out his arms and calls Apollo to account he is, by the poet's fiat, a living creature who is fallible and seemingly free. The poet has thus made him demonstrate the awesome disparity between mortal understanding and the natural and supernatural facts that a man must deal with, and this is why, while Pindar's Pelops leaves us feeling vaguely exalted, Bacchylides' Croesus plants a kind of terror in us.

Needless to say, Bacchylides does not always arrange for this kind of drama in his mythic scenes. The Heracles of Ode 13 was not like Croesus at all, but was in fact even more iconic than Pindar's Pelops. Theseus too, when he dove from the deck of Minos' ship, did so with a justified confidence very much like that of the Tantalid, and even the Proetus of Ode 11, though he thought for a moment of suicide, did not appear as a tragic figure but only as an element in a mythic meditation on the meaning of the city. All of these figure were viewed externally and, though they moved, the scenes in which they appeared were not truly dynamic, but were instead mere frames for a meaning that happened to be rendered in gesture. There are, however, two more Heracles songs and another piece about Theseus in which action is depicted as truly mobile—uncertain and fluctuating and dependent upon human decision and resolve.[4] In these three songs mortal will is conditioned by mortal ignorance and adapts itself to fate with something less than ease, producing fictions where the meaning cannot be posted like a motto, and scenes that are apprehended not as poetic teaching but as vital experience.

Because of its dialogue form the Theseus poem, usually called Dithyramb 18, is the easiest place to start, though of the three it is the least tragic. It is not an epinician ode, nor is there any convincing sign of a Dionysiac purpose, though the piece seems to be meant for public performance at Athens under city sponsorship.[5] The one thing that is certain is that it has been heavily influenced by the theatre, for the poet has provided no invocation, no *envoi*, no description of the present festivity, and no third-person narrative voice. The myth is all, in this song, and the myth is rendered exclusively in direct mimetic speech that is delivered as an exchange between a chorus costumed as young soldiers of the past and a solo performer dressed as a legendary king.[6] The spectacle evidently began with a military alert played upon a trumpet, at which signal the chorus and the single dancer entered, very probably from opposite sides of the dancing space. The soldier performers were the first to sing (18.1 ff.):

Α′ ⟨ΧΟΡΟΣ⟩ 1 Βασιλεῦ τᾶν ἱερᾶν Ἀθανᾶν,
τῶν ἁβ⸍ροβίων ἄναξ Ἰώνων,
3 τί νέον ἔκ⸍λαγε χαλκοκώδων
σάλπιγξ πολεμηΐαν ἀοιδάν;
5 5 ἦ τις ἁμετέρας χθονὸς
δυσμενὴς ὅρι᾽ ἀμφιβάλλει
στραταγέτας ἀνήρ;

8 ἢ λῃσταὶ κακομάχανοι
9 9 ποιμένων ἀέκατι μήλων
10   σεύοντ᾽ ἀγέλας βίᾳ;
11 ἢ τί τοι κραδίαν ἀμύσσει;
φθέγγευ· δοκέω γὰρ εἴ τινι βͱροτῶν
13 ἀλκίμων ἐπικουρίαν
καὶ τὶν ἔμμεναι νέων,
15 15 ὦ Πανδίονος υἱὲ καὶ Κρεούσας.
Β′⟨ΑΙΓΕΥΣ⟩ 1 Νέον ἦλθε⟨ν⟩ δολιχὰν ἀμείψας
κᾶρυξ ποσὶν Ἰσθμίαν κέλευθον·
3 ἄφατα δ᾽ ἔργα λέγει κραταιοῦ
φωτός· τὸν ὑπέρβιόν τ᾽ ἔπεφͱνεν
20 5 Σίνιν, ὃς ἰσχύϊ φέρτατος
θνατῶν ἦν, Κρονίδα Λυταίου
σεισίχθονος τέκος·
8 σῦν τ᾽ ἀνδροκτόνον ἐν νάπαις
9 Κρεμμυῶνος ἀτάσθαλόν τε
25   Σκίρωνα κατέκτανεν·
11 τάν τε Κερκυόνος παλαίστραν
ἔσχεν, Πολυπήμονός τε καρτεράν
13 σφῦραν ἐξέβαλεν Προκό-
πτας, ἀρείονος τυχών
30 15 φωτός. ταῦτα δέδοιχ᾽ ὅπᾳ τελεῖται.
Γ′ ⟨ΧΟ.⟩   1 Τίνα δ᾽ ἔμμεν πόθεν ἄνδρα τοῦτον
λέγει, τίνα τε στολὰν ἔχοντα;
3 πότερα σὺν πολεμηίοις ὅ-
πͱλοισι στρατιὰν ἄγοντα πολλάν;
35 5 ἢ μοῦνον σὺν ὀπάοσιν
36   στείχειν ἔμπορον οἷ᾽ ἀλάταν
ἐπ᾽ ἀλλοδαμίαν,
8 ἰσχυρόν τε καὶ ἄλκιμον
9 ὦδε καὶ θρασύν, ὃς τ⟨οσ⟩ούτων
40   ἀνδρῶν κρατερὸν σθένος
11 ἔσχεν; ἢ θεός αὐτὸν ὁρμᾳ,
δίκας ἀδίκοισιν ὄφͱρα μήσεται·
13 οὐ γὰρ ῥάιδιον αἰὲν ἔρδοντα μὴ ᾽ντυχεῖν κακῶι.
45 15 πάντ᾽ ἐν τῶι δολιχῶι χρόνωι τελεῖται.
Δ′ ⟨ΑΙΓ.⟩   1 Δύο οἱ φῶτε μόνους ἁμαρτεῖν
λέγει, περὶ φαιδίμοισι δ᾽ ὤμοις
3 ξίφος ἔχειν ⟨∪∪_∪__⟩
ξεστοὺς δὲ δύ᾽ ἐν χέρεσσ᾽ ἄκοντας
50 5 κηΰτυκτον κυνέαν Λάκαι-
ναν κρατὸς πέρι πυρσοχαίτου·
χιτῶνα πορφύρεον

8 στέρνοις τ' ἀμφί, καὶ οὔλιον
9 Θεσσαλὰν χλαμύδ᾽· ὀμμάτων δὲ
55 στίλβειν ἄπο Λαμνίαν
11 φοίνισσαν φλόγα· παῖδα δ᾽ ἔμμεν
πρώθηβον, ἀρηΐων δ᾽ ἀθυρμάτων
13 μεμνᾶσθαι πολέμου τε καὶ
χαλκεοκτύπου μάχας·
60 15 δίζησθαι δὲ φιλαγ'λάους Ἀθάνας.

Cho.   King of our holy Athens,
        lord of luxurious Ionians,
    why did the brazen-voiced trumpet
        just now sing out the call to war?
    Has some enemy captain
        broken across our borders
        leading an army in?
    Have marauders with evil schemes
        come to kill stubborn shepherds
        and take away our flocks?
    What threat sinks its claw in your heart?
        Speak, for I do believe,
    if ever a mortal man had, you have
        brave young allies beside you,
    son of Pandion and Creusa!

King.   Just now a herald came on foot
        from the tortuous Isthmian path
    to tell of unspeakable deeds done
        by a prodigious man. Mighty Sinis
    he killed—strongest of men
        he was, grandson of Cronus and son
        of the Lytaean earthquake-maker!
    This man has slain the murderous
        sow of the meadow of Cremmyon;
        has killed dread Sciron as well;
    has captured the wrestling school
        that Cercyon ran, while Procoptes
    has dropped the hideous mattock
        Polyphemus made, faced with one
    stronger than he! The end of these deeds I fear.

Cho.   Who does the messenger say that he is?
        Where from, and what is his company?

Has he come armed for war,
  commanding a body of men,
or does he come single with
  no one but servants, like
  a merchant who travels abroad—
this man who is strong and brave
and fearless enough to break
  the overpowering strength
of so many enemies? Surely some god
  has sent him out to punish injustice
for on his own a man of deeds
  now and again must fail. All things
fulfill their ends within the coils of time.

King.   Two [men], he says, accompany the unknown one.
  Down from his gleaming shoulder
hangs a sword with an ivory hilt,
  polished javelins in his hands,
and a Spartan dogskin cap
  covers his ruddy curls.
  A purple shirt is wrapped
round his body and over that
a woolen mantle from Thessaly; from his eyes
  a spark of Lemnian fire
flashes red. He is a boy
  scarce grown, eager for games
of Ares, wanting war
  and the battle clash of bronze. He comes
seeking Athens where splendor is.

How did the performance end? When singers were allowed to make their farewells to patron or audience, and so to get their feet back on the ground of actuality, they could simply march out of the dancing space. These performers, however, were different from those of every other song that survives from Pindar and Bacchylides, because when their song finished they were still caught in their fictional situation, still on the razor's edge. If they simply turned and took themselves off, the effect must have been curiously anticlimactic, and it may be that their exit was covered by another more urgent trumpet call, or a warning roll of drums. Some have even supposed that just as the music stopped a group of actual ephebes burst in, ready to perform the exercises of their annual review.[7] Whatever the drill of the performing chorus, however, the poetic fact is that when this song ends the powerful stranger it has described seems to be just out of sight. The rapid, geographic sequence of his adventures[8] has launched him toward Athens; the king's description has made him almost visible, and so, when the music stops, the silence is filled with the sense that this youth who is too strong, and too eager for war, stands just outside the gates.

The young man who is out there knows that he has arrived at his goal (he has asked the way, 60), and he also knows his own capabilities, for they have been proved by a series of tests tailored to his temper and his strength. He is ready for his fate, suitably dressed,[9] adequately armed, appropriate to the hour, and a song that stood outside with him, at the gates of Athens, could have recreated a moment of heroic opportunity consciously seized. That, however, is just the song that Bacchylides decides not to compose. He wants his chorus within the gates, on the side of the wall where there is uncertainty, apprehension, and fear. Suppose, he seems to say, that Athens first heard of Theseus' deeds without knowing who their author was? And then he makes a song that forces the confusion of its fictional Athens upon its actual audience, keeping listeners ignorant of who the present king is until the end of the first strophe, and unable to reject the idea of inimical invasion until the monstrous names begin, in the fifth line of the second stanza. The performance thus embodies and enforces a moment in which ordinary certainties are assailed by something beyond expectation. When the unexercised parts of men's natures respond to an awesome and ill-defined challenge of this sort, tragedy can ensue, but Bacchylides in this song is more interested in another sort of effect. He is at work to make the invisible more perceptible than the visible, and so he sketches but does not exploit the tragic potential of his chosen situation.

What Bacchylides chooses not to do can perhaps best be appreciated by comparing his scene to the formally almost identical one from Aeschylus' Seven Against Thebes (182–244). There again a king and a chorus meet in a city that has just received news of a threatening presence outside its walls. There, however, action is at once in question, as the two parties dispute over the best response to be made. When the Aeschylean king leaves the stage, he means to take hold of the coming event and shape it, and meanwhile both he and the chorus have been shown to be, not a typical soldier-ruler and a typical group of city women, but a man unique in his mixture of arrogance and statesmanship and women remarkable for their persistent hysteria.

The Bacchylidean scene by contrast shows neither motion nor decision. Its dialogue suggests a play, but the stunning effect of this piece comes from the fact that in a situation that calls for action, no one makes a move. What is more, though the nameless messenger who would naturally bring this news has been replaced by a particular king, there is no characterization here. Aegeus has found a violence in the stranger's adventures that is awesome in its quantity, while the men have discovered a quality in the killings that they guess to be justice (41–2), but the effect of this difference is to enrich the portrait of the external Theseus, not to discriminate between the characters of the two parties who are before our eyes, for in the end the two responses are exactly the same. The king repeats his information as if he were telling a nightmare that still has hold of him; he makes no gesture, he only says, "I am afraid" (30). The young men stare into his dream and, finding something supernatural there (41), join him in his fixed trance. No one for an instant considers the stranger outside as a force to be resisted; all see him as a sign to be studied, or perhaps a punishment to be endured. And so the song ends, like the beginning of Cavafy's best-known poem.[10] The city waits, but it does not deck itself out or prepare scrolls for its "barbarian," it only stands frozen in its expectation.

The ostentatiously dynamic form of Dithyramb 18 is used paradoxically to convey a condition of paralysis, for in this scene the only actor is somewhere else. Movement and ethos are absent, and yet there is a third, eminently tragic element that is present, for this poetic scene fairly overflows with irony. Theseus, like the barbarians of Cavafy's poem, has a double aspect and the audience—joined with the poet in a conspiracy of superior knowledge—understands many things that the soldiers and the king do not. First and foremost, the audience knows who this stranger is and so they know that the king who dreads the coming of a destroyer is about to open his gates to one who is much more than a friend. That is positive irony in its plainest form, and it is sharpened by the theatrical detail of Theseus' ivory sword hilt (48), which will serve as the tell-tale token in a scene of happy recognition to be played soon between Aegeus and his unexpected son.[11] The spectator feels the joy of that coming scene even now and so he almost smiles at the king's present fear, and yet he also knows further truths that feed an opposite response. Because he is a monster-killer, the stranger seems to the young men to be a bringer of justice, and so he will be for Athens. He will "punish the unjust" (42) in the archaic sense by killing the bull of Marathon and the Minotaur, in a melodramatic sense by driving Medea away, and in a truly Athenian sense by organizing the city and giving it law. His coming will make his city indeed a place that loves what is splendid (*philaglaous Athanas*, 60), not merely one that loves luxury (2). Nevertheless, all the world knows that this monster-killer is fated to be a father-killer too. The story of the dark sail that Theseus forgot to replace when coming home from Crete was at least as old as Simonides,[12] and so the audience that watched this performance knew that finally Aegeus' general fears would be particularly confirmed. "All things fulfill their ends within the coils of time," says the chorus, once it has glimpsed a fateful purpose in Theseus' sequence of killings (45), and the audience hears the echoed *teleitai, teleitai* that joins their observation to the fears of Aegeus (30).[13] The king dreads a stranger who might attack his city, but he should dread the son who will save Athens, and the complexity of his error is the source of a pervasive and truly tragic irony. The song does not imitate action, and so it is not tragic in the Aristotelian sense, but it does imitate mortal blindness and the innate ambiguity of all worldly events, and to this extent it treats the stuff that tragic action is made of.

Another song (Dithyramb 16), apparently a winter paean,[14] keeps the conventional form of the choral lyric but gives clear expression to the poet's sense of tragedy by showing mythic mortals who are at once free and enslaved, powerful and helpless, magnificent and small. There are two such figures and Bacchylides shows one in a moment of action, the other in a moment of decision, both suffused by the fate that manipulates them even as they give it its shape:

1 . . .]ιον . ιο . . . ἐπεί
ὅλκ]άδ' ἔπεμψεν ἐμοὶ χρυσέαν
3 Πιερ]ίαθεν ἐ[ὔθ]'ρονος [Ὀ]ὐρανία,
πολυφ]άτων γέμουσαν ὕμνων
5 5 . . . . .]νειτις ἐπ' ἀνθεμόεντι Ἕβ'ρωι
. . . . . ἀ]γάλλεται ἢ δολιχαύχενι κύ[κνωι
7 . . . . .]δεῖαν φρένα τερπόμενος
8 . . . . . .]δ' ἵκηι παιηόνων
ἄνθεα πεδοιχνεῖν,
10 10 Πύθι' Ἄπολλον,
τόσα χοροὶ Δελφῶν
σὸν κελάδησαν παρ' ἀγακ'λέα ναόν,
1 πρίν γε κ'λέομεν λιπεῖν
Οἰχαλίαν πυρὶ δαπτομέναν
15 3 Ἀμφιτρυωνιάδαν θρασυμηδέα φῶ-
θ', ἵκετο δ' ἀμφικύμον' ἀκτάν·
5 ἔνθ' ἀπὸ λαΐδος εὐρυνεφεῖ Κηναίωι
Ζηνὶ θύεν βαρυαχέας ἐννέα ταύρους
7 δύο τ' ὀρσιάλωι δαμασίχθονι μέ[λ-
20 λε κόρᾱι τ' ὀβ'ριμοδερκεῖ ἄζυγα
παρθένωι Ἀθάνᾱι
10 ὑψικέραν βοῦν.
τότ' ἄμαχος δαίμων
Δαϊανείρᾱι πολύδακ'ρυν ὕφα[νε

25 1 μῆτιν ἐπίφ‌ʲρον᾿ ἐπεὶ
    πύθετ᾿ ἀγγελίαν ταλαπενθέ‌α,
3 ᾿Ιόλαν ὅτι λευκώλενον
    Διὸς υἱὸς ἀταρβομάχας
    ἄλοχον λιπαρὸ[ν] ποτὶ δόμον πέμ[π]οι.
30 6 ἆ δύσμορος, ἆ τάλ[αι]ν᾿, οἷον ἐμήσατ[ο·
    φθόνος εὐρυβίας νιν ἀπώλεσεν,
8 δνόφεόν τε κάλυμμα τῶν
    ὕστερον ἐρχομένων,
    ὅτ᾿ ἐπὶ ῥοδόεντι Λυκόρμᾱι
35 11 δέξατο Νέσσου πάρα δαιμόνιον τέρ[ας.

str.   Ourania sends me a golden ship
           freighted with songs . . . . .
        [. . . Apollo is absent,
        whether at flowery Hebrus,
        whether among the bent-necked swans . . .
        When he returns, the Delphic chorus
        will sing for him. Until that time]

ant.   we sing how he left Oechalia
           once it was tamed by fire—
        Amphitryon's bold-willed son—
           and came to the wavewashed cliff
        where from his spoils he began to kill
        nine bellowing bulls for cloud-lord Cenean Zeus,
        two for the earthtamer king of the sea,
           and for Athena, the grim-eyed
        virgin, a single yoke-free
        horned cow.
        Meanwhile an incontestable power
        wove for Daianeira's mind

ep.   a tear-filled meditated scheme
           as she learned the harsh grief-laden news
        of white-armed Iole,
        how Zeus' strife-bold son
           brought her home as his favored wife.
        Oh hard-fated, desolate, dread in her plan!
        The wide rage of jealousy ruined her
        but also the dark disguise
           worn by the future when
           one day in rosy Lycormē she
        took the godsent marvel Nessus gave.

This single triad evidently held the whole song,[15] its now damaged strophe given over to the occasion, which was Apollo's wintertime absence from Delphi, its antistrophe and epode filled with a tale meant to please the god, wherever he might have gone. We have, in other words, all of the myth that the poet meant us to have in two stanzas that, though they do not respond metrically, are cleanly posed against one another and artfully linked by enjambment. One concerns a man, the other a woman, and each of these is named so that the tale will be experienced in its swift entirety with the sure knowledge that these are Heracles and Daianeira, hero and wife, victim and assassin.[16] Indeed, the speed of the song almost superimposes the second upon the first, the woman upon the man, and it is plain that the poet's intention lay exactly there, in the simultaneity of the two moments that he chose for choral evocation.[17]

In the Heracles passage we are asked to perceive only an externalized motion which is attended by a violence that seems to be borrowed from nature. The first word of the tale is a verb of movement that ostensibly turns the hero away from the city he has besieged and destroyed, but also turns him towards the "house" that is mentioned later (29), in connection with Iole and Daianeira. He has "tamed" Oechalia with fire;[18] he comes to a place where waves strike from all sides,[19] and there he is in the act of killing loud beasts for the lords of air and water, while he gives the least possible recognition to the virgin goddess of civic culture, his usual friend and protector. The invidious moderation of his gesture towards Athena seems to refer to his having just burnt a city and stolen its virgin princess, and the poet has caused a sense of Athena's temporary alienation from him[20] to mix itself into the nameles power that is mentioned next, the daimon that links Heracles to his death just as it links antistrophe to epode. As daughter of Metis and goddess of women's skills, Athena is the patron of weaving,[21] and so when Bacchylides specifies the action of the daimon as that of weaving (*huphane*, 24), he reminds us not only of the robe that Daianeira has made (though not yet poisoned) but also of the divinity who would normally supervise all such work.

As the epode begins, the song passes from a masculine, outdoor scene to a feminine interior, and at the same time the quality of its observation changes radically. It is no longer external action but an internal realm of intellect and emotion that we are now asked to perceive, and it is no accident that the first words of the new stanza are *metin epiphron'* (25),[22] a thought-out ruse or show of skill. The first verb is one of inquiring and learning (*puthet'*, 26), and the "news" that is its object is emotionalized as "full of griefs to be suffered" (26). The fact that Iole is to arrive[23] is offered only as a piece of information contained in Daianeira's mind, for the poem has as nearly as possible moved inside the consciousness of this character. She is in the act of deciding, but it is not the substance of her decision that the song will describe, for that is knowledge that the poet and the audience already share. Daianeira will put an end to all the violent natural motion that is occurring even now in the antistrophe—of this we are sure. But how could a woman's mind have the power to destroy? That is the question that the poet has set himself to answer in the space of thirteen lines.

At first glance, this woman whose mind is invaded by a supernatural power is like a Homeric warrior whose rage comes from outside, leaving him without responsibility. Bacchylides, however, has made a Daianeira who is not epic but tragic, for he lets both passion and the past join the daimon in shaping her decision. The poet insists upon Daianeira's suffering and the evil portion that will come to her, even as he asks us to consider the enormity of her scheme (30),[24] and the sequence of thought at this point tells us that she too was destroyed by the woven plan (*emēsato . . . apolesen*, 30–31). Evidently her own plan claimed her as its responsible author, and evidently it was more enormous than she knew, which means that the daimon who made it made use of an agent at least partially blind. This notion is no sooner broached, however, than it is combined with another, for it seems that the daimon exploited her own private passion, too. Indeed, in its penultimate lines the song extends its view of Daianeira's decision by proposing two more defining forces, one deriving from the woman herself, the other from the nature of the world.

The first additional force is jealousy, and though it is to a degree universalized by its epithet (*eurubias*, 31, "whose ability to violate is broad") the preceding reference to Iole makes it clear that this destructive power has developed within Daianeira's own passionate self.[25] Linked with this biographical and very human jealousy, however, is an impersonal, universal force that originates in the way the world experiences time. The poet calls it "the veil that covers things to come" (32–3), and with this concept of tomorrow's obscurity added to that of *phthonos* he achieves a causal analysis that is perfectly double and wholly secular. Jealousy and the inscrutability of the future destroy Daianeira, but are these two natural forces replacements for the supernatural daimon, its equivalent, or possibly its worldly agents?[26] For an instant we do not know, but Bacchylides does not mean to leave us in doubt. In his two final lines he brings to life one more mythic moment, and with his last word he provides a new idea that caps and clarifies all that has gone before. The moment is the one in which Nessus died; the word is *teras*, an omen or portent (35), and the idea is that of a destined design.

The hiddenness of the future does not, after all, act upon every human life as it did upon Daianeira's—not even when it is paired with jealousy. Most people are passionate and uncomprehending, but only a few destroy (or save) something of power and magnificence with their blind decisions. These few are the executors of schemes invented by gods (or by daimons) and recognized by poets, after the fact, because of the sublime authority of their patterning. A system of omens or portents is characteristic of such divine schemes, for signs guide or tease destiny's agents through the complexities of their functions, and the same signs allow the fullness of the supernatural plan to be retrospectively understood. In this present case, Bacchylides points to such a sign in the philtre that the centaur gave to Daianeira, for that was the motif whose repetition had patterned the divinely ordained scheme of Heracles' death, a death that was in turn only a part of the larger design of his entire fate.

In the song's "today" Daianeira blindly and willingly takes the daimonic *mētis* into her mind, but she has already blindly and willingly taken it into her hands on the day long ago when she took from the monster Nessus the poison that she now will use.[27] That sunken moment is made to touch the surface of Bacchylides' poem just at its close, where proper names and roses give it an immediate reality and cause it to join, as an equal third, in the poetic conflation of the moment of Heracles' victory sacrifices with the moment of Daianeira's decision. Immediacy comes with the singer's evocation of the sensual and the natural, but nevertheless the singers label the gift of the past as a marvelous sign. What Daianeira received was not just a philtre, not just a poison, not just the means of Heracles' death, but proof that goods were in charge, shaping every incident of that hero's life and preparing its inevitable end.

Nessus is named in the last line, but he did not compound the deadly marvel that he gave; for that, a series of previous actions were necessary. Typhon and Echidna had to mate, producing the monster Hydra who in turn had to become a pet of Hera's. Heracles had to kill Hydra and tip his arrows in her bile. Then his arm had to draw his bow, the bow had to shoot forth an arrow, and the arrow had to touch Nessus in the river—only then could the centaur offer his "heaven-sent" sign to Daianeira.[28] There are four elements present in this sequence—monstrous nature, Heracles' strength, the disfavor of certain gods, and the magical favor of others—and they summarize the special destiny that belonged to Heracles. Consequently the words *daimonion teras* leave us, at the end of the song, with a recognition of deepest causes that is much like the recognitions of tragedy. We understand that it is not Daianeira, not Nessus, not even Hydra who is about to wrap Heracles in his cloak of death. The destructive force, the daimon, is the hero's own fate, strangely designed by the gods. The power that ultimately directs such dynamic fates is the same power that has made Delphi a place of signs, and consequently this myth of a sign that could not be read in the past, though it is magnificently instructive now, is precisely appropriate to a song that calls upon Apollo to return to his seat of prophecy.[29]

9. HERACLES AND MELEAGER

For Bacchylides, deeds performed in contest and celebrated in song were the models for (and the replicas of) fine deeds of every sort. Questions of knowledge, freedom, and fate could arise even inside the artificially defined athletic space and, more important, success there could be recognized as the cleanest possible example of the god-willed reversal that might come at any time, whatever a man's actions might be. This meant that awe, rather than joy, was the emotion proper to victory, and so it is not surprising to find that Bacchylides' sense of tragedy sometimes entered even into the making of an epinician song. It is, in fact, in Ode 5, a long and sumptuous piece that he made for Hieron,[1] that the double evaluations of tragedy are most evident, for there the poet shows mortal deeds that are at once superb and meaningless, wrought willingly but blindly in a universe the gods have designed for unknowable purposes.

The occasion of Ode 5 was more than brilliant, for Pherenicus, the finest animal in the tyrant's stable, had continued his astonishing career by giving Hieron an Olympic crown to match earlier ones from Delphi. Bacchylides responded to this extraordinary event with an extraordinary passage in which he paid direct tribute to the superlative strength of the horse and to his moment of supreme exertion (37–49; cf. 182–189). Then, after the briefest gnomic pause (50–55), this commissioned poet moved his dancers on into a long mythic demonstration of the inefficacy of strength, however superlative, and of exertion, however supreme. Even when these animal virtues are joined to human will and excellence and guided by human choice, they can be reduced to nothing or diverted from their course by gods intent upon carrying out some design of their own. So says this song that was meant to please the most powerful man of its time.

A′   1 Εὔμοιρε [Σ]υρακ[οσίω]ν
      ἱπποδινήτων στρατα[γ]έ,
    3 γνώσηι μὲν [ἰ]οστεφάνων
      Μοισᾶν γλυκ[ύ]δωρον ἄγαλμα, τῶν γε νῦν
  5 5 αἴ τις ἐπιχθονίων,
      ὀρθῶς· φρένα δ᾽ εὐθύδικ[ο]ν
    7 ἀτ｜ρέμ᾽ ἀμπαύσας μεριμνᾶν
      δεῦρ᾽ ⟨ἄγ᾽⟩ ἄθ｜ρησον νόωι·
    9 ἢ σὺν Χαρίτεσσι βαθυζώνοις ὑφάνας
 10   ὕμνον ἀπὸ ζαθέας
   11 νάσου ξένος ὑμετέραν
     ἐς κλυτὰν πέμπει πόλιν,
   13 χρυσάμπυκος Οὐρανίας
     κλεινὸς θεράπων· ἐθέλει {δὲ}
 15   γᾶρυν ἐκ στηθέων χέων
   1 αἰνεῖν Ἱέρωνα. βαθὺν
    δ᾽ αἰθέρα ξουθαῖσι τάμνων
   3 ὑψοῦ πτερύγεσσι ταχεί-
    αις αἰετὸς εὐρυάνακτος ἄγγελος
 20 5 Ζηνὸς ἐρισφαράγου
    θαρσεῖ κρατερᾶι πίσυνος
   7 ἰσχύϊ, πτάσσοντι δ᾽ ὄρνι-
    χες λιγύφθογγοι φόβωι·
   9 οὔ νιν κορυφαὶ μεγάλας ἴσχουσι γαίας,
 25   οὐδ᾽ ἁλὸς ἀκαμάτας
 26 11 δυσπαίπαλα κύματα· νω-
    μαῖ δ᾽ ἐν ἀτ｜ρύτωι χάει
   13 λεπτότ｜ριχα σὺν ζεφύρου πνοι-
    αῖσιν ἔθειραν ἀρίγ｜νω-
 30   τος {μετ᾽} ἀνθρώποις ἰδεῖν·
   1 τὼς νῦν καὶ ⟨ἐ⟩μοὶ μυρία πάντᾱι κέλευθος
    ὑμετέραν ἀρετάν
   3 ὑμνεῖν, κυανοπ｜λοκάμου θ᾽ ἕκατι Νίκας
    χαλκεοστέρνου τ᾽ Ἄρηος,
 35 5 Δεινομένευς ἀγέρωχοι
    παῖδες· εὖ ἔρδων δὲ μὴ κάμοι θεός.
   7 ξανθότ｜ριχα μὲν Φερένικον
    Ἀλφεὸν παρ᾽ εὐρυδίναν
   9 πῶλον ἀελλοδρόμαν
 40) εἶδε νικάσαντα χρυσόπαχυς Ἀώς,
B′   1 Πυθῶνί τ᾽ ἐν ἀγαθέᾱι·
    γᾶι δ᾽ ἐπισκήπτων πιφαύσκω·

3 οὔπω νιν ὑπὸ π'ροτέ[ρω]ν
ἵππων ἐν ἀγῶνι κατέχ'ρανεν κόνις
45 5 πρὸς τέλος ὀρνύμενον·
ῥιπᾶι γὰρ ἴσος βορέα
7 ὃν κυβερνήταν φυλάσσων
ἵεται νεόκ'ροτον
49 9 νίκαν ῾Ιέρωνι φιλοξείνωι τιτύσκων.
50 ὄλβιος ὧιτινι θεός
11 μοῖράν τε καλῶν ἔπορεν
σύν τ᾽ ἐπιζήλωι τύχᾱι
13 ἀφ'νεὸν βιοτὰν διάγειν· οὐ
γά‚ρ τις‚ ἐπιχθονίων
55 π‚άντ‚α γ᾽ εὐδαίμων ἔφυ.
1 δῦναί π]οτ᾽ ἐρειψιπύλαν
ἄνδρ᾽ ἀνίκ]ατον λέγουσιν
3 ἔρνος Διὸς] ἀργικεραύ-
νου δώματα Φερσεφόνας τανισφύρου,
60 5 καρχαρόδοντα κύν᾽ ἄ-
ξοντ᾽ ἐς φάος ἐξ Ἀΐδα,
7 υἱὸν ἀπ'λάτοι᾽ Ἐχίδ'νας·
ἔνθα δυστάνων βροτῶν
9 ψυχὰς ἐδάη παρὰ Κωκυτοῦ ῥεέθ'ροις,
65 οἷά τε φύλλ᾽ ἄνεμος
11 ῎Ιδας ἀνὰ μηλοβότους
πρῶνας ἀργηστὰς δονεῖ.
13 ταῖσιν δὲ μετέπ'ρεπεν εἴδω-
λον θρασυμέμνονος ἐγ-
70 χεσπάλου Πορθανίδα·
1 τὸν δ᾽ ὡς ἴδεν Ἀλκμή⟨ν⟩ιος θαυμαστὸς ἥρως
τ[ε]ύχεσι λαμπόμενον,
3 νευρὰν ἐπέβασε λιγυκ'λαγγῆ κορώνας,
74 χαλκεόκ'ρανον δ᾽ ἔπειτ᾽ ἔξ
75 5 εἵλετο ἰὸν ἀναπτύ-
ξας φαρέτ'ρας πῶμα· τῶι δ᾽ ἐναντία
7 ψυχὰ προφάνη Μελεάγ'ρου,
καί νιν εὖ εἰδὼς προσεῖπεν·
9 ,,υἱὲ Διὸς μεγάλου,
80 στᾶθί τ᾽ ἐν χώρᾱι, γελανώσας τε θυμόν
Γ′   1 μὴ ταὔσιον προΐει
τραχὺν ἐκ χειρῶν ὀϊστόν·
3 ψυχαῖσιν ἔπι φθιμένων·
οὔ τοι δέος.'' ὣς φάτο· θάμβησεν δ᾽ ἄναξ

85 5 Ἀμφιτρυωνιάδας,
   εἶπέν τε· „τίς ἀθανάτων
  7 ἢ βροτῶν τοιοῦτον ἔρνος
   θρέψεν ἐν ποίᾳ χθονί;
  9 τίς δ᾽ ἔκτανεν; ἦ τάχα καλλίζωνος Ἥρα
90 κεῖνον ἐφ᾽ ἁμετέρᾳι
  11 πέμψει κεφαλᾶι· τὰ δέ που
   Παλλάδι ξανθᾶι μέλει.‛‛
  13 τὸν δὲ π|ροσέφα Μελέαγ|ρος
   δακ|ρυόεις· „χαλεπὸν
95 θεῶν παρατ|ρέψαι νόον
  1 ἄνδρεσσιν ἐπιχθονίοις.
   καὶ γὰρ ἂν πλάξιππος Οἰνεύς
  3 παῦσεν καλυκοστεφάνου
   σεμνᾶς χόλον Ἀρτέμιδος λευκωλένου
100 5 λισσόμενος πολέων
   τ᾽ αἰγῶν θυσίαισι πατήρ
  7 καὶ βοῶν φοινικονώτων·
   ἀλλ᾽ ἀνίκατον θεά
  9 ἔσχεν χόλον· εὐρυβίαν δ᾽ ἔσσευε κούρα
105 κάπ|ρον ἀναιδομάχαν
106 11 ἐς καλλίχορον Καλυδῶ-
   ν᾽, ἔνθα πλημύρων σθένει
  13 ὄρχους ἐπέκειρεν ὀδόντι,
   σφάζε τε μῆλα, βροτῶν
110 θ᾽ ὅστις εἰσάνταν μόλοι.
  1 τῶι δὲ στυγερὰν δῆριν Ἑλλάνων ἄριστοι
   στασάμεθ᾽ ἐνδυκέως
  3 ἓξ ἄματα συν̄εχέως· ἐπεὶ δὲ δαίμων
   κάρτος Αἰτωλοῖς ὄρεξεν,
115 5 θάπτομεν οὓς κατέπεφ|νεν
   σῦς ἐριβ|ρύχας ἐπαΐσσων βίᾳι,
  7 Ἀ[γκ]αῖον ἐμῶν τ᾽ Ἀγέλαον
   φ[έρτ]ατον κεδ|νῶν ἀδελφεῶν,
  9 οὓς τέ|κεν ἐν μεγάροις
120)___ .....]ς Ἀλθαία περικ|λειτοῖσιν Οἰνέος·
Δ´   1 ..... ὤ]λεσε μοῖρ᾽ ὀλοὰ
   ......]ς· οὐ γάρ πω δαΐφ|ρων
  3 παῦσεν] χόλον ἀγ|ροτέρα
   Λατοῦς θυγάτηρ· περὶ δ᾽ αἴθωνος δορᾶς
125 5 μαρνάμεθ᾽ ἐνδυκέως
   Κουρῆσι μενεπτολέμοις·
  7 ἔνθ᾽ ἐγὼ πολλοῖς σὺν ἄλλοις

128   Ἴφικλον κατέκτανον
   9 ἐσθλόν τ᾽ Ἀφάρητα, θοοὺς μάτρωας· οὐ γὰρ
130   καρτερόθυμος Ἄρης
   11 κρίνει φίλον ἐν πολέμωι,
     τυφ┘λὰ δ᾽ ἐκ χειρῶν βέλη
   13 ψυχαῖς ἔπι δυσμενέων φοι-
     τᾶι θάνατόν τε φέρει
135 __ τοῖσιν ἂν δαίμων θέληι.
   1 ταῦτ᾽ οὐκ ἐπιλεξαμένα
     Θεστίου κούρα δαΐφ┘ρων
   3 μάτηρ κακόποτ┘μος ἐμοὶ
     βούλευσεν ὄλεθ┘ρον ἀτάρβακτος γυνά,
140 5 καῖέ τε δαιδαλέας
     ἐκ λάρνακος ὠκύμορον
   7 φιτ┘ρὸν ἐξαύσασα· τὸν δὴ
     μοῖρ᾽ ἐπέκ┘λωσεν τότε
   9 ζωᾶς ὅρον ἀμετέρας ἔμμεν. τύχον μὲν
145   Δαϊπύλου Κλύμενον
   11 παῖδ᾽ ἄλκιμον ἐξεναρί-
     ζων ἀμώμητον δέμας,
   13 πύργων προπάροιθε κιχήσας·
     τοὶ δὲ πρὸς εὐκτιμέναν
150 __ φεῦγον ἀρχαίαν πόλιν
   1 Πλευρῶνα· μίνῦθεν δέ μοι ψυχὰ γλυκεῖα·
     γνῶν δ᾽ ὀλιγοσθενέων,
153 3 αἰαῖ· πύματον δὲ πνέων δάκ┘ρυσα τλά[μων,
     ἀγ┘λαὰν ἥβαν προλείπων.
155 5 φασὶν ἀδεισιβόαν
     Ἀμφιτ┘ρύωνος παῖδα μοῦνον δὴ τότε
   7 τέγξαι βλέφαρον, ταλαπενθέος
     πότ┘μον οἰκτίροντα φωτός·
   9 καί νιν ἀμειβόμενος
Ε´ 160)__ τᾶδ᾽ ἔφα· „θνατοῖσι μὴ φῦναι φέριστον
   1 μηδ᾽ ἀελίου προσιδεῖν
     φέγγος· ἀλλ᾽ οὐ γάρ τίς ἐστιν
   3 πρᾶξις τάδε μυρομένοις,
     χρὴ κεῖνο λέγειν ὅτι καὶ μέλλει τελεῖν.
165 5 ἦρά τις ἐν μεγάροις
     Οἰνῆος ἀρηϊφίλου
   7 ἔστιν ἀδ┘μήτα θυγάτ┘ρων,
     σοὶ φυὰν ἀλιγκία;
   9 τάν κεν λιπαρὰν ⟨ἐ⟩θέλων θείμαν ἄκοιτιν.“
170   τὸν δὲ μενεπτολέμου
   11 ψυχὰ προσέφα Μελεά-
     γ┘ρου· „λίπον χλωραύχενα

13 ἐν δώμασι Δαϊάνειραν,
νῆϊν ἔτι χ'ρῦσέας
175 ___ Κύπ'ριδος θελξιμβρότου."
176 1 λευκώλενε Καλλιόπα,
στᾶσον εὐποίητον ἄρμα
3 αὐτοῦ· Δία τε Κ'ρονίδαν
ὕμνησον Ὀλύμπιον ἀρχαγὸν θεῶν,
180 5 τόν τ᾿ ἀκαμαντορόαν
Ἀλφεόν, Πέλοπός τε βίαν,
7 καὶ Πίσαν, ἔνθ᾿ ὁ κ'λεεννὸς
πο]σσὶ νικάσας δρόμωι
9 ἦλθ]εν Φερένικος ⟨ἐς⟩ εὐπύργους Συρακόσ-
185 σας Ἱέρωνι φέρων
11 εὐδ]αιμονίας πέταλον.
χρὴ] δ᾿ ἀλαθείας χάριν
13 αἰνεῖν, φθόνον ἀμφ[οτέραισιν
χερσὶν ἀπωσάμενο͞ν,
190 ___ εἴ τις εὖ πράσσοι βροτῶ[ν.
1 Βοιωτὸς ἀνὴρ τάδε φών[ησεν, γλυκειᾶν
Ἡσίοδος πρόπολος
3 Μουσᾶν, ὃν ⟨ἂν⟩ ἀθάνατοι τι[μῶσι, τούτωι
καὶ βροτῶν φήμαν ἔπ[εσθαι.
195 5 πείθομαι εὐμαρέως
εὐκλέα κελεύθου γλῶσσαν οὐ[__◡_
197 7 πέμπειν Ἱέρωνι· τόθεν γὰ[ρ
πυθ'μένες θάλλουσιν ἐσθλ[ῶν,
τοὺς δ μεγιστοπάτωρ
200 Ζεὺς ἀκινήτους ἐν εἰρήν[αι φυλάσσοι.

1 str.   You, high-fortuned man, over Syracusan
cavalry the captain,
you will know the blue-crowned
Muses' gift, sweet recompense,
if ever mortal did, so rest
your just, unfearing mind
from high concerns and turn
your thoughts this way
to where deep-waisted Graces oversee
the weaving of a song,
friend's tribute sent from sacred isle
to your more famous town.

Himself Ourania's slave
 and not without renown,
 he would his loud chest-notes pour out

ant.   in praise of Hieron. Steep air
  the eagle cuts
with swift and tawny wing,
 high messenger
of great-voiced Zeus, the king,
 and bold in knowledge of
his overbearing might, as small
 shrill birds sink down in fright.
Not fenced by broad earth's peaks
 nor by the untiring sea,
though tall waves boom,
 he navigates the changeless void
lifted high on slender plume
 and wheeling with the wind,
 bright sight for eyes of men.

ep.   So with me: ten thousand paths
  open as I sing the high success
won from dark-haired Nikē and
 from bronze-girt Ares too by
you who are the lordly sons
 of Deinomenes. May god not tire in grace!
Pale-maned was Pherenicus when he won
 beside the flood of Alpheus,
the wind-swift running of his race
 watched by gold-limbed Dawn

2 str.   who saw the same at holy Pythia.
  My hand on earth I testify:
not once did dust of swifter horse
 defile him as he plunged
towards that contested goal,
 but like a northwind blast
that answered to a rider's touch
 he struck his mark and sent
a new-coined victory to gracious Hieron.
 Blessed he who gets from god
some portion of the splendid things,
 envied for his luck
within a lifetime spent at ease!

No creature on this earth
is happy without let.

ant.   They say the undefeated
city-smasher, son of Zeus
white lightning's master, once
went down to slender Korē's house
to take the fierce-toothed dog
of Hades back to light—
it was Echidna's greedy child.
Down there he saw the souls
of wretched men beside the stream of Cocytus
whirled like leaves when sudden wind
spins up along Mount Ida's
bright sheep-feeding crags.
A single ghost among them
overshadowed all—Porthaon's heir,
bold to resist and ready with his spear.

ep.   Alcmenē's wondrous hero son saw him
as he glimmered in his armor; at once
he fit the shrieking string into his bow,
opened up his pouch,
made choice, and took
a bronze-tipped arrow out. Close
came Meleager's recognizing ghost
and spoke:
"Son of highest Zeus,
hold off, placate your heart

3 str.   and do not send a vain
swift arrow from your hand
among these wasted souls!
They are no cause for fear." Wonderstruck,
Amphitryon's son replied:
"What god or man
put forth so fine a sprig
and in what land?
Who killed you? Surely rich-sashed Hera
means to send the same
man against my head—but let
fair-haired Athena trouble over that!"
Then Meleager weeping
answered him, "God's plans
are hard to overturn

ant. for men who walk the earth,
      else horsedriving Oeneus, my father,
would have stopped the rage of Artemis,
      white-armed and flower-crowned,
with prayers and promises
      of many goats
and red-flanked cows in sacrifice.
      Instead, the never vanquished goddess
hugged her wrath and sent a fierce boar,
      shameless in its battle-ways,
into the plain of festive Calydon
      and like the ocean surge
it tore at orchards with its tusk,
      eviscerated sheep and men
      if any came its way.

ep. Against this enemy we noblemen of Greece
      made ceaseless war
for six long days and when
      Aetolian triumph came from god
we buried all the men that screaming pig
      had charged and killed.
Ancaeus and strong Agelaus too were dead,
      my brothers, brought to birth
in famous halls, children to Althea,
      fathered by my father, Oeneus.

4 str. And now a baleful fate destroyed
      many other men, for that dread-minded one
had not yet checked her rage—the huntress
      girl that Leto bore. For the gleaming skin
we fought remorselessly
      with battle-hardened Curetēs
and that was when I killed
      (with others) Iphiclus and noble
Apharetēs, rash brothers of my mother.
      Ares in his heavy anger
fails to know the friend among the enemy;
      the arrow leaves the hand, blind,
and flies towards souls of hostile cast
      carrying its freight of death
      where doom would have it brought.

ant. Unremembered was this truth
      when she—dread-minded girl

of Thestius, my evil-fated mother—
　　planned my death without a pang of fear.
She burnt the short-lived branch
　　taken from its inlaid box
and chanted spells above the torch
　　that fate had set as my life's
boundary. The body of
　　fair fallen Clymenus,
Daïpylus' brave son, I by chance
　　was stripping of its arms
where we had met ouside the walls
　　(the enemy had fled into
　　the ancient well-built citadel

ep.　　of Pleuron). Then and there my own sweet soul
　　　　grew weak! I knew my force was gone.
Aiai! I wept my last breath out, wretched,
　　and left bright youth behind."
They say Amphitryon's bold-
　　shouting son only this once
wet his eye in pity
　　for a suffering man. Then,
answering, he said:
　　"For mortals, never to be born

5 str.　　were best—never to have looked
　　　　upon the sun. But no deed comes
from such complaint. A man should speak
　　of things he means to do.
Is there still within the halls
　　of warlike Oeneus
a daughter yet unwed
　　whose look is like your own?
I wish to make her my rich bride."
　　To him staunch
Meleager's ghost then said,
　　"I left at home a tender-throated
child called Daïaneira,
　　not yet wise
　　in golden Aphrodite's magic ways."

ant.　　White-armed Calliopē,
　　　　halt the well-built chariot

just here! Sing Cronian Zeus,
  Olympian captain of the gods, sing
everflowing Alpheus, sing
  the might of Pelops, and sing
Pisa where the flying hooves
  of famous Pherenicus
raced and won and then brought home
  to towering Syracuse
the bloom of bliss for Hieron!
  For truth's sake praise is
imperative, while envy must
  be thrust away with both hands
  when a man does well.

ep. Boeotia's poet, Hesiod,
  servant of sweet Muses,
said, "Where gods give honor,
  there should mortal praises follow."
I obey, and easily my tongue
  keeps to the path of truth
and sends fair fame to Hieron,
  from which the stalks of noble deeds
will flower up, and these may mighty father Zeus
  guard in safety and in peace.

Because of the scale of the piece, Bacchylides can give an entire triad and one more stanza to the initial task of bringing the moment of Olympic victory into the moment of Syracusan festivity, and his use of this extra performance time is in every way extraordinary.[2] To begin with, he purposely complicates the mixing of victory times and places with festival times and places by adding another set—a moment of Cean composition.[3] In consequence, the notes that issue now from the mouths of boys in Sicily seem also to be issuing from the "deep chest" of the poet on his island, earlier, when he first received Hieron's commission and felt the commands of the Charites and Ourania. Next, this detachment of the act of praise from ordinary geography and time is extended and transformed by means of a stanza-long metaphor, as the eagle praise-song moves through space with an effortless motion that repeats the tyrant's easy triumph over care (6–7), the poet's easy pursuit of justice in the tyrant's praise (195–7), and Pherenicus' easy rush toward his victorious goal (46).[4] The praise-eagle is even associated with Zeus, and this dangerous suggestion of alliance with god is matched in other parts of the opening passage. The first lines contain an invocation addressed, not to a god or a Muse but to Hieron himself, as if he were an equivalent, and the long passage ends with lines that greet the same triumphant ruler as "Blessed!" much as if he had received a grant of immortality.[5]

The enormity of Hieron's bliss is of course formally reduced by the application of a gnomic saying (55), but the song still claims to come almost as a message from Zeus, and the extreme exaltation of this opening passage seems to prepare for a positive myth that will be likewise bliss-filled and exalted. That, at any rate is probably what Hieron expected, but what follows is a double myth filled with death and doom in both its parts. What is more, the poet makes his chorus call attention to the apparent inappropriateness of their material by pretending to have gone too far. "Stop the song," they cry (176), bringing the mythic section to its end, and this abrupt reassertion of their own existence is a poet's trick for making sure that his listeners, and especially his patron, will take special notice of the effect he has just contrived.

The self-conscious halt brings the song back to Zeus and Olympia and back, also, into the known paths of epinician song, for the technique is conventional. Pindar does the same sort of thing, often pretending to have digressed in order to insist upon the crucial bit in the myth he has just cited.[6] Nevertheless, the situation in Ode 5 is distinctly non-Pindaric, for here it is no mere point of mythic information that is being emphasized, and no ordinary transition from narrative to occasion that is being made. The name of Daianeira is what the chorus ostensibly turns away from at the beginning of the fifth antistrophe, averting their faces because that name promises death for Heracles. It is much more than Daianeira and death, however, that they are insisting upon, for the slight pause between strophe and antistrophe has been filled with the power indicated by the final syllables of Meleager's speech wherein Aphrodite has been named. Every listener has received an intimation of her magic, along with a momentary sense of having understood the way that human fates are made, and it is this divine presence (and this human recognition) that Bacchylides marks with his emphasized call upon Calliope to stop the myth just here.

The effect of the mythic passage is thus very much like that of tragedy, and so indeed are the means, for in these stanzas two stories have been represented in a scene of mimed speech that ends in a deed of decision. Obviously, the poet means to mix the unrelated deaths of Meleager and Heracles in his listeners' imaginations, but instead of telling first one and then the other (as with the Nemean lion and the Aeginetan heroes), or one within the other (as with the founding of Tiryns and the madness of the Proetids), he presents the two simultaneously by the device of a dialogue. Each hero belonged to his own province of mythic geography, but it was not hard to make them meet since Meleager was one of the better known residents of Hades and Heracles had visited that place; some even said that he had spoken there with the hero of Caly-don.[7] Easy enough to set the two talking, but this alone could not effect the mixing of the two death stories since, though the shade could tell the visitor about his own end, the living man could not respond in kind. Events not yet experienced had to be brought into the passage, and the epic way to do this would have been to give Meleager the power of prophecy. This, however, would have produced an instructed Heracles instead of an unknowing one, and it would also have created a scene as static as that between Aegeus and the garrison in Dithyramb 18, and so Bacchylides made another choice. His Heracles unwittingly tells his own future, not in words but by exerting his will in a death-bearing ac-tion that is filled with irony.

In spite of its different mode of performance, the mythic encounter of Ode 5 is very much like a tragic-messenger scene. Meleager as deutera-gonist reports, and Heracles as protagonist responds,[8] the first offering the audience the epic pleasure of hearing a finished tale well told, the second providing the very different dramatic pleasure of watching an as yet unfinished event take shape. Heracles' preeminence is established by first mention; then the persistence of his appetite for action and the in-tensity of his response to Meleager are immediately displayed in a char-acteristic gesture. He believes that his ultimate fate is a thing to be settled between Hera and Athena, but nevertheless to see danger is for him the signal to prepare his bow, and the instant in which he behaves as an archer is curiously prolonged. There is suspense as he strings his weapon, then carefully opens his pouch to select an arrow, but the detail only serves to emphasize the uselessness, and consequently the true sig-nificance of the gesture.[9] This is an instant that displays the man and also ironically prefigures what is to come, and so it is important to watch Heracles as he picks the arrow he would use when there is no need to fear. At the end of the episode he will once again exercise his seeming power to choose, but then he will pick the bride all listeners know he ought to fear, and they will understand that though he has acted freely he has had no choice at all.

The scene as a whole belongs to Heracles, but the voice and history of Meleager occupy most of its length.[10] The answers to the two questions that launch him—whose son is he and how did he die?—could have been given with a single name, but this is the poet's one chance for a full picture of a death, and it is also a chance to put one of the most famous Hellenic stories into the mouth of its own hero, and so the tale is told expansively. At the same time, of course, it is told selectively, since the content of an epic is to be distilled into this one speech, and as always the poet indicates his largest intentions by the cut that he gives to his original materials. The Meleager traditions were rich in episode and character,[11] but the poet trimmed away the entire Homeric exemplum of withdrawal, persuasion, and late return to battle, and he also lopped off the figures of the wifely Cleopatra and the unwifely Atalanta.[12] For his song he wanted only Meleager's death, and with careful selection he gave that death a particular form.

There were two current versions of Meleager's end, one in which the agent was Apollo, another in which Althea acted, and within the second of these there were alternate methods, since the mother could kill with a Homeric curse, or she could burn the fairy-tale brand. By choosing Althea over Apollo and the brand over the curse, Bacchylides achieved a story that turned on the collaboration of a beast, a female relative, a magical implement, and fire—just the scheme required by his ironic intention of making his two heroes similar. The tale is pared down to these essentials, and so, as Meleager's speech unwinds no listener can fail to remember that Heracles too, after killing monsters, will eventually be undone in a moment of triumph, destroyed by a woman's magic, his body finally plunged into fire. The woman who kills him will be wife, not mother, and she will act for Aphrodite, not Artemis, but nevertheless the two fate-patterns are seen to fit one upon the other with a grotesque accuracy.

When Melaeger's speech is considered more closely, however, a second and subtler intention can be recognized in the peculiarities of its stylistic details. To begin with, this favorite epic tale fails, in Meleager's mouth, to offer the expected epic pleasures. It had been the story of a hunt, and its central beast had supplied archaic painters with a favorite motif,[13] but in this lyric telling the boar of Calydon is never pictured at all. He signals divine rage and he erupts as pure violence, "boiling" with strength (*plemuron*, 107, cf. *eurubian*, 104) but he has suffered a curious disembodiment and no one of his epithets is visual. What is more, though he is the cause of six days' fighting (111 f.) and the noisy maker of corpses (116), he himself is never killed at all—he simply disappears, in the modest phrase that Meleager uses to mark the close of one phase of his story, "when some power gave the advantage to the Aetolians" (113-4).

As well as a boar to the painters, the epic hunt at Calydon had offered to the bardic singers a chance to repeat the names and describe the equipment of great men who had lived before the Trojan War.[14] Meleager, however, speaks here only of "Aetolians" who seem to have no names, no weapons, and no former deeds to be recounted, when he reports that the "nobles of Greece" assembled for the hunt (111). For his purposes, the only men who need to be directly named are his own kinsmen and the youthful "perfect" opponent (an ally of his kinsmen) whose body he was stripping before the walls of Pleuron. This does not mean, however, that he tells the story with himself as chief actor, for in sixty lines of narrative there is only one physically active first-person verb, the "I killed" that stands at the very centre of the tale (128).

Meleager makes us feel that only the gods have been truly active, for every human deed that he reports has been immediately influenced by a supernatural power (Artemis, 99; *daimon*, 113; *moira*, 121 and 143; Ares, 130). Furthermore, his own single action, the killing of his uncles that was the immediate cause of his destruction, becomes curiously abstract.[15] Its author locates it in the *terrain vague* of an unspecified battlefield; he does not bother to make it occur at any particular moment, not even on any particular day, nor does he say whether it was done with ease or with difficulty. "Along with many others, I killed Iphiclus and noble Apharetes," is the speaker's weary phrase. He killed from a distance, without intention, or decision, or passion, and he explicitly refuses all responsibility for this nongesture by calling it the undiscriminating work of Ares and fate. Deprived of all sensual reality (like the boar and the hunt), Meleager's one deed thus seems to have been performed by a hero who was already little more than a ghost.

Coming after this somnambulistic act of killing, the one deed in the entire account that seems to depend in any way upon human will gains an almost shocking quality of passion, and it is much more sharply delineated. Althea is indoors, in a place specific enough to contain a bit of decorated furniture (141); more important, she is endowed with a mind, and the psychic, ethical nature of her action is four times emphasized in the four lines that introduce her. She is "dread-minded" (137) and "unafraid" (139), and she "refuses to consider" (136) the chancy nature of battle as she "resolves upon" (139) the destruction of her son. She knows what she does,[16] but Meleager makes it plain in the telling that she too is only a mortal piece in a divine game, for she does not destroy directly. A fateful magic must extend her power before she can kill, and that magic inhabits an object—the brand—given her by the same *moira* that has been in operation along with the rage of Artemis and the daimon of Aetolian victory throughout this version of the hunt and the war with the Curetēs.

Naturally Meleager makes no didactic statement about Althea's place in the larger pattern of Artemis' vengeance, nor about her relevance to the shape of Heracles' fate, but the poet plays his own game with these notions by manipulating the sound *da-i*, which means "torch" and, by extension, war and destruction. Artemis was *daïphrōn* (122) when she prolonged her anger after the killing of the boar,[17] and consequently the Althea who is *daïphrōn* now (137) seems to be an extension of that same divine "fiery-mindedness" as she performs her act of burning.

What is more, the shared epithet looks forward to the name that will be produced, like the answer to a riddle, at the end of Bacchylides' scene in hell—Daïaneira, she who will destroy her man and give him to the fire. (This key sound is also reiterated in the central passage in the perfectly gratuitous name given to Meleager's victim's father, Daïpylus.)[18] By such means, the torch that Althea makes of Meleager's life illuminates events that are yet to come in the life of Heracles.

In the final section of the ghost's tale the listener is taken outside again, to a spot endowed now with the reality of a place-name. He is shown a Meleager who for the first time seems to be acting for himself (though not, be it noted, in finite verbs—his movement is expressed in participles which depend upon chance, *tuchōn* ... *exenarizōn* ... *kichēsas*, 144–8). He is proving his vitality by despoiling a corpse and the listener is asked to look even at the dead man and to notice his name, for at last the storyteller has come to the moment that he wishes to fix and make memorable. There has evidently been motion—the enemy has fled (150) and Meleager has followed—but the instant for which the whole story has been preparation is one in which motion stops and knowledge comes. With the gesture of conquest incomplete, the corpse beneath him still unspoiled, the hero perceives the decline of his own forces and now, but only now in this tale, he knows what he is doing (152). He knows that he is dying young (154), yet nevertheless dying in weakness instead of in strength, and for this he weeps.[19]

In spite of its epic content and Homeric vocabulary,[20] the narrative of Meleager's ghost has a lack of prodigality, a disciplined emphasis, indeed, that is wholly unlike anything in Homer. And in spite of its functional likeness to a messenger speech from Attic tragedy,[21] the narrative has a subjectivity and also an analytic tendency that cannot be matched in the extant plays. In one sense it is only ostensibly a narrative, in fact a lament, but in another sense it is an almost abstract demonstration of man's slavery to supernatural forces and fate. The ghost who speaks weeps and cries out *aiai*, reviving tears and the cry with which he earlier greeted the end of his life, and what he bewails, now as then, is not death but the abandonment of a youth that should have been heroic but was not. By his own telling he died without a deed to claim as his own, never having willed or chosen or decided, always having been perfectly unfree. Fate had used him, magic had made him its victim, and even the fact that he was destroyed by what he calls "the mind of the gods" (95) fails, in this tale, to lend him any true magnificence since the rage of Artemis was not directed against him, but took him only as his father's proxy. And so Meleager weeps forever because his end was woman-made and passive—pathetic, but not tragic.

In his weakness, Meleager offers a conceptual contrast to the city-sacker who confronts him, but his tale nevertheless demonstrates a formal likeness between the two heroes. His account has been shaped by the poet for purposes of irony, and it succeeds in including a fearful glimpse of a future that is fully known to the audience. As soon as he saw Meleager "glimmering in his armor" Heracles knew him as his own equal, and their likeness is verbally enforced—both young men are to be marveled at (71; 84), both are described as saplings or twigs (58; 87), and Meleager wears the epithet that had belonged exclusively to Heracles in Homer's songs (*thrasymemnōn*, 69).[22] Heracles' question, "Who could have killed you?"[23] thus in effect asks how he himself can die, as he in a sense knows (89 ff.), but he does not know that the speech that follows has application to himself as well as to Meleager. He continues in ignorance to the end of the scene, but the spectator who hears the name of Daianeira, after such a narrative, understands perfectly. That name means death, and it forces the congruency of the two tales—the told and the untold—directly into his consciousness as an experienced proof of the symmetry that heaven likes to give to its most dread designs.

The recognition of the fate of Heracles, hiding within the fate of Meleager, creates an emotion of mixed terror and awe, and meanwhile it lends a new magnificence to the living hero. He arrived in the song as a popular and archaic figure, a sacker of cities and the son of Zeus who could make a mock-rueful reference to the persecutions of Hera,[24] but now he has a more solemn significance. This man famous for his strength, his appetites, and his labors must be something much more, if his destiny has been so well prepared and so splendidly prefigured, and the audience knows that the Athena whom he expects to supervise the details of his death will in fact take him past death and on to Olympus and his final marriage with Hebe (Hes. *Cat.* 229 MW). "For mortals, it were better not to be alive," he says (160 f.), but everyone in the audience remembers that though he is mortal now, he will not be so always.[25]

Awe and terror, however, are only half of the poetic achievement of this passage, for there are other emotions that derive, not just from the juxtaposition of the two stories, but from verbal style, arrangement of scene, and above all from a kind of ethical portraiture. The poet hints at Heracles' divine nature with the unwitting gnome that he puts into his mouth, but in the lines immediately preceding he has managed to give his human nature a form that communicates directly with our senses. Heracles has listened to Meleager's speech without taking in its cold ironies or grasping its formal identification of this other story with his own—how could he understand these things?[26] What he *has* taken in, however, is a warm sense of another man's grief, and he has also, for the first time in his life, made the identification between himself and the rest of mankind. His response is characteristic in that it comes in action instead of words, but it is also, for him, unique. The chorus has just breathed out Meleager's life in Meleager's voice, as they described his weeping (both in Hades and at Pleuron). Then, without pause, they change focus and shift their angle of observation, catching our attention with a wholly altered mode of delivery. *"They say,"* they announce at the beginning of line 155, and this sudden objectivity tells us that Meleager is no longer speaking, while the *phasi* itself marks what is coming as a truth already hallowed by remembrance[27]—"They say that then and only then did Amphitryon's son wet his eye in pity for a suffering man."

Heracles' unparalleled tear, viewed from afar and sparkling in its web of destiny, is a triumphant poetic effect that begins to be tragic because it depicts both the character and the fate of the man. The earlier emphasis upon the enchanted puppet-like quality of Meleager makes this spontaneous tear seem to be wholly free, the product of a human essence that destiny cannot touch. And yet Heracles weeps in this free fashion just at the moment when the poet's ironies have made us feel the mesh of the future as it settles upon him, and consequently he seems to weep freely for himself and his own unfreedom as much as for the ghost. The boar, the woman, the magic, and the fire have outlined fate's design, but this unique action stands against them all as a sign of vital anarchy. The design is enormous and the action very small, but together they represent Bacchylides' solution to a problem that was both philosophical and aesthetic. He cannot show a man who escapes from his fate, because everyone knows that no such man has ever lived and that Heracles, in particular, did not escape. On the other hand, he cannot for a second time display the gods' crude extinction of a man's vital flame without seeming to subscribe to a pessimism that is both gloomy and unhellenic.[28] At this impasse, Bacchylides' solution is to make of his Heracles a genuinely tragic figure who proves both his freedom and his unfreedom in a single further action.

Heracles says that for mortals the best thing would be not to be. He goes on at once, however, to add that such reflections are bootless since speech is valuable only when it fixes what a man will do. And then he proceeds to use speech in exactly that way. He is looking at Meleager's ghost—a shadowy disembodiment of his own future—and as he admires it, weeps for it, and identifies himself with its mortality, he finds that he longs for it with something like love. For him, to feel a want is to act upon it, and so he asks straightaway for the living female equivalent, an unwed girl whose form is like the phantom's own. The response produces the name of Daianeira, and the mythic section of Bacchylides' song is done, but not before the syllables "golden Aphrodite, enchantress of men"[29] have been sung (175). Daianeira as yet knows nothing of this goddess but Heracles does, and she has been with him just now in Hades as he made his free and passionate choice of the death he would have met anyway. She exists both in heaven and in men's flesh, being both a goddess and the surge of physical desire, and so she can reconcile the irreconcilable by simply fusing the hero's autonomous will with the implacable force of his fate. Like Althea and Daianeira she uses magic, but hers is not the sordid manipulation of tokens or poisons—it is an enchantment that even Zeus submits to. Under her influence Heracles has fallen in love with his own future and in so doing he has bent himself to the fate that he must endure, but he has also freely followed the swerve of his own soul. He has acted, for he has decided and chosen, and he has exercised man's single freedom—the freedom to turn toward, or away from, what will in either case inevitably come.

With Aphrodite still in the air the chorus turns self-consciously back to Zeus, Olympia, Alpheus, Pisa, Pherenicus, Syracuse, and Hieron (178–186), as if these masculine names were a counterspell that could ward off her power. Let us remember the other side of existence, they seem to say, the side Zeus loves, where there are no baneful women, no enchanted deaths, and where the moving feet of a racehorse can bring the flower of happiness. Hieron is on earth, not in Hades; he has not died young nor has he fallen into the power of witches. He has, however, followed Heracles' example, for he has chosen, decided, and moved himself about; he has deeds that he can call his own. His superlative good fortune at the games and in battle (33–4) teaches him that he, like Heracles, is one whom the gods would honor (193), and so he may believe that, whatever fate has in store for him, his is one of the magnificent and tragic lives guided by Zeus' will.[30] And finally, though the death of the rushing boar suggests death for the fleet Pherenicus, while the deaths of the heroes remind the tyrant that he, like all men, will die, the poem has evoked one vital figure that seems to survive. The eagle of praise, being outside of time, will whirl and swoop forever over the heads of men, carrying Hieron's fame in this and other songs. Meanwhile, on earth and within time, the deeds of Hieron, thus praised, will keep their vitality like some root or bulb, and will send up perennial shoots in the form of fresh actions of Syracusan valor, which Zeus can be expected to guard from wind and storm (197–200).

The singers have associated Hieron's fame with the unforgettable fame of not one but two mythic heroes; they have left his deeds rooted in quietude and full of promise for the future. The tyrant was probably more than satisfied, but certain modern critics have suggested that the plant-like fruitfulness that seems to be the poem's final promise is in fact a threat.[31] What Bacchylides really says, according to this view, is that happiness won from a horse is as short-lived as a flower petal, and that men and their virtues are like tender plants in a world where nature is as destructive and as full of *phthonos* as a wild boar.[32] Why he should have sent such a message to the victorious Hieron, and why Hieron should have cared to see it performed at his banquet are questions that present themselves, but in this case they need not be asked, for there is in the song itself no syllable to suggest that Bacchylides meant to devalue the growing, leafy, sprouting images that he used. Quite the contrary, since the unspoken meanings of his narrated myth all work to identify the vegetable world with a form of human culture that the gods have willed and made permanent.

In its fundamental effect, the myth of Artemis, Oeneus, and Calydon takes care of a final phase in the discrimination of cultivators from hunters. The particular distinction being made is between cultivator-warriors who fight (like hunters) against an invader, and cultivator-warriors who fight (like animals) among themselves. There is a proper "shame of battle" which animals do not have (105) but which warriors must recognize, and the men of Calydon demonstrate it while they fight (like hunters) against the boar. When, however, they quarrel over the shameless beast, they demonstrate the violation of *aidōs* in its extremest form, for they kill members of their own families, and as soon as this happens their culture destroys itself. These imperfect cultivator-warriors have been living as horsemen (97) in a city surrounded by vineyards, orchards, and meadows where cattle and sheep grazed (108–10), and they know the ritual uses of domestic animals in sacrifice (100 f.).[33] Inside their city are houses (119) that hold furniture (141) and, also brothers and uncles and cousins (119–20), peacefully discriminated in respect to the women and the central hearth. This culture of men who have left off hunting has evidently functioned for some time, but it self-destructs when kin-war breaks out. As soon as a man kills his uncles, a woman unmothers herself, obliterates her husband's son, and attacks the peaceful hearth with the cut wood and the fire that were its own symbols. This world breaks down without *aidōs*.

By constructing an aberration, the myth locates the vital principle at work in the culture it would comprehend, and consequently it conveys a warning but also an assurance to all who live in the era of cultivation. The settled society that knows vines, crops, and domesticated animals no longer hunts Artemis' wild beasts for its food, but it does still cut her forest trees for fire,[34] and it does still owe her honor. If it makes her angry, the community will be invaded by bestiality, but if it offers correct and timely ritual satisfactions to the divinity of the abandoned hunt, and meanwhile pursues its new occupations according to the inhibitions of *aidōs*, such a society can produce not only sons who know their fathers and warriors to defend the fields, but also cities with well-built walls (149–50), and dancing choruses (106) like the one that is singing this present song. The Calydonian tale thus outlines a rich and urbane civilization based upon vines and cultivated fields, and taken on this level it reveals a perfect appropriateness to the occasion of Ode 5, for what better mythic augury could be found for the "master of Syracusan cavalry" who rules in an island whose chief boast is its grain? His city knows how to honor Artemis; he himself is a brother who has respected kinship's bonds; moreover, he is one who understands the ways of choruses (3–6). The glory that such a man has won (with the aid of Ares and Nikē) may well be thought of as rooted (like a vine-stalk) and ready to bear perennial fruit, for Zeus gives it promise of protection with this present Olympic victory. Of course Hieron will die, but the ways of field culture will endure under divine patronage, and so will the deeds of this horseman who is a civilized warrior.

APPENDIX: ODE 1

A single example of Bacchylides' way with a local legend is offered by Ode 1—or rather, would be offered if that song were not so severely damaged. It is an ode made to celebrate the victory of a boy named Argeius, the same who was sung in the short chant for the victory night that is called Ode 2, but this time the scale is generous. There seem to have been eight triads (though Snell's 47–56 could conceivably be moved to the space preceding his 111, in which case his gamma triad would be eliminated),[1] but whether there were eight or seven, all except the last three are extremely fragmentary, and consequently anything said about the song as a whole is largely hypothetical. Of a certainty there was an opening apostrophe to the Muses—"Lyre-famed virgin daughters of far-ruling Zeus"—and we can read at the close an extended system of gnomes, beginning, "I say and I shall say . . ." (159 ff.).[2] Between these, after an early identification of Isthmia as the victory place (6, and perhaps 13–14, though this apostrophe to the "gates of Pelops' land"[3] need not stand just here in the ode), there was to all appearances just one myth, developed in three (or two) triads and coming to its close just as the penultimate strophe begins its direct praise of the victor and his father (140). In the ruins of the mythic section, the names Minos (113), Dexithea (118), and Euxantius (125),[4] with what must be Macelo in line 73, identify the story as an obscure Cean foundation legend which tells how the island's first city was built by Cretans, but ruled by the son that a local heroine had borne to King Minos.[5]

In later times Dexithea is found in association with a complex tale of the gods-come-to-visit type.[6] She and Macelo (daughter and mother according to Callimachus)[7] and another female of the family are the only ones on the island of Ceos to offer hospitality to Zeus and a companion god, either Poseidon or Apollo.[8] In consequence, the island is destroyed by earthquake and flood and only Dexithea (or she and one of the others) is saved. In these later tales, the inhospitable men to whom the gracious women are foils are identified as Telchines,[9] members of the evil magical race that had been evicted from Rhodes,[10] and consequently their destruction is doubly motivated. There is also an available sentimental elaboration in which Macelo, though able to save herself with the others, chooses to stay behind with the damned because she is married (or is about to be), and so is blasted with the enemies of the gods, though she had earned an escape (schol. ad Ovid, *Ib*. 475).

It looks as if there had originally been two old tales that were simple and separate. One, the story of a local nymph loved by Minos, allowed the Ceans to claim (in logical self-contradiction) that they were at once authochthonous and descendants of the Cretans. The other, the story of a disaster[11] from which only a handful survived thanks to their virtue, was the local version of the ubiquitous flood myth, and it allowed the Ceans to feel that their ancestors had been specially chosen by the gods to live under an altered dispensation. For some reason, however, early tradition also reported an occupation of the island by certain Telchines, after their departure from Rhodes. The notoriety of such inhabitants lent a glamor to the place, but one hardly wanted to admit creatures who were not quite human as one's grandfathers, and the local story-tellers' way of having the best without the worst was to identify the pre-disaster islanders with these men of terrible skill. The Telchines had settled and presumably taken local wives, but later they had been totally eliminated by the Olympians at the time of the great cataclysm. Who then were the handful that must, in a disaster tale, survive? They were the least harmful of the ancient race (representatives perhaps also of the oldest indigenous population, the nymphs), which is to say that they were women. When the gods who had decided to send the Telchines back to Tartarus were brought on the scene as visitors, the magicians could confirm their enmity to the Olympians with one more offense, while the women of one household could save themselves by their unique hospitality. In some such way the Cean disaster myth took on its special local form, and the prominence that it necessarily gave to its female figures allowed some enterprising raconteur to fuse the two major local legends by calling one of the hospitable Telchine women Dexithea, thus making her the mother of Minos' Cean son. There is no way of knowing when this fusion occurred; all one can say is that it was not the work of Bacchylides, for Pindar referred easily to a legend in which the mother of Euxantius had been spared, with her household, when Zeus and Poseidon sent the rest of the island to Tartarus by the combined might of the lightning bolt and the trident (*Pa.* 4.35 ff.).

Pindar showed his characteristic tact by leaving the notorious Telchines unnamed and offering no explanation of why all but a single household had to be destroyed. He could suppress the fantastic and disreputable details because for his purposes only the fact of the mother's escape was relevant, being a sign that Euxantius was fated to remain in Ceos as its ruler. Bacchylides, just as characteristically, decided to sing some of the matters that Pindar left to silence—this much, at any rate, is obvious to anyone who studies the scraps of his song. First of all, by mentioning Macelo, he identified the inhabitants who perished as Telchines, for hers is the name most closely associated with that of Damon, king of the Cean magicians. What Bacchylides said of the Telchine offenses we have no way of reconstructing, but the coming of the gods was almost certainly narrated (they may have arrived in the chariots of 1.19), along with the women's reception of them.[12] And the women, as a reward, are warned of the coming disaster, for one of them recounts a dream that commands them to leave their ancient city and go to a place by the sea (K13 = 47–57).[13] They go, and three days after (after the dream? their departure? the cataclysm?) Minos arrives, "masters" Dexithea (118), and departs again leaving colonists behind (119 f.). Nine months later Euxantius is born to become chief of the island (125 ff.), and then the whole story is summed up. Destruction came to the Telchines, but the daughters of the king escaped to the new city which was to be the Cean capital (138–40).[14]

By telling the story in this way Bacchylides makes the coming of the Cretans and the destruction of the magicians appear as two aspects of the same divinely directed event. He also pictures that event as a fateful shift of habitation, from upland to shore, and his emphasis upon the sunniness of the new city (55) leaves one with the sense that the uplanders had dwelt in shadow. The island thus moves from a phase of darkness into one of light as Ceos becomes a place where nature and Zeus are respected and men live like Greeks. The new life of Ceos is marked by the birth of a child since this is the tale of the beginning of a new era, but the notable thing about Bacchylides' song is that it concerns itself with the mother instead of the Cretan father of the newborn son. All of its emphasis is placed upon the previous epoch, for there was evidently something of importance that the woman Dexithea abandoned when she left the mountains, yet paradoxically passed on to Minos' son. An ordinary gods-come-to-visit story would have shown that through her the Ceans had abandoned ignorance and impiety, just as an ordinary local nymph and visiting-hero story would have shown that Dexithea had passed on her own earth-born quality to her son and his descendants. In this special case, however, the heritage that is renounced and yet claimed is the opposite of ignorance, more dreadful than impiety, but also far more interesting than mere authochthony.

The Telchines whom Dexithea's father[15] represents were more like daimones than men and the one essential fact about them was that they were dangerous. As masters of metallurgy they had extensive magical powers and a peculiar relation to water; they were form-changers who never took on a wholly human aspect (in later times they were thought to be something like seals), and they liked to live in caves.[16] More important, they had powers that made them the rivals of the Olympians, for they could create and destroy life. Like most smiths they could heal,[17] but as craftsmen, they could also make creatures of metal that moved, while as agents of chaos they had been known to kill the fertility of the earth by pouring on water from the Styx.

In a sense, then, Bacchylides' myth of the elimination of the Cean Telchines by Zeus parallels the Rhodian myth in which these same powers were driven off when Helius took that island under the Olympian dispensation. In this Cean version, however, there is an insistence upon the permanence of something Telchinian, for a strain of daimonic cleverness is preserved and passed on[18] to the future inhabitants through a child whose name is Euxantius, or Wool-Carder.[19] The craft of the magical form-changing metal-workers is thus not wholly lost; it is instead domesticated by being contained in a feminine mold, and then it is "mastered" by a representative of an Olympian-sponsored, city-centered culture. The exploit of Minos with Dexithea is in other words presented as a doublet of the exploit of Zeus, when he got the best of Metis by simply incorporating her ruse.

How did the telling of such a myth in such a way serve the epinician purpose? First of all it is a myth that belongs to the victor's locality, one that will make all Ceans feel proud. Next, it is one that places a high value upon hospitality, and hospitality is what the poet and all his listeners are at this moment enjoying, at the patron's family hearth. On a much grander level, it is a myth of the creation of culture, one that praises the general Hellenic order which has as one of its parts the holding of games like those at Isthmia. And finally, it must be significant that the father of the present victor (who presumably commissioned this song) is famous not only for his generosity to his guests, but also for his skill in the art of medicine (149–50). Such skill is related to magic: it is like the traditional power of smiths to heal, but it has been domesticated, and it is the gift of the same god that Bacchylides chooses as author of the present victory, for Apollo is its Olympian patron now (147 ff.).

NOTES

INDEX OF PASSAGES

INDEX OF SUBJECTS

ABBREVIATIONS

Periodical titles are abbreviated according to the practice of *L'Année Philologique* and are not included in this list.

ABV	J. D. Beazley, *Attic Black-Figure Vase Painters* (Oxford, 1956)
ARV	J. D. Beazley, *Attic Red-Figure Vase Painters* (Oxford, 1963)
Arch. f. Relig.	*Archiv für Religionswissenschaft* (Freiburg)
CIA	*Corpus Inscriptionum Atticarum* (1828–77)
CVA	*Corpus Vasorum Antiquorum*
Ditt. Syll.	*Sylloge Inscriptionum Graecarum*, ed. W. Dittenberger (Leipzig, 1883)
DK	H. Diels, *Die Fragmente der Vorsokratiker*, ed. W. Kranz (Berlin, 1956)
Eph. arch.	*Ephemeris Archaiologikē* (Athens)
FGH	*Die Fragmente der griechischen Historiker*, ed. F. Jacoby (Leiden, 1957)
FHG	*Fragmenta Historicorum Graecorum*, ed. K. Müller (Paris, 1848–74)
IG	*Inscriptiones Graecae*
IGM	*Inscriptiones Graecae Metricae*, ed. T. C. Preger (Leipzig, 1891)
Mon. Inst.	Monumenti, annali e bullettini. Instituto di correspondenza. Archaologisches Institut des Deutschen Reichs
PLG	*Poetae Lyrici Graeci*, ed. Th. Bergk (Leipzig, 1900)
PMG	*Poetae Melici Graeci*, ed. D. L. Page (Oxford, 1962)
PSI	*Papiri Graci e Latini* (Pubblicazioni della Società Italiana, 1912–)
RE	Pauly-Wissowa, *Real-Enclopädie der classichen Altertumswissenschaft*
Relig. Vers. u. Vor.	*Religionsgeschichtliche Versuche und Vorarbeiten* (Giessen)
Roscher *Lex.*	W. H. Roscher, *Ausführliches Lexikon der griechischen und römischen Mythologie*
SLG	*Supplementum Lyricis Graecis*, ed. D. L. Page (Oxford, 1974)
SMSR	*Studi e Materiali di Storia delle Religioni* (Rome)

NOTES

INTRODUCTION

1. E. Wallis Budge, *By Nile and Tigris* II (London, 1920), pp. 345 ff.
2. F. G. Kenyon, *The Poems of Bacchylides, from a Papyrus in the British Museum* (London, 1897); *The Poems of Bacchylides.* Facsimile of Papyrus DCCXXXIII (London, 1897).
3. F. Blass, *Bacchylidis Carmina cum fragmentis* (Leipzig, 1905).
4. R. C. Jebb, *Bacchylides. The Poems and Fragments* (Cambridge, 1905).
5. V. Inama, *RIL* ser. II 31 (1898) 20.
6. U. von Wilamowitz, *Bacchylides* (Berlin, 1898), p. 8. Compare the more recent remark of G. Kirkwood, "The Narrative Art of Bacchylides," *The Classical Tradition. Literary and Historical Studies in Honor of Harry Caplan*, ed. L. Wallach (Ithaca, 1966), p. 98: "many might wish that the modern fragmentary recovery of Greek poetry in the form of papyri had brought us Simonides or Stesichorus rather than Bacchylides."
7. R. Fagles, *Bacchylides. The Complete Poems* (New Haven, 1961). There is also now a good German translation with accompanying Greek text; H. Maehler, *Bakchylides Lieder und Fragmente* (Berlin, 1968).
8. A. Severyns' book (*Bacchylide, essai biographique*, Liège, 1933) is principally concerned with the poet's life, so that the one long critical work remains that of B. Gentili, *Bacchilide. Studi* (Urbino, 1958), a sympathetic and learned study of Odes 3 and 5.
9. Ode 1 is treated in the Appendix, and so the two major songs left undiscussed are Odes 15 and 19. Of 15 only the end survives and the fiction, deriving as it does from the *Cypria*, is beyond our control. *Il.* 3.203 ff., with its emphasis upon Odysseus, is no help (nor is Ov. *Met.* 13.197) and there is no way to guess what the Bacchylidean chorus had created as preparation for Menelaus' final, very Solonic words. Ode 19, on the other hand, seems to have been complete in its single triad, and it treats a very familiar story, but its sense breaks precisely at the moment of highest significance. Without knowing just how the poet engineered the release of Io from Argus, we cannot judge his particular intention in bringing this release into contact with the birth of Dionysus and the different sort of release that he brings.

1. THE CHORAL MODE

1. Socrates was supposed to have said, "They who honor the gods best with dancing are best at war" (Athen. 14.628 F). Compare the opinion of Plato (*Laws* 7.803 E): "A man must spend his life in certain pastimes—sacrificing, singing, and dancing—so as to win the favor of the gods and be able to repel the enemy in battle." In one of Laurens Van der Post's books a modern Matabele chieftain talks about a boy's education: "He also had to learn how to sing and above all to dance, for dancing and singing were the best

ways he had of showing gratitude for the good things of life. Song and above all dancing were the surest ways of helping a man to endure the great trials of his existence; they were needed at birth, marriage and before war to strengthen the heart. Also after war they were needed to exorcise the spirit of death in him, and at the moment when the final loss of his shadow was upon him and those he loved, to drive away the power of death and revive the desire to live." On shamanistic dances, see J. P. Roux, "La danse chamanique," *Les danses sacrées* (Paris, 1963), pp. 283 ff.

2. On the importance of repetition in magic, see W. Deonna, "Unité et diversité," *RA* 23 (1914) 1, 39 ff; "Essai sur la genèse des monstres," *REG* 28 (1915) 312 ff.; J. Jannoray, "Nouvelles inscriptions de Lebadée, *BCH* 64–65 (1940–41) 48 note 2; J. Marcadé, "Hermes doubles," *BCH* 76 (1952) 616. On incantation in general, see F. G. Welcker, "Epoden oder das Besprechen," *Kleine Schriften* III (1850) 64–88; F. Pfister, "Epode," *RE* Supp. IV (1924) 323–44; Th. Hopfner, "Mageia," *RE* XIV col. 343 ff.; F. B. Jevons, "Graeco-Italic Magic," *Anthropology and the Classics*, ed. R.R. Marett (Oxford 1908), pp. 94 ff.

3. For outright magic in epinician, see for example, the attempts to send messages to the dead at *P. O.* 14.20 f.; *I.* 7.31; *N.* 4.85–88; *I.* 8.62–65; *O.* 8.72–76; *N.* 5.50–54.

4. Wedding dances are mentioned at *Od.* 23.135; *Il.* 18.492; Hes. *Sc.* 274; some of Sappho's wedding songs seem to be choral (111 V for example) and she describes choral celebrations for Hector and Andromache (44 V). As examples of field magic, note 858 *PMG*, a paean that calls on the Euros to fertilize Spartan fields, and Diehl II. vi. 279, the Dictaean hymn that calls for full wine jars, fleecy flocks, and standing crops (see M. West, "The Dictaean Hymn to the Kouros," *JHS* 85, 1965, 149–159). *Il.* 567 describes dancing at the wine-making season and 871 *PMG* is a women's song for an Elean wine festival; for the spring, Pollux describes a flower festival for Hera at Argos (4.78), and the Homeric hymn for Gaia (30.14–15) describes the same sort of flower-bearing dance; one at least of Stesichorus' Oresteia performances was meant for spring (34, 35 *PMG*). Euripides (*IA* 1467 ff.) describes the placation of Artemis with danced paeans, and at Rhegium the anger of Artemis was assuaged with annual sequences of such performances (B. Pace, "Artemis Phacelitis," *Misc. Orsi. ASSO* 16–17, 1921, 8–17). Apollo was made joyful by the performance of the Deliades (*h. Ap. Del.* 147; cf. E. *HF* 687 ff. and, not of Delos, *Il.* 1.470–71), and Dionysos by the processions of the *ithyphalloi* (851 *PMG*). Pausanias mentions coming-of-age choruses at Olympia (5.16.4) and Athenaeus (139 D) refers to dancing at the Hyacinthea (see A. Brelich, *Paides e Parthenoi* I, Rome 1969, p. 115 ff.); probably Alcman's *Partheneion* was meant for a celebration of the same sort (see C. Calame, *Les choeurs de jeunes filles en Grèce archaique* II, Rome, 1977). Aristotle speaks of choral performances at the funerals of Cypriote kings (fr. 476 Rose), and in early Sicyon choruses were assigned to the festivals for the hero Adrastus (Hdt. 5.67). In general, see T. B. L. Webster, *The Greek Chorus* (London, 1970), pp. 46–94.

5. Compare what Thomas Hardy says of the bonfire builders, in chapter 3 of *The Return of the Native:* "It was as if these men and boys had suddenly dived into past ages and fetched therefrom an hour and deed which had before been familiar with this spot." Jacques Borel expresses the same notion with a different metaphor when he is describing the world of Jammes: "Un

univers comme sans couture entre le dedans et l'en dehors, ou le passé le plus amorti affleure sans cesse le present le plus vivace" (F. Jammes, *De l'Angelus de l'aube à l'Angelus du soir*, Paris, 1971, p. viii).

6. For examples, see P. *O.* 1.17; *O.* 3.5; *P.* 8.20; *parth.* 94b.6 ff.; 107 ab; cf. the popular Bacchic song, 851b *PMG*. Compare Rose's comment on A. *A.* 26, *A Commentary on the Surviving Plays of Aeschylus* (Amsterdam, 1957–8) where he cites as further examples A. *Supp.* 822, 514; S. *El.* 1209; *OC* 854; E. *Ba.* 504; *Andr.* 577–8; Ar. *Nu.* 1145. A parallel from the ancient dance songs of Egypt is cited by H. Wild, "Egypte," *Les danses sacrées* (Paris, 1963), p. 62.

7. The spectator of *P. N.* 5, for example, saw and heard a singing chorus of Aeginetans who took on themselves the character of, and sang the song of, the Muses at Peleus' wedding.

8. A comparable effect could be achieved through the decoration of festival buildings. So, for example, the frieze of the Parthenon generalized and idealized the actual processions that would pass beneath, while the metopes introduced mythic moments and the pediment gave a cosmogonic permanence to the complex of temple and ceremony. Similarly at the archaic Hera temple at Foce del Sele, some of the metopes depicted festival dancers dancing for Hera while others showed scenes from myth (P. Zancani-Montuoro and U. Zanotti-Bianco, *Heraion alla foce del Sele* I. Rome, 1961, pp. 123 ff., pl. XLI–LIX; some suppose the dancers to be mythic also, for example, see E. Simon, "Die vier Büsser von Foce del Sele," *JDAI* 82, 1967, 275–295).

9. D. L. Page, *Alcman. The Partheneion* (Oxford, 1951); A. Garzya, *Alcmane. I Frammenti* (Naples, 1957). See also the commentary of P. Oxy. 2389 = 1 schol. B. *PMG*.

10. Eusebius and the Suda offer three possible periods of activity for Alcman: 672–68 BC, 659–8, 611–10. M. West, "Alcmanica," *CQ* 15 (1965) 188–202, chooses the last of these, giving the *Partheneion* a date between 620 and 570, after the Second Messenian war and the Lycurgan reforms; in this opinion he was preceded by P. Janni, "Alcmane," *Stud. Urb.* 33 (1959) 162–72, and he is followed by F. D. Harvey, "Oxy. pap. 2390 and early Spartan history," *JHS* 87 (1967) 62 ff., and Calame, *Choeurs de jeunes filles* II, p. 22. There was, however, a firm ancient tradition that made Alcman precede Stesichorus in the list of choral poets, and consequently either of the two earlier periods would seem to be preferable. For the culture of pre-Lycurgan Sparta, see E. Homann-Wedeking, "Vom Spartanischen Art und Kunst," *AA* 8 (1958) 63–73; F. Stoessl, "Leben und Dichtung" *Eumasia. Festgabe E. Howald* (Zurich, 1947), pp. 92–114.

11. The goddess has been identified as Artemis, Aphrodite, Helen, Phoebe, Eileithya, or Demeter. The occasion is usually described as a festival of fertility or of girls' coming of age, but B. Gentili, "Il partenio di Alcmane e l'amore omo-erotico femminile nei tiasi spartani," *QU* 22 (1976) 59–68, imagines it to have been a homosexual wedding between two girls. On the many problems of the Louvre fragment, see H. Diels, "Alkmans Partheneion," *Hermes* 31 (1896) 339 ff.; U. von Wilamowitz, "Der chor der Hagesichora," *Hermes* 32 (1897) 251 ff.; H. Jurenka, "Epilegomena zu Alkmans Partheneion," *Philol.* 56 (1897) 399 ff.; C. M. Bowra, "The occasion of Alcman's Partheneion," *CQ* 28 (1934) 35 ff.; B. A. van Groningen, "The enigma of Alcman's Partheneion," *Mnem.* 3 (1935–6) 241–61; J. A. Davison, "Alcman's Partheneion," *Hermes* 73 (1938) 440–58; A. Garzya, "Sul

nuovo Alcmane," *Maia* 3 (1962) 209 ff.; M. L. West, "Alcmanica," *CQ* 15 (1965) 188–202; A. P. Burnett, "The Race with the Pleiades," *CP* 59 (1964) 30–33; A. F. Garvie, "On the Deity," *CQ* 15 (1965) 185–7; T. G. Rosenmeyer, "Alcman's Partheneion Reconsidered," *GRBS* 7 (1966) 321 ff.; C. O. Pavese, "Alcmane. Il Partenio del Louvre," *QU* 6 (1967) 113 ff.; M. Puelma, "Alkmans gr. Parth. frag.," *MH* 34 (1977) 1–55; and most extensively, Calame, *Choeurs de jeunes filles*, II.

12. As a non-Greek parallel to a metaphorical race of the sort proposed by Burnett, *CP* 59 (1964) 30–33, one might cite the celebration of the Mescalero Apaches in honor of girls who had reached womanhood. On the first and last dawns of a four-day festival the Sun-Greeting Ceremony occurred; in this the girls raced to the east just as the sun rose, circling a basket of ritual items four times, and a chant was sung for each turn. On the night previous to the final race there was dancing until dawn, and in the course of the last Sun-Greeting ceremony each girl took a feather from the basket and ran with it to her own hut where she remained for four days. When she came out on the fifth, she was ready to be married.

13. On this passage see M. West, "Alcman and Pythagoras," *CQ* 7 (1967) 11–14.

14. If *ate sērion astron* is taken as modifying *aueiromenai*, then the many pale Pleiades are compared to the single brilliant Dog Star, and the sense is probably astronomical: the Pleiades rise now like Sirius in its most significant rising, i.e. its heliacal rising; see Burnett, *CP* 59 (1964) 30–33. It is possible, however, that it is the robe that is being compared, like certain Homeric garments, to a heavenly ornament.

15. Compare the description of a Spartan girls' festival at E. *IT* 1136–51, where the chorus dreams of taking wing and flying home:

> I'd circle with the maidens
> in their dance, I'd join
> that war of loveliness
> where perfumed curls contend,
> I'd wear my best embroidered cloak
> and let my loosened hair
> cast its shadow on my cheek!

16. The gift brought to the goddess may have been either a plough or a robe; both can be parallelled in other cults, but the latter seems far more appropriate as an object to be carried at a run. D. Boedeker, *Aphrodite's Entry into Greek Epic* (Leiden, 1974), p. 73, note 1, compares the bright garments of the Dawn Goddess in the Rig Veda and points also to the dawn robings of Circe and Calypso at *Od.* 5.228 and 10.541

17. For ancient references to this story, see Strabo 10.461; Diod. 4.33.5; schol. P. O. 10, 78ab; Plut. *qu. rom.* 90; for modern discussion, see C. Robert, *Die Griechische Heldensage* II, (Berlin, 1920), p. 545 ff.; Davison, *Hermes* 73 (1938) 442 ff. There were various traditional reasons for enmity between the sons of Hippocoön and Heracles and/or the Tyndarids: the Hippocoöntids fought for Neleus against Heracles (Apollod. *Bib.* 2.7.3); the Hippocoöntids refused to purify Heracles after his killing of Iphitus (Paus. 3.15.3); the Hippocoöntids offered rudeness to Helen (Plut. *Thes.* 31); the Hippocoöntids were rivals of the Dioscuri for the Leucippides (Euphorion ap. schol. Clem. Al. *Protr.* 1, p. 308 Stählin). Clement reported that Sosibius, the most famous ancient commentator of Alcman, stated that Alcman

somewhere mentioned a wound that Heracles received in an initial encounter with the sons of Hippoccoön; this wound is also reported by Pausanias (3.15.3) who tells elsewhere of its healing by Asclepius, after Heracles had taken refuge in a shrine of Demeter on the slopes of Taygetus (3.20.4).

18. Pavese, *QU* 6 (1967), 113 ff., argues that the whole mythic section is only a conventional foil in which the chorus uses a common rhetorical device to say, "I don't sing the Hippocoöntids, I sing only the beauty of Agido!"

19. If it should be the case that Alcman's Hippocoöntids were punished for an attack upon the Leukippides, who were to be the brides of Castor and Pollux (so Garvie, *CQ* 15, 1965, 185–187), then this mythic section might be thought to have brought another sort of divine power into the day since in later times at least the rape of these daughters of Apollo (Paus. 3.16.1) by the Dioscuri was taken as a figure for the rise of souls into the upper spheres of bliss; see J. Carcopino, *Le basilique pythagororicienne de la Porte Majeure* (Paris, 1926), p. 110. It should be noted in this context that the two nymphs, though they were associated with the introduction of the worship of Dionysus (M.P. Nilsson, *Griechische Feste* (Leipzig, 1906), p. 298 note 2), were seized while they danced in the festival of a goddess who may have been Artemis; see S. Wide, *Lakonische Kulte* (Leipzig, 1893), p. 324.

20. The fragment survives because it was posed as a metrical problem by Dion. Halic. (*comp.* 26.ii p. 140 f.), who dared anyone to detect its triadic structure. For discussion of its formal problems, see Wilamowitz, "Isyllos von Epidauros," *Phil. Unters.* 9 (1886) 140–146; Th. Bergk, *PLG* III⁴ 403–406; M. Garrod, "Simonidea," *CQ* 16 (1922) 117 f.; J. A. Davison, "Simonides fr. 13D," *CR* 29 (1935) 85 ff.; D. L. Page, "Simonidea," *JHS* 71 (1951) 133 ff.; G. Perotta, "Il Lamento di Danae," *Maia* 4 (1951) 81–117; C. O. Pavese, "Simon. 38.11.P," *QU* 4 (1967) 134–5.

21. Dionysus himself was sealed in a chest with Semele, according to Paus. 3.24.3–4, and in other sacred tales images of him were found in chests or washed up on the shore from the sea (Paus. 7.19.6–9). The appropriateness of the Perseus tale to Dionysus was clearly felt by Aeschylus, for he used it in his satyr play *Dictyoulkoi*.

22. For Asiatic and Indian versions of the tale, see M. E. Cosquin, "Le lait de la mère et le coffre flottant," *Revue des questions historiques* n.s. 39 (1908) 353–425 esp. 378; for other Greek versions, see F. Marx, "Bronzemünze von Elaia," MDAI (A) 10, 21 ff.; A. B. Cook, *Zeus* II (Cambridge, 1914), pp. 671 ff.; N. M. Holley, "The Floating Chest," *JHS* 69 (1949) 39 ff.

23. Whether or not we add a participle like *prophainōn* to line 17 (see C.M. Bowra *Greek Lyric Poetry*, Oxford, 1961, p. 338, note 1), the phrase *prosopon kalon* carries tremendous emphasis, coming as it does at the end of the complex rhetorical and emotional movement that begins nine lines before with Danaë's astonished, "You sleep!" For beauty's luminosity, cf. Phryn. 13 N²; E. *Ion* 475.

24. Compare Nohum Tate's lines for Purcell's "Blessed Virgin": "Whilst of thy dear sight beguil'd/ I trust the God but o!/ I fear the child!"

25. The present evil is disproportionate (*ametron*, unfathomed, 22), which means in archaic terms that it is unjust, but this truth has no place in Danaë's prayer, for with all her knowledge of her own innocence she knows too that she may be unwittingly unjust (26) and in need of god's forgiveness (27) simply because she is a mortal. On her concern over the form of her request, note the remark of M. Alexiou, *The Ritual Lament in Greek Tradition* (Cambridge, 1974), p. 161 (cf. notes on p. 235), that a standard

part of a request hymn is an expression of "anxiety that the speaker should fail to find words adequate to the occasion."

2. THESEUS' DIVE

1. Odes 15 to 28 were arranged in a more or less alphabetical order, which shows that Alexandrian editors thought they represented a single genre (unless they were simply "non-epinician"). Though only Odes 16 and 19 have any connection with Dionysus, they are usually all called dithyrambs, and Servius, ad *Aen.* 6.22, mentions the "twice-seven" men and girls of Ode 17 as coming "Bacchylides in dithyrambis." This description was, however, probably inspired merely by the heroic subject and narrative manner of the song, since these were thought of as dithyrambic ([Plut.] *de mus.* 10; Schol. Ar. *Av.* 917). See H. Jurenka, "Die Dithyramben des Bakchylides," *WS* 21 (1899) 216 ff., where 17 is called a paean; also R. Merkelbach, "Paonische Strophen bei P. und B.," *ZPE* 12 (1973) 45 ff.

2. The crane dance was one of the most famous of ancient choral performances but very little is known about it. We do not know whether it was dedicated to Apollo or Aphrodite (or Asteria-Delos, see below); whether it was a true choral performance, a dance to accompany the song of a single singer, or perhaps a dance that had no song at all. Pollux (4.10) specified a processional movement in single file, and Callimachus (*Del.* 307 ff. and schol.) suggests the possibility of flagellation as a part of the choreography (cf. Hesych. *Deliakos bōmos* and G. de Santerre, *Délos primitive et archaique*, Paris, 1958, p. 179). Robert and Nilsson proposed a summer dance that circled the horned altar which they thought of as dedicated to Aphrodite (de Santerre would have it sacred to Asteria-Delos), and F. Weige, *Der Tanz in der Antike* (Halle, 1926), p. 61, supposed a nighttime performance by torchlight. Among the many problems is that of reconciling the cranes of the title with Pollux's note about mimesis of the labyrinth, and some scholars have decided to ignore Pollux and posit a flapping of arms (Weige, ibid.) or a v-shaped formation (L. Sechan, *La danse grècque antique*, Paris 1930, p. 120 f.). Most, however, assume some sort of spiral dance; see L. Lawler, "The Geranos Dance," *TAPA* 71 (1946) 112–130; K. Kerenyi, *Labyrinth-Studien*[2] (Zurich, 1950), pp. 38 ff.; J. Duchemin, "Le thème du heros au labyrinthe," *KOKALOS* 16 (1970) 30 ff. J. N. Coldstream "A Figured Geometric Oinoche from Italy," *BICS* 15 (1968) 90, identifies the men and women's dance on a seventh-century vase from Euboea as the *geranos*, but this is denied by T. B. L. Webster, *The Greek Chorus* (London, 1970), p. 10, who believes that the lyre was essential to the crane dance and proposes the scene on a hydria of the Analatos painter instead. See also K. Friis Johansen, *Thésée et la danse à Délos*. Kgl. Danske Videnskab. Selskab. Ark. Kunst M. III. 3 (1945); E. Cohen, "L'autel de cornes et l'hymne à Délos de Callimaque" *REG* 36 (1923) 22: C. Calame, *Les choeurs de jeunes filles en Grèce archaique* I (Rome, 1977), pp. 108 ff.

3. To these Thesean innovations Plutarch would add games, the prize for which was a palm crown (*quaest. conv.* 8.724A; cf. Paus. 8.48.3).

4. The scene of Theseus' undersea reception makes its first literary appearance here, but it was already a popular vase-painting subject; see P. Jacobsthal, *Theseus auf dem Meeresgrunde* (Leipzig, 1911). Bacchylides has evidently added his own touches, for nowhere else is the dive treated, and only here and on the red-figure cup by the Briseis painter (*ARV*[2] 406.7)

does Theseus appear alone before Amphitrite. Most frequently the hero was received by Poseidon, either alone or with his wife; on a crater from Agrigento the god gives Theseus his hand (*Mon. Inst.* I. lii–liii; see R. Zielinski and A. Olivieri, *A proposito di Teseo e Meleagro in Baccilide*, Bologna, 1899); cf. *CVA Robinson* 25–27, TW 31–2 = *ARV²* 179, where Theseus and Poseidon shake hands in the presence of Nereus, a Nereid, and Amphitrite. The less frequent version omits Poseidon; on the cup by Euphronius (Louvre G 104, ca. 490 BC) Amphitrite presents a wreath in the presence of Athena and a tiny triton who supports a boyish Theseus; the same boyish figure is carried by a powerful triton in a terra-cotta cutout from Melos (Louvre MNC 746); cf. the frieze of the Briseis painter kylix mentioned above. Pausanias (1.17.3) mentions a painting by Micon in the Theseum which seems to have depicted a scene very much like the Bacchylidean one, but it is impossible to discern the actual content of the picture from his exegesis; see J. P. Barron, "New Light on Old Walls," *JHS* 92 (1972) 20 ff., esp. 40 and note 150, where all archaic and early classical representations of Theseus' introduction of Poseidon and Amphitrite are listed. (It is interesting to note that Attic vase painters knew a story in which Achilles was similarly received at the bottom of the sea, by Poseidon and Thetis, who gave him a diadem; see Roscher *Lex.* III, pp. 217 and 249.) Some observers have thought that the swimmer on the Francois vase was Theseus, but see Robert, "Theseus und Meleager bei Bakchylides," *Hermes* 33 (1899) 143, where it is pointed out that the painted figure swims from ship to shore; that he is a man, not a boy; that he has neither crown nor robe; that the ship is in port; that there are no girls on board; that the men do not look at the swimmer. On the extent of Bacchylides' innovations in this song, see E. Wüst, "Der Ring des Minos," *Hermes* 96 (1968) 526–38.

5. Compare the similar Homeric boasts and challenges on the subject of paternity (*Il.* 1.280 f.; 21.186; *Od.* 9.529). For an analysis of the language attached to the two antagonists, see G. W. Peiper, "Conflict of Character in Bacchylides' Ode 17," *TAPA* 103 (1972) 395 ff.

6. Note the pun between *boase* and Eriboea; it is repeated at 13.102, and H. Jeanmaire, *Couroi et Courètes* (Lille, 1939), p. 329, concludes that the name actually derived from a female ritual cry. Eriboea is pictured and identified on the Francois vase, and X. *Cyn.* 1.9 and Diod. 4.72 report her as the later wife of Telamon and the mother of Ajax. Pausanias, who calls her Periboea (1.42.2) makes her a Megarian princess and so, in her opposition to Minos, a reverse doublet of the lustful Scylla who betrayed her city and father to the same king (A. *Ch.* 611 ff.; Paus. 1.19.4; Apollod. 3.15.8).

7. See Housman's complaints about the careless treatment of Eriboea, "Critical notes on Bacchylides," *CR* 12 (1898) 218. Some scholars have insisted that she should have been the one to jump into the sea, but Jacob Stern notes how her cry of fear at 14 is balanced and replaced by the joyful *ololygmos* of the Nereids at 127 ("The Structure of Bacchylides' Ode 17," *RB Ph* 45, 1967, 42).

8. There has been much discussion of this ring and much distress over its loss. Pausanias (1.17.3) and Hyginus (*astr.* 2.5) refused to let it be lost, correcting Bacchylides by having the Nereids give it to Theseus, and two recent French scholars have erroneously reported that here in Ode 17 Theseus actually returns with the ring (J. Duchemin, *KOKALOS* 16, 1970, 52, and M. Detienne, *Maîtres de verité*, Paris, 1981, p. 36, who even makes it The-

seus' own ring: "il s'en va repêcher l'anneau qu'il vient de jeter au fond de l'ocean; il penetre dans le monde des dieux et il fait le preuve de sa qualité divine en surgissant des flots, sain et sauf, pourvu de sa bague."!) Usually moderns try to read a symbolic meaning into the disappearance of the ring; so Jane Harrison ("Notes Archaeological and Mythological," *CR* 12, 1898, 85 ff.) wanted the ring to be a symbol of Cretan matriarchy, a recognition token given to Minos by his mother; by this reading he would, by throwing away his ring, cast off his mother's definition of him. J. Baike, *The Sea Kings of Crete* (London, 1910) p. 256, argued that the ring in the sea confirmed Minos in his thalassocracy; cf. S. Reinach, *Cultes, mythes et religions* II (Paris, 1922), pp. 206 ff., and see the criticism of C. Blumlein, *Bursians Jahresberichte* 197 (1923), p. 51. More recently L. Gernet, "La notion mythique de la valeur," *Journ. de Psych.* 41 (1948) 430 ff., compared Minos' ring to the ring of Polycrates and tried to identify a rite that determined whether or not a ruler should continue in power. If the Polycrates parallel is instructive, it establishes a pattern in which the sea's return of the ring equals a fall from power, while the sea's keeping of the ring equals confirmation of rule. The story that Bacchylides tells would consequently be a conflation of two: one that confirmed Minos' power with the tale of the ring, another that promised Theseus' independence with the adoption by Amphitrite. (It is worth noting that, before Ode 17 was found, Robert thought that the story of Theseus' dive was archaic but that it was attached to the figure of Minos only in Hellenistic times; cf. *AA*, 1889, 142.) Considering the loss of the ring from a wholly different standpoint, Jacob Stern somewhat rashly concludes that as a poetic motif it proves that Ode 17 is "not serious," but instead a "reaction" against a "stereotyped set of bombastic tropes from the heroic ethos," *RB Ph* 45, 1967, 45).

9. Note Robert's contention that the normal place for this episode would have been the coast of Crete, *Hermes* 33 (1899) 134.

10. Some have thought that the ship was brought to a standstill at 87–9, but this is clearly not the sense of the lines; see below, note 11.

11. At 86–9 Minos orders that the ship should sail *kat' ouron*, "with the wind," which was its course already. Moira at the same time prepares a course that shall be "other," and since the ship does move onwards in the following lines, some of the early commentators tried to create an opposition by altering Minos' command; see, for example, E. Schwartz, *Hermes* 39 (1904) 641, who proposed *eneuse t' apsorron ischein;* cf. Housman, who read *katouron* and translated: "he ordered them to stop the ship which was running before the wind." This also is the sense found by A. Maniet, "Le caractère de Minos," *LEC* 10 (1941) 35 ff., while Peiper (*TAPA* 103, 172, 398) inexplicably supposes that Moira held the ship still, though Minos had commanded it to move. It is however plain that Jebb is right in reporting that Minos orders the helmsman to continue towards Crete; as Snell says in his commentary, "Iussit Minos nautas navis cursum dirigere ita ut vento secundo auferretur." This, in his mind will be a course that leaves Theseus behind; Moira, however, causes it to be "other," since she causes the ship to follow, on the sea's surface, the route of Theseus' undersea journey.

12. Bacchylides marks three moments at which men marveled with three parallel expressions (*taphon*, 48; *taphen*, 86; *thauma*, 123). Housman, who wanted a remorseful Minos, would have destroyed this sequence by reading *tachen* or *taken* at 86 (*CR* 12, 1898, 139).

13. Amphitrite was among the goddesses present at the birth of Apollo (*h. Ap.*

94) and some have thought that she had a cult on Delos before the coming of Apollo; see H. Gallet de Santerre, *Délos primitive et archaique*, pp. 150 ff.

14. For other versions of this miracle, see Stith Thompson, *Motif-Index* (Bloomington, 1932), D 1841.4; F. 930.1; compare too the marvelously refreshed costumes of the shipwrecked voyagers in Shakespeare's *Tempest*.

15. It is interesting to note that the lust that Aphrodite gives in str. 1, 8–10, is transformed into the fruitful love of Zeus and Europa in str. 2, 8–10 (=31–33). Minos' unseemly act of touching Eriboea is similarly transformed into the engendering act between Poseidon and Aithra (str. 1, 11–13/str. 2, 34–36).

16. As Aphrodite's gift, the wreath was proof that Olympus approved of Poseidon's marriage, and consequently a proof as well of a reconciliation between Olympians and the more ancient, watery, female powers. In its present state it also carries suggestions of immortality, since its magic is demonstrated by its unwithered condition (it is *amemphes*, 114) and by the fact that, though roses come from land, they have been kept under the sea. The roses themselves are symbols of Aphrodite (see the bibliography at A. P. Burnett, *Three Archaic Poets*, London, Cambridge, 1983, p. 263, note 88), and the crown explicitly looks forward to a marriage for Theseus. C. P. Segal, "Bacchylides reconsidered," *QU* 22 (1976) 107, reports the crown as a "sexually charged gift" (cf. Segal, "The Myth of Bacchylides 17," *Eranos* 77, 1979, 26), which may be a bit strong; this rose wreath is indicative of all the gracious pleasures of life that Aphrodite and the Charites can give. (The roses may be peculiar to Bacchylides; the wreath on the Euphronius cup may or may not be of flowers, but the one in Micon's painting was of gold.) The wreath has no place in the continuing tales about Theseus, and Robert was so disturbed by its disappearance that he invented his own mythic detail, causing this same wreath to be worn later by Theseus in the labyrinth, where it glowed in the dark. Others have supposed that it helped Theseus to win Ariadne (so B. Gentili, "Il ditirambo xvii," *AC* 6, 1954, 121–5), and some have thought that it was identical with the crown that Hyginus (*astr.* 2.5) records as passing from Theseus to Ariadne to Dionysus and then into the heavens in the form of stars, but that one was specified as decorated with gems and as having come from Thetis. On wreaths in general, see M. Blech, *Studien zum Kranz bei den Griechen* (Berlin, 1982), esp. pp. 265–7.

17. On this kind of regal heirloom, see Gernet, *Journ. de Psych.* 41 (1948) 430.

18. This adoption is as nearly as possible parallel to Hera's adoption of Heracles (Diod. Sic. 5.39), and consequently it carries a suggestion of divinization. Compare especially the wreath given to Heracles in some apotheosis scenes (P. Mungazzi, *Le rappresentazione vascolare del mito dell' apoteosi di Herakles*, Rome, 1925, IV, fig. 1; V, fig. 1, 2; VI, fig. 1; VII, fig. 2) and see the discussion of Robert, *Hermes* 33 (1899) 139. The notion of a return to life is also present, since a rite like that of adoption—a kind of *couvée*— was used in some places to reestablish the rights of one who had been presumed dead (Plut. *quaest. rom.* 5; Hesych. *s.v. deuteropotmoi*).

19. This robe may be a Bacchylidean invention, since it is never seen in pictorial representations of the scene of Theseus' reception. (Gentili, *AC* 6, 121–5, supposed that Bacchylides referred to the fringed scarf that Theseus wears on the Ruvo crater, but this is extremely improbable, since the robe is long enough to cling about Theseus' legs at line 124.) Certainly the robe

had a special significance for him, since it is the gift that he chooses to emphasize at the end of his song. It is purple, which means honor and royalty (cf. the purple robe given to Jason by Athena at AR 1.721 ff.) and in the present instance the color may be meant to remind the hearer as well of the purple sail which, according to Simonides (550 *PMG*), was to signify success to the waiting Aegeus. Robert (*Hermes* 33, 145) saw the robe as ceremonial and prefiguring the celebration at Delos; C. P. Segal, *Eranos* 77 (1979) 23 ff., argues that the symbolism of the robe is sexual ("the dark-red or purple robe ... recalls the veil which the Nereids gave Theseus' own mother, Aethra"), but how can a purple man's robe "recall" a golden woman's veil? The word used for this garment, *aiona*, may possibly indicate that it was made of linen (so K. Latte, "Randbemerkungen," *Philol.* 87, 1932, 271, and "Zur gr. Wortforschung II," *Glotta* 34, 1955, 192), but more probably it was used merely to give the garment an air of exoticism.

20. A trick of responsion establishes a kind of parallelism between Minos' "cosmic" marriage with Pasiphaë, Helius' daughter, and Poseidon's marriage with Amphitrite (50/116). Note the cosmic frame given to the scene of Theseus' undersea reception by the Kadmos painter on a vase from Bologna (*ARV*² 1184, 6), where Helius looks on and a star is depicted.

21. The word (*aithera*, 73) is a pun for Aithra, and so it was used in some of the foundation legends of Magna Graecia when an oracle called for rain to fall from a clear sky. If the pun is meant to be heard here, it reminds us that Theseus' existence is already proof that sea and sky (Poseidon and Aithra) need not be enemies.

22. The robe answers the question of Theseus' paternity structurally as well as imagistically: "if Poseidon engendered you ..." (ep. 1, line 11=57 ff.) corresponds to "the gods' gift shone about his limbs" (ep. 2, line 11=123 ff.).

23. Stern, in fact, complains of its prominence, asserting that Theseus' is an exaggerated response to a trivial gesture of the Cretan king's (*RBPh* 45, 1967, 43, note 1).

24. Stern, ibid., 41, finds everything before the dive "bombastic, virile, overly heroic," everything after "winsome, feminine and lyrical." Fortunately his insistence upon Bacchylides' satiric, anticonventional stance does not invalidate the close analysis that he makes of conceptual responsions between these two parts.

25. This is why the swimmers at Sphacteria were worth mentioning, though they were not of any strategic significance (Thur. 4.26). For girls swimming in an apparently secular situation, see an amphora of the Andocides painter: J. Boardman, *Athenian RF Vases: The Archaic Period* (London, 1975), fig. 4. One might also note Plut. *conv. vii sap.* 163A, where dolphins are said sometimes to swim and dive with children. In general, see R. Genouvès, *Balaneutiké. Recherches sur le bain* (Paris, 1962).

26. For Glaucus see also the schol. at AR 1.1310; schol. at E. *Or.* 364; Hyg. *fab.* 250, 273; *Et. Mag.* 685.40. Note the curious reversal of this idea in the case of the nearly immortal Hyperboreans: when they wished to die they wreathed themselves and jumped into the sea; *RE s.v.* 2834.

27. See L. R. Farnell, "Ino-Leucothea," *JHS* 36 (1916) 36 ff., who notes that there was a cult of Leucothea on Delos, citing *BCH* (1882) 25. Delos also knew the tale of Rhoio who, with Apollo's child, was washed up on the shore of the island in a chest (ibid., p. 44).

28. This was evidently the mythic accompaniment to the sacred bath of the

Eleusinian hierophants; see H. von Gaertringen, *De gr. fabulis ad Thraces pertinentibus quaest. crit.* (Berlin, 1886), pp. 31, 116a.

29. See also Callim. hymn 3, 189 ff. and schol. Ar. *Ran.* 1356. On Britomartis, see E. Strong and N. Joliffe, "The Stuccoes of the Underground Basilica," *JHS* 44 (1924) 65 ff.; R. Santyves, "L'anneau de Polycrate," *RHR* 66 (1912) 52. For other dives to escape sexual attack, see those of Apriate to escape Trambelos (Euphorion Thrax, ap. Parth. 26), Asteria to escape Zeus (Callim. *Del.* 36 ff.; Apollod. 1.4.1.1.), Argennos to escape Agamemnon (Ath. 13.80.603D).

30. Compare the ladies of Tanagra who were tossed into the sea to be eaten by Triton but were saved by Dionysus (Paus. 9.21.4). According to the schol. at Lyc. *Alex.* 791, Penelope was thrown into the sea by her parents when a girl, and was saved by birds.

31. Where nautical disasters were frequent, swimming came to be the equivalent of salvation; Odysseus invents an escape by means of a brief swim in his tale to Eumaeus (*Od.* 14.345–52); cf. E. *Hipp.* 469, where the nurse asks Phaedra how she will "swim out," that is, save herself, and note also the phrase at A. *Supp.* 408, where one is to dive into the depths of saving thought.

32. See, for example, the adventures of Menelaus at *Od.* 4.363 ff., and the many legends surrounding the figure of Glaucus, who was, according to Gernet, the embodiment of a rite of a "saut dans la mer ... associé particulièrement, semble-t-il, à un souvenir de prophètes specialisés dans la plongée rituelle" (*Journ. de Psych.* 41, 1948, 441). Unfortunately he offers no documentation.

33. For the Epidaurian Limera, see Pausanias 3.23.8; the proverb reported at Paus. 10.19.2 seems to reflect a ritual test for virginity by diving; cf. the mythic cases of Aerope and Alcyone, daughter of Sciron. See Pliny 31.23 and Philostr. *VA* 1.6, for Anatolian rites of *ordalie*. In general, see G. Glotz, *L'Ordalie dans la Grèce primitive* (Paris, 1904).

34. See, for example, the extraordinary (and fictitious) sea-washing of the image of Artemis at E. *IT*, 1041 ff. and 1191 ff. Images of Dionysus were thrown into the spring at Lerna (Plut. *Is.* 364 F); cf. O. Gruppe, *Mythol.*, 585.

35. Pausanias (10.32.6) reports cleansing leaps by priests in a cult of Apollo in Magnesia; compare Ael., *h. a.* 11.8 and Strabo 10.2.9, who notes that the jumpers were saved and that the ritual was apotropaic and effective for the whole community (cf. Gruppe, *Mythol.*, 287). For the sea as a source of cleansing and renewal, note also the idea that the stars dove into the ocean at dawn and reappeared the next night, refreshed; see E. Vermeule, *Aspects of Death in Early Greek Art and Poetry* (Berkeley, 1979), p. 134, fig. 6 A, an Attic red-figure bell crater on which the diving stars are figured as young boys.

36. This is the view of recent writers (see below, notes 39 and 41); Gruppe, however, ignored the rising and believed that all ritual leaps were essentially sacrificial, being leaps into Hades. He would link Theseus' dive, his throwing Sciron off the cliffs, and Aegeus' jump from the Acropolis, making them all versions of a rite in which an offering or victim is thrown into a hell mouth marked by white cliffs; see "Die eherne Schwelle," *Arch. f. Relig.* 15 (1912) 368 ff.

37. For the mystical, initiatory sense of the dive, see Plut. *de sera num. vind.* 22, where a young man whose life has been transformed by a fall and three

days of "death" describes his experience as like that of a pilot who jumps into the sea; he journeyed by way of an ocean of stars to the land of the souls of the dead, met an ancestor who greeted him and gave him a new name. (Unlike Theseus, however, Thespesios also saw punishments meted out to sinners.) Immersion represented a rupture of life, "un bref hiatus dans la succession des états de conscience" (M. Delcourt, *Oedipe*, Liege, 1944, p. 52), during which one's condition might be changed; at Eleusis the priests changed their names after a form of baptism, and initiates had some version of the same rite on 16 Boedromion (P. Foucart, *Recherches sur l'origine et la nature des mystères d'Eleusis*, Paris, 1895, p. 29).

38. Eupolis wrote a play called *Abaptai*, satirizing Alcibiades; see also Juvenal 2.9.92; Cicero *Att.* 6.1.18, and C. A. Lobeck, *Aglaophamus* (1829), pp. 1007 ff.

39. Charon of Lampsacus (FGH 2.262.7=Plut. *de mul. virt.* 255); Strabo 10.9 p. 452; Photius *Bibl.* 152 f. Bekker; see S. Wide, "Theseus und der Meersprung bei Bacchylides," *Festschrift für Otto Benndorff* (Vienna, 1898), pp. 13 ff. for a summary of ancient plunges. Gruppe (*Arch. f. Relig.* 15, 368 f.) argued that the Leucadian leap was sacrificial, but this seems unlikely in the presence of the waiting boats. Eitrem (*RE* sv. "Leukothea" 2303) recognized three sorts of leaps (sacrificial, cathartic and initiatory), but for Farnell (*JHS* 36, 39) all sea leaps derived from vegetation magic. Carcopino revived the theories of Glotz and argued that they reflected some form of the ordeal (*De Pythagore aux Apôtres*, Paris, 1956, 47 ff.), and G. Nagy has asserted that all such plunges are symbolic of the setting sun ("Phaethon, Sappho's Phaon and the White Rock of Leukas," *HSCP* 77, 1973, 137–77). Marie Delcourt, *Hephaistos ou la légende du magicien* (Paris, 1957), p. 117, associated the plunge into the sea with the magician's attainment of power and saw the action as essentially one of initiation, and this position has been expanded by C. Gallini, "Katapontismos," *SMSR* 34 (1963) 61–90.

40. J. Houbax, "Le plongeon rituel," *Mus. Belge* 27 (1923) 1–81; cf. E. Strong and N. Jolliffe, *JHS* 44 (1924) 65 ff., where other possible cult dives are discussed.

41. F. P. Badoni, *AA* 81 (1966) 364–5, fgg. 141–45 and *ASMG* 9 (1968) 65 ff., where the symbolic significance is taken for granted; cf. M. Napoli, "L'attività archaeologica nelle province di Avellino, Benevento e Salerno," *La Magna Grecia e Roma.* Atti dell' 8 Conv. di Studi Mag. Gr. 1968 (Naples, 1969) 139 ff.; R. Holloway, *AJA* 75 (1971) 73, where a date between 480 and 470 BC is assigned; cf. P. Somville, "La tombe du plongeur," *RHR* 196 (1979) 41–51, where there is discussion of a possible orphico-pythagorean context. Compare the more naturalistic scene from the Etruscan Tomba della caccia e pesca at Corneto, where the significance again may be initiatory, since the jumper jumps freely and there are friends in a little boat, waiting to take him up.

42. See P. Vidal-Naquet, "The Black Hunter and the Origin of the Athenian Ephebeia," *PCPhS* 144 (1968) 49–64, esp. 54 ff.

43. See Eitrem, *RE s.v.* "Leukothea" 2303 and also A. Brelich, *Gli eroi greci* (Rome, 1958), pp. 120 ff. For river-bathing as part of initiation ritual, note Paus. 7.19.4 (Patras) and 2.7.7 (Sicyon). For plunges in other sorts of initiations, note that the wolf men of Zeus Lycaeus began their nine forest years by diving into a lake (Paus. 6.8; Pliny *n.h.* 8.22; August. *CD* 18.17), and also that the Eumolpids, when they were initiated as hierophants at

Eleusis, were immersed in the sea (*CIA* III.900; *AE* 1883); see M. Foucart, *Les mystères d'Eleusis* (Paris, 1914), p. 173. H. Jeanmaire, *Couroi et Courètes*, p. 330, writes: "Une plongée, avec immersion plus ou moins prolongée, était, sans doute, l'une des épreuves par lesquelles se qualifiaient les novices. Il s'agit, en verité, de toute autre chose que d'un bain rituel, à valeur purificatrice ... l'equivalent symbolique d'une mort rituelle." He is, however, not summarizing evidence, but extrapolating from Ode 17. For water initiation in other cultures, see A. Brelich, *Le Iniziazione* (Rome, 1959–60), p. 137.

44. According to Nilsson, *The Mycenaean Origin of Greek Mythology* (Berkeley, 1932), p. 170, the dive also prefigures Theseus' descent to Hades with Pirithoos, and even the rape of Helen, for he sees all these as versions of an essential descent to the underworld in search of a vegetation goddess (cf. *The Minoan-Mycenaen Religion*, pp. 452 ff.).

45. This statement would, I presume, be categorically denied by H. Herter, since he insists that the dive is a late sixth-century invention with no mythic or cult associations whatsoever; see "Theseus der Athener," *RM* 88 (1939) 244 ff.; 289 ff., and *RE* Suppl. 13.1142 ff. Th. Zielinski, "Bacchylidea," *Eos* 5 (1898) 25–38, was even more concrete about the date and the purpose of this invention: he called it Cimonian propaganda meant to claim a special place for Athens in the Delian League.

46. By removing all supporting figures such as tritons, Bacchylides has emphasized the lonely mortality of the boy who had entered a strange element, and by eliminating his mythical sponsor, Athena, he has increased our sense of Theseus' courage and also made the exploit more easily assimilable to the pattern of a boy's initiation. For an analysis of Ode 17 as a commemorative reminiscence of an initiation rite, see Jeanmaire, *Couroi et Courètes*, pp. 273–75; 314 ff.; 324 ff.; see also A. Brelich, *Gli Eroi*, pp. 309, 128, and *Paides e Parthenoi* (Rome, 1969), pp. 376–7; cf. 471–2. Jeanmaire notes the association of Theseus with the ephebes in festivals characterized by military parades, gymnastic exercises, torch races, and contests of heralds and trumpets. For Theseus as ephebe, see also R. Merkelbach, "Der Theseus des Bak.," *ZPE* 12 (1973) 56 ff. It may be relevant that when Herodes Atticus changed the black chlamys of the ephebes to white, he explained his action as a reflection of the story of Theseus' two sails (*IG* II/III² 3606.20 ff.).

47. Within this particular fiction the dive may be conceptually related to Theseus' taking the throne, since it prefigures Aegeus' leap from the Acropolis (or into the sea, as at Hyg. *fab.* 242; Serv. ad *Aen.* 3.74; Suda, *s.v. Aigaion pelagos*); see H. Herter, *RE* Suppl. 13.1142 ff. However, for the story of the two sails Simonides (550 *PMG*) is the only archaic source, and there is no early account of Aegeus' leap; it is mentioned at Cat. 64.207; Lucan 2.612 and schol.; Diod. 4.61.4 f.; Plut. *Thes.* 17.4; 22.1; Paus. 1.22.5; Apollod. *epit.* 1.7. f.; Hyg. *fab.* 41.3; Schol. Dan. V *Aen.* 3.74; Accius (Ribbeck, *Rom. Tr.* 567); Ovid *Ib.* 495 f.; *Aetna* 584 f.; Sen. *Phaedr.* 1164 ff.; 1211 f.

48. M. Eliade, *De Zamolxis à Gengis Kahn* (Paris, 1970) pp. 81–130, trans. as *Zamolxis: The Vanishing God* (Chicago, 1972) pp. 76–130.

49. See also Stith Thompson, *Motif-Index* A 812 (and for related notions of diving to become strong, K 1051.3, diving to another world, F 153). Amerind examples are collected by E. W. Count, "The Earth Diver and the Rival Twins," *Proceedings of the 29th International Congress of Americanists* (Chicago, 1952), pp. 55–62. To these examples one might add the Aztec

creation myth in which, after men have emerged from the island in the lake, the priest must dive back into the lake to get underworld permission to build the shrine that will be their first act of settlement.

50. This is from a Yakut tale cited by Eliade, *Zamolxis*, p. 105.

51. See M. L. West, "Three Presocratic Cosmologies," *CQ* 13 (1963) 154–6; "Alcman and Pythagoras," *CQ* 17 (1967) 1–15; J.-P. Vernant, "Thetis et le poème cosmogonique," *Hommages à Marie Delcourt* (Brussels, 1970), pp. 38 ff.

52. There are other Greek stories which, though they are not concerned with Thetis or the first creation, nevertheless reflect this same way of thinking. The clod of earth that will spawn an island when dropped into the sea (P. *P.* 4) is conceptually related to the bits of sand brought up from the depths by creator divers, to become the seed from which the world is made. Rhodes, flowering up from beneath the waters (P. *O.* 7.69–70) also proves that the Greeks did indeed think of the sea as the source of creation, as do the stories of gods or magical objects that appear from the waters: e.g. Aphrodite herself (*Theog.* 191 ff.); Dionysus and Semele (Paus. 3.24.2); Pelops' bone (Paus. 5.13.5–6). It may be too that the story of the creator-apprentice who fails has influenced the tale of Icarus and the magician-creator, Dedalus. In general, for the survival of bits of pre-Hellenic water-based mythology and belief, see C. Picard, "Les Néréides funeraires de Xanthos," *RHR* 103 (1931) 5–28.

53. For the Thetis legend, see the bibliography cited in Burnett, *Three Archaic Poets*, p. 196, n. 38, and for a persistent Hellenic association of Nereids with creation, see C. Picard, *RHR* 103 (1931) 5–28.

54. Note that Hephaestus, in imitation of a cosmic creator, wrought sun, stars and moon on the shield that he made for Achilles (*Il.* 18.483 ff). In a repetition of this mythic model, the tripod of the Seven Sages, originally made by Hephaestus, was fished up out of the sea and used as a divine wedding gift (D.L. 1.27.33; Plut. *Solon* 4). Similarly, a pledge might be fixed by throwing an anvil or a lump of iron into the sea, the action probably being a form of self-curse: May we lose the metallurgical science brought up from the sea (as we lose this anvil) if we break this oath. On this kind of oath, see H. Jacobson, "The Oath of the Delian League," *Philol.* 119 (1975) 256–8.

55. The story is reported in three slightly different forms; one, attributed to Anticleides and presumably deriving from Ephorus (Athen. 11.466 C–D 781) equips Enalus with a golden vase; another, preserved by Plutarch (*conv. vii sap.* 20.163), reports the miraculous convoy of cuttlefish, the bringing up of the stone, and its dedication; this version also contains the motif of salvation by dolphins, which is repeated by Plutarch at *de soll. anim.* 36, p. 984E, who cites Myrsilus (=*FHG* IV 459), where Enalus is brought back to Lesbos by a dolphin.

56. Athenian tradition made Minos a tyrant and the conqueror of Greece (e.g. A. *Cho.* 619; E. fg. 386 N; Plut. *Thes.* 15–16), but as Zeus' representative he was also thought of as a lawgiver on earth and a judge in the underworld (e.g. *Od.* 19.178; 11.568) cf. J. Souilhé, *Plato. Oeuvres complètes* XIII² (Paris, 1930), pp. 77–81, on ps. Plato, *Minos.* The two aspects of his reputation were so contrary to one another that Diodorus (4.60) posited two men, a good Minos followed by his evil grandson. Strabo likewise reflected the double tradition by citing Ephorus on the Zeusian origin of Minos' laws, then reporting his own opposite opinion that Minos was a tyrant (10.4.8 and 19).

57. The dolphin's face and habits made him a good emblem for friendship between land (and air) and sea, and dolphins were often reported as the saviors of particular men: Arion (Hdt. 1.23–24); Coeranus (Archil. 192W; Plut. *sollert. anim.* 36 p. 984 f; Phylarchus, ap. Athen. 13. 606ef); Melicertes (Paus. 1.44.8; 2.1.8; 2.3.4); Taras and Phalantus (Paus. 10.13.10); Icadius (Serv. ad *Aen.* 3.332); Enalus (Pl. *de soll. anim.* 984E). See O. Klement, *Arion, mythologische Untersuchung* (Vienna, 1898), and Welker, *Kl. Schr.* I, p. 90.

58. For a possible contradiction, see above, note 19.

59. Farnell, *Cults* IV, p. 254, notes that the horned altar, associated with Theseus' arrival at Delos, was thought of as the oldest altar on the island, and that this association lent Theseus the aspect of founder even of the most ancient parts of the ceremonies there.

60. Compare the song that greeted the birth of Apollo (*h. Ap.* 119), and more particularly the paean that greeted his rebirth from the sea in dolphin form (*h. Ap.* 445). At Athena's birth Olympus, earth, and sea all moved and cried out (h. 28.9 ff.), and Alcaeus, in his hymn for Apollo, caused a song of the local waters to greet the god when he approached Delphi, bringing it music and dance (307 [1]c V). Compare also E. *Ion* 1074, where, when Iacchus comes, the Aether of Zeus, the stars, the moon herself, and the fifty daughters of Nereus all dance in honor of Kore and her mother. Similarly at E. *HF* 787 ff., the chorus of old men, recognizing the divinity of the Heracles who has returned to them, call for a song in which the nearby springs and mountains shall join. Egyptian parallels are described by H. Wild, "Egypte," *Les danses sacrées* (Paris, 1963), p. 38.

61. For this meaning of *aglaothronos* cf. P. *O.* 13.96 (of the Muses), *N.* 10.1 (of the Danaids) and Sappho's *poikilothronos* (1.1 V), all clearly derived from *throna* (flowers), real or embroidered (see schol. at *Il.* 22.441). See G. Lieberg, *Puella divinia* (Amsterdam, 1962), p. 22, and the bibliography cited in Burnett, *Three Archaic Poets*, p. 250, n. 53.

62. Compare this effect to the one produced by P. *N.* 5, where a chorus singing about the song of the Muses confounds itself with that heavenly company. Similarly, the chorus that calls upon Echo at the close of P. *O.* 14 (21 ff.) will leave a perceptible echo in the air. C. Robert, *Hermes* 33, 145, found it "sehr hübsch" that the paean of the Athenian men and maids "unmittelbar die Anrufung des Gottes durch seinen eigenen Chor ausschliesst."

3. THE EPINICIAN BURDEN

1. According to early epic Heracles performed a victory song with the gods after the Gigantomachy (*Titanomachia* fr. 5 K). Pindar (*N.* 8.50–51) asserts that the victory song is older than the quarrel of Adrastus with the Cadmaeans, and Hesychius reports that the *Kallinikos* was danced when Cerberus was brought up from Hades.

2. Simonides is often reported as the inventor of choral epinician; see A. Lesky, *Geschichte der griechische Literatur* (Bern, 1957–8), pp. 219 ff. There are, however, fragments from Stesichorus that seem to come from formal victory odes (7/512 *PMG*).

3. For choral songs greeting warrior victors, note Pausanias 4.16.6, where the Messenian women sing the victory of Aristomenes in 684 BC, throwing flowers and crowns and describing his deeds. Sosibius reported (ap. Athen. 678b) that the victory of Thyrea in 547 BC was celebrated at Sparta by

putting palm branches into the hands of the dancers in the *gymnopaidiai*, and Sophocles suggests that a proper response to Heracles' victorious return to Trachis will be men's choruses singing Apollo and women's singing Artemis (S. *Tr.* 207 f.; cf. *Ant.* 151–3; E. *HF* 77 ff.; Ar. *Lysist.* 1275). For later times, see Demosth. 19.128, and Lucian's parody of such ceremonies, *ver. hist.* 24. In general, see R. Lonis, *Guerre et religion en Grèce* (Paris, 1979).

4. For the theory that epinician is in essence the thanks of the group, see H. Gundert, *Pindar und seine Dichterberuf* (Frankfurt am Main, 1935), pp. 30 ff., and W. Kraus, "Die Auffassung des Dichterberufs," *WS* 68 (1955) 84.

5. Heidelberg Sl *ABV* 51.1; Copenhagen NM 109 *CVA* 3, pl. 101.2 = *ABV* 135 Group E; see T. B. L. Webster, *The Greek Chorus* (London, 1970), pp. 15–16.

6. For *kōmos*: Sim. 519 col.ii.2 *PMG*; B. 11.12: 13.74; P. *O.* 4.9; 6.98; 8.10; 14.16; *P.* 3.73; 5.22; 5.100; 8.20; 8.70; *N.* 3.5; 9.50; *I.* 2.31; 6.58; 8.4. For *kōmazein*: P. *O.* 9.4; *P.* 4.2; 9.89; *I.* 3.8: 3.90b; 7.20; *N.* 2.24; 9.1; 10.35; 11.28. Compare the comastic phrase of Simonides said to come from a victory song for a chariot team (512 *PMG*).

7. Cf. P. *O.* 9.1; see the testimony at Archil. 324W and also Jebb's discussion of B.7.

8. If the song was indeed performed at Isthmia, this means that the poets sometimes at least went to the great festivals and made songs like this on the spot in the hope of receiving larger commissions later. In this case Bacchylides evidently succeeded, for he composed a very long and surely expensive ode (Ode 1) for performance when this same son of Pantheides returned to Ceos.

9. Lachon, l. 1 *lache*, l. 2. Compare the elaborate conceit of P. *I.* 8, where the chorus pretends to be an informal group of young men out on the town, who have just heard the news of the victory.

10. The banquet itself was usually consecrated to one of the aristocratic hero-cults; on banquet as icon of contact between nobles and heroes, see J.-M. Deutzer, "Aux origines de l'iconographie du banquet couché," *RA* (1971) 2, 215–58.

11. The idea of the debt nevertheless remained strong and found expression in Pindar's many phrases according to which victory put the poet and the world in general into a condition of indebtedness, the payment being song; see *nikas apoina*, *I.* 8.4.

12. Note the phrase at P. *O.* 8.54, in which the chorus (or the poet) "reruns" (*anedramon*) the *kudos* of its victor. The *kudos* came from god via the victory (so Bacchylides speaks of *Nika pherekudēs*, 13.59; cf. l. 160); this had to be translated into *kleos* so that it could be spread among men (cf. e.g. P. *P.* 4.66; 2.52). In general, see M. Greindl, *KLEOS KUDOS EUCHOS* (diss. Munich, 1938). Once it had been sung, the victor's glory became report or reputation (*phēmē*) and in this form it could travel even beyond the present company (P. *N.* 5.1 ff.).

13. Cf. P. *I.* 7.38.

14. Cf. B. 3.9 ff.

15. Cf. P. *P.* 5.20, 46, 94; *P.* 9.4 (*olbios*); B. 3.10. On *makarismos* and the notion of god-like bliss, see P. Lévêque, "La religion grècque de la première moitié du 1er millénaire," *PP* 28 (1973) 47 ff.

16. According to tradition, sacred choruses were sometimes drawn from just one part of society—from a certain age group or a certain clan—but the

community at large was thought of as represented in the leader, who was generally appointed by the city; see B. Snell, *Dichtung und Gesellschaft* (Hamburg, 1965), p. 127.

17. It is worth noting that this change will have been parallel to that made in the dithyramb at Corinth, when Arion first taught the Dionysiac chorus, substituting a learned song for the traditional cries and improvisations; see Hdt. 5.67.

18. Note Plato's warning against making hymns and encomia for the living (*Lg.* 802a).

19. See Plut. *Lyc.* 8–26, where there is also mention of a kind of blame (*psogos*) that could be danced by a chorus of young girls. On early praise and blame, see M. Detienne, *Les maîtres de verité* (Paris, 1981), pp. 19 ff.

20. These generalities are meant to apply to the eighth and the seventh centuries; Detienne's attempt to reconstruct a split between religious and military praise in the Mycenaean courts remains fascinating but wholly speculative (ibid., pp. 16 ff.).

21. Cf. e.g. *Il.* 1.70; Hes. *Theog.* 32 and 38; Detienne (ibid., p. 15) says of the poet, "il a le privilège d'entrer en contact avec l'autre monde." See also the discussion of J. P. Vernant, "Aspects mythiques de la mémoire en Grèce," *Journ. de Psych.* (1959) 5 ff.; also in *Mythe et pensée* (Paris, 1965), pp. 55 ff.

22. Empedocles 121 Diels (+158), *pros ton tēs Alētheias leimōna*, shows that this way of thinking is older than Plato (*R.* 621; cf. *Phdr.* 248b); note also the *Lethēs pedion* at Ar. *Ran.* 168, and the *pedion alētheias* at Plut. *de defectu oraculorum* 22.422B.

23. For the meaning of *aletheia* as *a + lēthō* = "Unverborgenheit," see the accumulated arguments of W. Luther in *Wahrheit und Lüge* (Leipzig, 1935); "Der frühgr Wahrheitsgedanken," *Gymn.* 65 (1958) 75–107; "Wahrheit, Licht und Erkenntnis," *Archiv für Begriffsgeschichte* 10 (1966), 1–240. To these may be added the observations of E. Heitsch, "Die nicht-philosophische *ALETHEIA*," *Hermes* 90 (1962) 24–33 and "Wahrheit als Erinnerung," *Hermes* 91 (1963) 31 ff.; H. D. Rankin, "*A-LETHEIA* in Plato," *Glotta* 41 (1963) 51–54 (discussing the playful *alē + theia* of *Crat.* 421b); M. Detienne, "La notion mythique d'Alētheia," *REG* 73 (1960) 27–35 and *Maîtres*, pp. 24 ff.; J. Svenbro, *La parole et le marbre* (Lund, 1976), pp. 141 ff.

24. See for example, Theogn. 214; Plut. *de E ap. Delphi* 394A.

25. As an emblem of the new anonymity in battle note the disappearance of the shield design in the early classical period; see J. D. Beazley, *Attic Vase Paintings*, Boston II (Oxford, 1954), p. 79. On the collectivity of hoplite war and the disappearance of recognized deeds of *aristeia*, see Lonis, *Guerre et religion*, and W. K. Pritchett, *The Greek State at War* II (Berkeley, 1974), pp. 276 ff.

26. For example, Ibycus 282 *PMG*; Pindar 108B.

27. Compare P. *P.* 1.85; *kressōn gar oiktirmou phthonos.* See the discussion of H. Fränkel, *Wege und Formen*[2] (Munich, 1960), p. 67 note 3, and on *phthonos* in general, W. Steinlein, *Phthonos* (diss. Erlangen, 1944); E. Milobenski, *Der Neid in der griechische Philosophie.* Kl. Philos. Studien 29 (Wiesbaden, 1964).

28. Note the similar sentiments at P. *P.* 1.85; Hdt. 3.52; Aesch. *Ag.* 939.

29. *Phthonos* was the basis of the good *eris* that Hesiod praised at *Erg.* 24–26.

30. Cf. Heraclitus B 121, when the Ephesians banned their most prominent citizen.

31. Democ. B 245: *phthonos gar stasios archēn apergazetai.*
32. Note the statement of Sotades (fr. 10 Powell = fr. 13 D²): *ho penēs eleeitai, ho de plousios phthoneitai / ho mesos de bios kekramenos dikaios estin.*
33. Aristides (*Or.* 28 K[49D]62) describes early athletes: ". . . in a sense they praise themselves since they commission poets, giving them silver, and then, when they finally receive the victory song, they sing themselves to the accompaniment of flute and chorus." The scholiast at P. *I.* 2.22 says that Pindar was paid by the line and got double rates when he praised the charioteer as well as the victor. For a somewhat simplistic discussion of the significance of poets' wages, see S. Gzella, "The Problem of the Fee," *Eos* 59 (1971) 189 ff.
34. Xenophanes (schol. ad Ar. *Pax* 697 = 21 B 21 DK) calls Simonides a skinflint, *kimbix*, and the same point is made in the famous story of his salvation by the Dioscuri (Quintillian *Inst.* 11.2.12; Cicero *de orat.* II. 86.352–3), as well as by the anecdote about his ode for the mule team of Anaxilas (Arist. *Rhet.* 111.2/1405b23–7 = 515 *PMG*); Aristotle speaks of him as "hanging around the gates of the rich" (*Rhet.* 1391a 8–12; cf. Plat. *R.* 6.4/489b). On this tradition, see W. J. Slater, "Simonides' House," *Phoenix* 26 (1972) 231 ff.; Svenbro, *La parole et le marbre*, pp. 141 ff.
35. Stobaeus, *flor.* 3.10.39 p. 417. On the shift from prize to wage, see L. Gernet, "La notion mythique de la valeur en Grèce," *Journ. de Psych.* 41 (1948) 415 ff.
36. Athenaeus (14.656d) preserves a story of Simonides' taking the gifts of Hieron and selling them for money.
37. The comparison of poet to artisan is said to have originated with Simonides (Plut. *de glor. Ath.* 346) but it became a favorite with Pindar; cf. e.g. P. *P.* 3.113: *tektones hoia sophoi harmosan,* etc.; cf. the figures from artifacts at O. 6.91; *N.* 7.77–79; fr. 179. It may be that the actual techniques of composition and memorization changed at this time, if it is true that Simonides introduced new mnemonic devices. See Svenbro, *La parole et le marbre*, 141 ff., esp. 160 ff., and also M. Detienne, "Simonide de Ceos," *REG* 77 (1964) 405 ff.
38. If the fragment of Oxy. pap. 2432 (= Sim. 54 *PMG*) is correctly attributed to Simonides, then we find him listing *kerdos* along with Aphrodite and *philonikia*, as an obstacle to the attainment of noble virtue. On the attribution, see C. M. Bowra, "Simonides or Bacchylides?" *Hermes* 91 (1963) 257–67, where Bacchylidean authorship is (wrongly, I think) urged.
39. Note Theocritus 16.42 ff., where the poet remarks that many rich men would be unremembered if it were not for Simonides. Detienne (*Maîtres*, p. 26) puts it this way: "Le poète n'a plus pour mission que d'exalter les nobles, de louanger les riches propriétaires qui developpent une economie de luxe, de dépenses somptuaires, s'enorgueillissent de leurs alliances matrimoniales et tirent vanité de leurs quadriges ou de leurs prouésses athletiques." See also L. Gernet, "Les nobles dans la Grèce antique," *Annales d'histoire economique et sociale* (1938) 36–43.

4. BEARING THE BURDEN

1. This notion works backwards as well, for fresh deeds revive the memory of older ones (B. 2.6).
2. Pindar is sometimes characterized as a pro-Spartan reactionary, but see the remarks of E. Will, *Doriens et Ioniens* (Paris, 1956), pp. 58 ff., who argues

that Pindar's praise for old Laconian forms of government is not praise of Sparta but of the ideal of *eunomia*.

3. There are opening invocations of divinity at P. *O.* 4 (Zeus); *O.* 12 (Tyche Soteira); *N.* 7 (Eleithyia); *N.* 11 (Hestia); *I.* 5 (Theia); cf. *I.* 3.4 and *I.* 6.4 for quasi-invocations of Zeus, and *O.* 2.13 for one that comes a little later in the song. Indirect opening allusiions to Demeter and Kore are found in Ode 3 of Bacchylides, to Castor and Pollux in P. *O.* 3. It was the opinion of W. Schadewaldt, *Der Aufbau der Pindarischen Epinikion* (Halle, 1928), p. 276, that Pindar's victory odes were truly "ritual" and hymnic, whereas Bacchylides' invocations were simply conventional.

4. A version of this is Bacchylides' call upon Zeus to validate his claim about the number of victories gained, at 8.26. Less direct are phrases like that at 14.20–21 where along with the victor the singers sing the place of victory that is sacred to a god—there, the *temenos* of Petraian Poseidon.

5. For song as libation, see P. *I.* 6.9; as an ex voto, see *P.* 4.67, where from the *kudos* given to Arcesilaus by Apollo the song offers back a golden fleece for the Muses.

6. Cf. 13.70 ff., "You, son of Lampon, shading your locks with full-flowered crowns (bring honor to the city of Aegina)"; a slightly different version appears at 11.10: "Thanks to you, Nike, bands of fine-limbed youths and the joys of feasting take possession of Metapontum, city honored by the gods." For city praise in Pindar, see e.g. *O.* 7.93–4; *O.* 5.4; *P.* 8.38; *I.* 7.1 ff. and especially the opening of *P.* 12, where Acragas is begged like a divinity (and confounded with Persephone) to accept the Pythian crown.

7. In effect, the "time alone will tell" gnome (B. 13.205; cf. e.g. P. *O.* 1.33) is a way of looking at the inevitable death of the praised. Gnomes could also be used to placate the gods by reminding victors that they could not hope to pass the bounds of mortality; e.g. *O.* 1.113; *O.* 3.445; *O.* 5.25; *P.* 3.59 ff. Gnomes had a purely structural use as well, in ripe epinician, for they often served as links between passages of disparate function, allowing the poet to pass, for example, from a mythic section to an occasional one, or vice versa (as at 3.75; 5.50). See P. A. Bernardini, "Linguaggio e programma poetico in Pindaro," *QU* 4 (1967) 80 ff.

8. See for example the sequence at *P.* 8.88 which moves from the common to the idiosyncratic; cf. *O.* 9.100 ff.

9. Note Farnell's glum judgment (*CR* 12, 1898, 343): "He moralizes like the others on the divine government of the world, but his words do not strike home; he speaks without profound or original conviction and without the glow of inspiration."

10. This is surely the right reconstruction; Fraenkel's *brachys gar to terpnon* is ill-suited to the thought of the passage that follows.

11. When lines 6 and 17 are compared it becomes evident that *symphora* and *theos* (daimon) are working at cross purposes: chance "sets upright" even the base, but god "sets right" him who works well, helping him to superlative excellence. This opposition was not perceived by Wilamowitz, who read the passage as a single onrolling statement about what the gods give, finding in it a restatement of the archaic assertion that a man's quality (whether he was *esthlos* or *kakos*) depended upon his fortune or misfortune (*Sappho und Simonides*, Berlin, 1913, pp. 183 ff.). Wilamowitz also argued that *dikaios* in l. 11 meant having a sense of "fair play" (p. 185). The whole passage, however, makes it clear that justice has here its much older sense of natural suitability and appropriateness.

12. This is the companion concept to one of Pindar's, i.e. that suffering dies under the weight of good fortune (*O.* 2.19 f.; cf. the physician *euphrosyne* at the opening of *N.* 4).

13. Compare in particular Solon's Elegy for the Muses, where the thought likewise moves from the best that the gods give to the best that men can do. The two poems obviously belong to the same convention, but it is wrong to suggest (as does E. Romagnoli, "Appunti sulla gnomica Bacchilidae," *SIFC* 7, 1899, 163 ff.) that Bacchylides is simply a slavish imitator of Solon.

14. One can glimpse a traditional ranked list just beneath the surface of his statement, however, for *kubernasen . . . machais . . . choroi . . . thalias* suggest that sailing might be capped by soldiering, soldiering by singing, and singing by lordly hospitality.

15. Cf. Simonides 516 *PMG.*

16. The complexity of this apparently very simple passage can be appreciated when it is compared with the similar passage at B.1. 159. Analysis yields the following sets of parallel statements.

1. *ploutos*	keeps company with	cowards
14. Events	exalt	the *kakos*
1. enriched cowards	bloat up	their hearts
14. man of excellence	has *dikē* in	his heart
1. *theos*	warms the heart of	*eu erdōn* with *elpis*
14. *theos*	sets upright	*eu erdōn*
1. man of health and moderation	contests with	the first
14. man who understands *kairos*	is equal to	the victor
1. man who pursues *aretē*	with toil and sense of true *elpis*	ends *orthos*
14. man who pursues *aretē*	with justice and sense of *kairos*	ends *orthos*

Thus, where the system of Ode 1 emphasizes a god-given hope that leads towards success and good fame, that of Ode 14 emphasizes a human sense of *dikē* which lets one understand opportunity and leads likewise to success when god is willing. The parallelism between *elpis* and *kairos* is of course perfectly reasonable, since they are in part simply the subjective and the objective aspects of the same opportunity. The full statement of the gnomic passage at 1.159 ff. can be summarized in this way: "What wins highest glory? Some say wealth (some say health), some say pleasure," (cf. Sim. 584 *PMG*) "but I say *aretē*. Wealth is to be eliminated because it consorts with cowards and it leads men astray with false hope. Health is eliminated because it is a prerequisite to pleasure, which means that pleasure must be more important. Pleasure, however, has no content, no achievements, but is all pursuit. Could pursuit be the highest glory, then? Well, there are two kinds, the light-minded pursuit that brings lightweight results in one's lifetime—that can't be the highest!—and the virtuous pursuit that brings true success in life and glory after death. It is only when virtue is added to pursuit that the result is glory, and consequently virtue is the answer to the problem."

17. When Pindar says that song is like a hot bath after toil (*N.* 4.4), or like the spells that can render exertion painless (*N.* 8.50–51) he is using the vocabulary of hygiene to suggest that praise "heals" the act of victory, bringing it out of the phase of physical strife as if from a painful symptom.

18. Compare the more extreme abstraction of a very similar passage from Pindar (*O.* 9.91 ff.):

> Never failing himself but taking
> opponents with sharp feints that shifted the scales,
> he left the circle to such a shout—
> fair himself and the doer of deeds supremely fair!
>
> Also amongst the Parrasian throng
> he showed himself as a marvel
> during the games for Zeus Lykaios . . .

19. To a certain degree, this poetic discussion of the poet's means and modes must have been a conventional part of the epinician style, for both Pindar and Bacchylides seem to have found the deliberative trope of the thousand paths of song in the works of their predecessors; cf. P. *I.* 4.1–3; *I.* 9.47; B. 5.31; 19.1, and see O. Becker, "Das Bild des Weges," *Hermes Einzelschriften* 4 (1937), p. 96.

20. On this contrast see B. Gentili, *Bacchilide* (Urbino, 1958), p. 17.

21. Fame (*doxa*) is here given the sea's epithet, *akamata*, as if it copied the sea's eternal motion. For the thought as a whole, compare B. 5.193–4: "whom the gods honor, him does fame of mortal tongues pursue."

22. At 12.1 ff. the Muse guides the poet's mind as a pilot might a ship; at 16.1 she freights his mind with golden hymns. If the interjection at 5.276 is meant literally, the Muse there supervises the choice of mythic subject (cf. 19.1 ff.) and starts and stops his narration. The poet on the other hand evidently chose or "found" the correct mythic episode, though he depended upon the Muse to jog his memory (15.47). The poet was also presumably responsible for the deployment of gnomes, prayers, references to the victor's family and city, etc. And meanwhile the Charites lent his song conviction (9.1 ff.), the ability to command honor (19.5 ff.), and the power to bewitch (15.49–50). Compare P. *N.* 3.10 ff. where the Muse is asked to "begin" (*archē*) the hymn, while the poet partakes of it or keeps it company (*koinasomai*).

23. As if in answer to Pindar's worry over poetry's ability to deceive (*O.* 1.28b–29, cf. P. *O.* 7.53, where *sophia* may be accompanied by evil *dolos*), Bacchylides announces that *sophia* (poetic wisdom) does not sound out a thieving word among men (fr. 26).

24. Pindar likewise says that silence is inappropriate to the victor: *P.* 9.92; *N.* 9.7; *I.* 2.44; fr. 240 S; cf. *O.* 9.103–4. He believes, however, that suffering and examples of an evil fate, as well as mythic motifs that suggest blasphemy, should be "blamed" with silence (e.g., *O.* 13.91). (It is amusing to note that silence *was* considered to be the proper decoration for female virtue; Aesch. *A.* 611; Soph. *Aj.* 293; fr. 64.4P; Thuc. 1.45.2.).

25. Cf. Theogn. 1183; also 799 and 801; P. *O.* 74.

26. On this passage, see R. Merkelbach, "Ba. 13.205 und 59," *ZPE* 12 (1973) 90–91.

27. Cf. Democritus B302: *ton phthonon eipen helkos einai alētheias;* also Philolaus, who couples *phthonos* and *pseudos* (Stob. *I.* 16.20=B11 *Vors.* I. 412.9 ff.). Gorgias (B6 *Vors.* II. 285.13) compares the Nemesis of the gods with the Phthonos of men; cf. Plato *Phaedr.* 247a; Soph. *Philoct.* 776; Hdt. 1.32.4; Aesch. *Ag.* 750 ff.

28. R. Wind (*Bacchylides' Odes 5, 17, 18,* diss. Iowa, 1964) supposed this gesture to be literally apotropaic, and this may have been Bacchylides' meaning; see E. Riess "Studies in Superstition," *AJP* 24 (1903) 427. The exaggerated gesture may also be the necessary response to that tendency to violence that Bacchylides recognized in *phthonos* at 13.199. P. T. Brannon reads these lines as if they concerned the envy of the gods: "the poet is . . . fearful that he may overstep the limits of true praise, that he may fail to keep Hieron in a purely human category and thus expose him to the envy of the gods" ("Hieron and Bacchylides," *CF* 26, 1972, 264). This, however, is surely wrong, for one meets possible envy from the gods with gestures of supplication, self-abasement, worship, but *not* with an aggressive wrestler's stance. On this passage see also M. Lefkowitz, *The Victory Ode* (Park Ridge, 1976), pp. 89–90.

29. Bacchylides does not simply liken himself to an eagle; the eagle image figures Hieron as well as the poet because it expresses the idea *ainein Hierōna* (16). Thus, when the eagle trusts in his strength and rises above smaller birds in ll. 21–22, he is like Hieron in the same position in the strophe (6–7), resting in his justice, listening to his own praise, and separating himself from cares. The controlling notion, however, is that praise-song is like the eagle, and this is stated in the responsion of the *agalma* of the Muses phrase (4) with the phrase that names the eagle of Zeus (19). One may note also that in ll. 10–11 of the strophe, the poet is sending the poem from his island across water, and in the responding phrase of the antistrophe the eagle is crossing waves (25–26). On these lines, see A. Bonnafée, "L'Aigle dans B. v. 26–30" *ZPE* 9 (1972) 35 ff.; also W. J. Verdenius, "Two Notes," *Mnem.* 28 (1975) 63.

5. HIERON AND CROESUS

1. Hieron won at Delphi in 482 with a horse, in 474(?) with a horse, in 470 with a chariot; he won at Olympia in 476 with a horse, in 472 with a horse, and in 468 with a chariot.

2. The sequence of wealthy words is as follows: *olbion,* 8; *plouton,* 13; *chrysos,* 17; *aristos olbon,* 22; *chrysaoros,* 28; *chrysodinas,* 44; *chryson,* 65; *bathyplouton zoan,* 82; *kerdeōn hypertaton,* 84; *euphrosyna d'ho chrysos,* 87; *olbou . . . anthea,* 92.94.

3. Kenyon thought that Delphi was the scene of the present performance, for he took Ode 3 to be, not a true victory ode, but one specially made to accompany the dedication of Hieron's second tripod.

4. The meanings of the word *bruein* are various; the central idea is of being full to overflowing, and so there is often an association with containers filled with liquid, a seed-pod teeming with seeds, a bud bursting with flower. For Bacchylides the word seems also to have light in it (suitable either to a sense of liquid or of petal-sheen), for at 13.175 he sets it against the concepts of night and darkness and being hidden: Areta, *brouousa* with fame, becomes *pasiphanēs.* See also 6.9, where boys wearing leafy crowns are described as *stephanois etheiras/ neaniai bruontes.*

5. According to Theopompus (*FGH* 115 F193= Athen. 231e–232b), it was not easy for Hieron to find enough gold.

6. Note the inscription on the votive helmet from the spoils of Cumae (Ditt. *Syll.* 910): *Hiaron ho Deinomeneos kai toi Syrakosioi.*

7. Punning was a common ancient practice, especially punning on proper names, which was a technique for getting at the true quality of the thing, place or person denoted (Pl. *Crat.* 435d). Elsewhere in Bacchylides there is a pun between Lachon and *lache* at 6.1–2; between Eriboea and *boaso* at 17.14 and at 13.102; between Koresas and *korai* at 1.48 and 117; between Lousos and *lyssas* at 11.96 . . . 103. There is also play between Daïaneira and the compounds *daîphrōn* and *daïpylou* at 5.137 and 145 (see the remarks of P. T. Brannon, "Hieron and Bacchylides," *CF* 26, 1972, p. 242); cf. the echo between Phema at 10.1 and *pephatai* at 10.52, and the sequence *ni-kasas . . . Pherenikos . . . pheron . . .* at 5.183–5. Probably also in *Pa.* 4 there is a reference to the popular punning etymology which took Asine from *sinomai;* see W. S. Barrett, "Bacchylides, Asine and Apollo Pythaieus," *Hermes* 82 (1954) 432. As playful, I would cite also the phrase *alampei nuktos* at 13.175, where the victor's father is named Lampon, and also the *mathe mython* phrase at 26.14. In Pindar, there are puns between Ajax and *aietos* (*I.* 6.53); Themis and *tethmos* (*O.* 8.21); *Laos* = man and *laos* = stone (*O.* 9.46); Opous and *ōpasen* (*O.* 9.66); Pagon and *pēgnumi* (*O.* 10.50); Hieron and *hierōn* (fr. 105S). In other early poetry one might note Hesiod *Theog.* 901, where the *Horai erg' oreuousi;* the puns on the name Krios (Simon. 22D = 13B Hdt. 6.50); the word-play of Stesichorus' line, *hote ēros ōrai keladei chelidon* (211 *PMG*), which is not unlike Eumelus' *katharan kitharin* (696 *PMG*); and all the *dys-* compounds in Aesch. *Pr,* a play much about Zeus. City names were often punned, as for example Gela with *gelan* and Himera with *himeros, hemera* and even *chimaira.* The fact that puns might be made between kappa and chi words is proved by the frequent association of Kronos and *chronos,* as for example in Pherecydes *Cosmology* (DK 7A8). For puns and plays on words in general, see Ar. *Rhet.* III.11 6=1412a; E. S. McCartney, "Puns and Plays on Proper Names," *CJ* 14 (1918–19) 343–58; W. D. Woodhead, *Etymologizing* (Toronto, 1928); W. B. Stanford, *Greek Metaphor* (Oxford, 1936), p. 54; J. C. Kamerbeek, *The Plays of Sophocles. Ajax* (Leiden, 1953), pp. 95–96; G. Dimock, "Names of Odysseus," *Essays on the Odyssey,* ed. C. Taylor (Bloomington, 1963), p. 72; see also the remarks of E. R. Dodds ad E. *Ba.* 367 and of Platnauer ad E. *IT* 32.

8. Because Croesus is an historical and not a mythic figure Bacchylides showed a certain daring in choosing him, though as Jane Harrison long ago pointed out, the man who has been depicted in vase painting has been virtually mythologized (*CR* 12, 1898, 85–86; cf. H. Jurenka, "Der Mythos in P. O. 1 und B. 3," *Philol.* 59, 1900, 313–14). It has often been assumed that Bacchylides is here simply expanding the Pindaric reference to Croesus at the end of *P.* 1, which was composed in 470, but the vase paintings prove that there was a general vogue for Croesus legends at this time. The rationalized version of Herodotus likewise makes it plain that a well-known and luxuriant legend was being ordered and synthesized, and a comparison of that narrative (Hdt. 1.85 ff.) with Ode 3 reveals the trends that are especially characteristic of the Bacchylidean telling; cf. C. Segal, "Croesus on the Pyre," *WS* 5 (1971) 40 ff. Unlike Herodotus' chained Croesus (1.86; cf. 90), the Croesus of Ode 3 is free, and consequently more noble in his choice

of death; the same nobility is evident also in the defiant equality of his final address to heaven, in contrast to the plea for salvation voiced by the Herodotean king (1.87). In addition, Bacchylides suppresses all suggestion of the motif of the misleading oracles that is so important to Herodotus: the poet's Apollo is a receiver of gifts, a giver of salvation and victory, but not an oracle-speaker. Bacchylides also suppresses Solon and Cyrus, so that Croesus may stand alone and the story may emphasize piety, not wisdom. The story as Bacchylides found it may have contained elements of an ordeal by fire, for this is hinted at in Herodotus (see Glotz, *L'Ordalie,* pp. 104 ff. for other examples) but if so, the poet has strictly eliminated all traces of them. His Croesus is freely moving, active, and as much as possible like Heracles, who also chose a death by self-immolation. For some reason, later tellers of the Croesus story abandoned the pyre; Ctesias (fr. 29 Muller) has the king chained again and again in chains that fall from him in the Dionysiac fashion until he is at last released by Cyrus and treated as a holy man. On the Croesus legend in general, see O. Regenbogen, "Die geschichte v. Solon u. Kroisos," *Kl. Schriften* (Munich, 1961), pp. 101 ff.; J. A. S. Evans, "What happened to Croesus?" *CJ* 74.1 (1978) 34 ff.

9. Since the Louvre vase (G197; see Beazley, *Handbook,* p. 398) shows him alone on his pyre, critics often ask why Croesus is here presented in this female company. (One proposed answer was that this is an Oriental motif—a harem!) The poet's reason would seem to be obvious, however, for the women serve the same function as a tragic chorus would, their ordinary gestures and sentiments setting off what is extraordinary and heroic in the king.

10. Compare E. *Tro.* 428, *pou d'apollōnos logoi?* The same sort of phrase is also used by Pylades at Aesch. *Ch.* 900.

11. Cf. the imitation at E. *Tro.* 287: *aphila ta prōtera phila.*

12. It sounds as if a popular riddle had asked: "When is death most hateful?" Answers like, "In youth," or "In prosperity," are all capped by the present phrase, "When it's right in front of you."

13. The audience would think at once of Heracles, taken up from his pyre by Athena, but they would also remember the more secular version of the same event, when Alcmena was released from the pyre on which her husband had placed her, for there as here a sudden rainstorm put out the fire. (For a vase-painting of Alcmena's escape, see Cook, *Zeus* III, 506 ff.).

14. For the Hyperborean land as a version of heaven, see *Epigonoi* fr. 3K; schol. P. *O.* 3.28: Plin. 4.12.189; Roscher *s.v.,* I. 2835. The Hyperboreans provide one more Apolline note, for they were associated with the legendary foundations of Delos (Paus. 5.7.2), and Alcaeus had caused Apollo to visit them before going to Delphi (307a V); an early, possibly Hesiodic, tradition reported that Apollo had sent Asclepius to live among them (ps. Eratosh. *Catast.* 29 p. 154R). They may also add a western and Pythagorean touch, for there were cults of Apollo Hyperboreus in Croton and Metapontum (Ael. *VH* 2.26; Hdt. 4.23) and the archaic coinage of Caulonia perhaps showed Heracles (who in western legend had a Hyperborean wife, DH I.43) capturing a deer and discovering the olive among the Hyperboreans, as told in P. *O.* 3 (I. Cazzaniga, "Testi e Monumenti," *PP* 23, 1968, 371–83).

15. J. Defradas, *Les thèmes de la propagande Delphique* (Paris, 1954), p. 225, suggested that this page was called Habrobatas, a name known from Hdt. 7.224, but the Louvre vase calls him Euthymos. His appearance there, with

a name, suggests a version of the story in which a loyal friend was asked to play the Philoctetes role and set the fire. O. Crusius thought that the page represented a lover of Croesus, and Blass assumed that he must be a eunuch, but in fact nothing at all is known about the vase-painter's Euthymos. What we do know is that Bacchylides has chosen to include him and has chosen also to give him an epithet that connotes Lydian luxury and fastidiousness (cf. E. *Tro.* 820 of Ganymede, and Aesch. *Pers.* 1029 of the Persians; note also his *habrodiaitōn Lydōn* at *Pers.* 41 and cf. his fr. 60 and also Hdt. 1.155). In the present song, this boy who walks so elegantly is a reminder of what Croesus has been in the past and also a promise of the ease that awaits him in the future, while in the immediate scene he adds a touch of decoration that prepares for the imminent delight of escape.

16. For the notion of purifying gold in fire, cf. P. *N.* 4.79-85.

17. Compare Pindar, fr. 108S. A god may combine gold and water in the streams of Pactolus and then add blood, and in the same way a god may mix water with fire so as to darken the brilliance of flame. The god does not, however, shadow the brightness of Croesus' *aretē*; rather, he combines it with the enduring brilliance of life beyond the boundaries of the world. C. P. Segal, "Bacchylides Reconsidered," *QU* 22 (1976) 110 ff., somehow finds a foreboding pessimism and a sense of mutability in the divine action of extinguishing Croesus' fire; see likewise M. Lefkowitz, who describes this as "an ode that concentrates on death and defeat" (*The Victory Ode*, Park Ridge, N.J., 1976, p. 139). Attitudes of this sort can only be maintained by those who refuse to believe in Apollo's part in the miracle and there is no word in the song to suggest that such disbelief would be tolerated by the poet.

18. Croesus' golden gifts at Delphi are listed by Herodotus (I. 50) as gold and silver beds, gold ingots, a golden lion, craters and jars of gold offered on a pyre; he also gave a golden shield for Athena Pronaia (I. 92). Elsewhere he offered a golden tripod to Apollo Ismenos at Thebes, and golden cows and columns at Ephesus.

19. The transition from Hieron to Apollo is made by way of a gnome, but the text at this point is very uncertain (71-74). Hieron has just been described as excellent in three areas, horsemanship, politics and the arts, and in the damaged passage the chorus clearly either summarizes or caps these virtues with something more general. The movement of thought is, "in the past you knew or acted in manner A, but now you seek B," and the key to B lies in the word *ephameron*, followed as it is by *brach* [*ys estin*] life or pleasure. Hieron now seeks something that is consonant with a knowledge of the ephemeral brevity of life, and this makes *kairia* a likely opening for line 74 (so Jebb; cf. E. *Rh.* 339, *kairiōs skopeis*). Like all the seekers after excellence in the gnome of Ode 14, Hieron brings a just response to the opportunity of the moment, and this suggests that perhaps what he did before was seek some greater or more long-lasting power. Schwartz suggested *hos rō*] *maleai pot* [*e cheiri nōmōn*, which is the basis of the translation offered. In l. 75, then, *elpis* with a positive value supplies the link-notion between the wisdom of Hieron and that of Apollo: the reason why a man can continue to seek the appropriate, pious pleasures of the day, while yet knowing his own ephemeral condition, is that winged hope warms his view (*noema*, 75; *gnomas*, 79) of life.

20. For the myth of Admetus, see A. Lesky,"Alkestis, der Mythus und das Drama," *SB Akad. Wien* (Ph. Hist. Kl.) cciii:2 (1925) 1-86. On the num-

ber fifty, see Roscher, *Die Zahl 50 in Mythus, Kult, Epos und Taktik* (Liepzig, 1917); H. Thiry, *"PENTAKONTAKEPHALOS KER-BEROS" Philol.* 119 (1975) 138, and G. Germain, *Homère et la mystique des nombres* (Paris, 1954), p. 21, where fifty, among men, is said to mean "more than moderate abundance."

21. The reference is to an Attic scolion (Aristoph. *Pelargoi* 430 Kock) that was evidently well known in conservative circles. Compare the similar advice attributed to Theognis and Mimnermus: *dikaios eōn tēn sautou phrena terpe.* Another part of the thought is paralleled in Epicharmus 267 Kaibel: *hōs polun zēsōn xhronon chōs oligon, houtō dianoou.* B. Lavagnini, "ADME-TOU LOGOS," *RFIC* 65 (1937) 372-3, argued that Apollo's words ended with l. 82, so that this final exhortation came from the chorus instead of the god, but this seems extremely unlikely since the last two lines serve as a kind of farewell to Admetus.

22. Some would follow H. Fränkel and introduce the idea of pleasure in line 74, writing *brachy gar to terpnon;* likewise, one of Jebb's suggestions was to read *terpsin hasycha skopeis* at 73-4. Since notions of pleasure and happiness are so strongly emphasized in this final section, it is hard to understand how J. Peron can report that the end of the song is "franchement negative ... une vision pessimiste" ("Crésus et Méléagre chez Bacchylide," *REG* 91, 1978, 335).

23. Compare Sappho 16.5V and P. *O.* 8.59-60 (cf. *O.* 2.83-85), likewise placed in the middle of demonstrations. Here in Ode 3 the phrase serves as a transitional announcement, instructing the listener to be ready to apply his own gnomic wisdom to the gnomic passage that is about to begin.

24. That this was a familiar priamel is proved by P. fr. 222S, and this means that Bacchylides was not simply imitating the opening of P. *O.* 1, but instead manipulating bits of wisdom that were familiar before Pindar ever expressed them. The conventional opposite opinion has recently been restated by D. Campbell (*Greek Lyric Poetry,* London, New York, 1972, p. 415): "When he modelled 3.85 ff. on the opening of Pindar's first Olympian, a foolhardy undertaking, he botched the job." On the combination of several priamels, and the omission of certain understood elements, see Burnett, *Three Archaic Poets,* pp. 281 ff.

25. Gold mediates between the realms of permanence (nature and god) and of impermanence (man), since unlike air and sea it is a medium of exchange between men and a means of approach to god, when it takes the form of dedications. It becomes a part of men's deeds and therefore a part of their virtue, since virtue must express itself in deeds, and ultimately it becomes a part of their happiness, since happiness must be based in virtue. Before the priamel's characteristic shift in evaluation terms was understood, critics were wont to complain because Bacchylides failed to say that gold was *more permanent* than the other two elements; see Campbell, *Greek Lyric Poetry,* p. 415: "The weakness of *euphrosuna d' ho chrysos,* where the sense required is 'gold is indestructible' shows that Bacchylides was distressed in this rare atmosphere." A far better understanding of the passage is exhibited by R. Wind, "Bacchylides and Pindar," *CJ* 67 (1971) 9-13.

26. Note E. Schwartz, "Zum Bakchylides," *Hermes* 39 (1904) 631, who argued that the golden *euphrosyna* of l. 87 referred specifically to "Festes-freude."

27. *Pace* G. Kirkwood who concluded about this ode: "Nothing in the thought or structure ... commands special admiration." He found a "heavy-handedness about the application of the myth ... something faintly inept

about the dominant intrusion of Apollo," though he thought the Croesus episode was "lively and engaging" ("The Narrative Art of Bacchylides," *The Classical Tradition, Studies Harry Caplan*, Ithaca, 1966, p. 108).

28. The idea of song as repayment is a favorite one with Pindar, who likes to use specific metaphors of money, debt, or profit for poetry; song is *lytron* (*I.* 8.1; *P.* 5.106), *apoina* (*I.* 3/4.7; *I.* 8.4; *N.* 7.16; *O.* 7.17; *P.* 2.14), *poina* (*P.* 1.59); *misthos* (*N.* 7.63; cf. *I.* 1.47). Bacchylides by contrast uses the much softer concept of *charis*, which may be anything lovely, and may also be as well an initial benefaction as the return made for such a benefaction.

29. At l. 96 the syntax is ambiguous, since *kalōn* could be a gen. pl. noun or a m. s. nom. participle: if a noun, it could be construed with *alatheiai* or with *charin*, and if with *charin*, it might be taken adverbially ("thanks to fine deeds"), or as a gen. of price ("a return for fine deeds"). However, since this statement is the complement of the one that preceeds and acts as its preface, it is possible to follow the poet's intention. He has just said:

| *siōpa* | *ou pherei* | *kosmon* | *eu praxanti* |

which yields two logical variants:

| 1. *siōpa* | *pherei* | *kosmon* | to one who fares or does badly |
| 2. speech PRAISE | *pherei* sound | *kosmon* | *eu praxanti* |

The continuing statement has to do with song, and consequently can be seen to follow this second variant pattern:

| *hymnēsei tis* | . . . . | *charin* | *kalōn* = *praxanti kala* |

The idea of sound is expressed in *hymnēsei* and this means that there is no need to use *kalōn* as a participle of sounding (*pace* Fränkel, *Dichtung und Philosophie*,[2], Munich, 1962, p. 530 note 44). The notion that does need expression is that of success, good fortune, faring well, and consequently it makes sense to take *kalōn* as a noun representing the deeds of the one who is *eu praxas*, and to associate it with the *charin* that represents the song that is an adornment (on song as *kosmos*, cf. P. O. 11). This rules out the adverbial usage of *charin* ("thanks to fine deeds" or—a much longer shot— *aēdonos charin*, "thanks to the nightingale," as urged by L. Woodbury, "Truth and Song," *Phoenix* 23, 1969, 331-35: "By right of those glories that have been made manifest in the outcome of the contest there shall be a song of praise about them and by grace also of the honey-voiced nightingale of Keos"). R. Merkelbach, "Ba. 13.205 und 59," *ZPE* 12 (1973) 90, takes the *kalōn* as a noun signifying the deeds, i.e. the victory, of Hieron, and he associates it with the phrase *syn alatheiai*, translating: "Wenn der Sieg (*ta kala*, cf. 2.6 und 9.82) überall bekannt gemacht wird, wird Mann die Gabe (das Lied) der honigsüssen Keischen Nachtigall singen." This would seem to be the best solution unless one is ready to suppose that *charin* controlled two genitives, one of price and the other of source, in which case *syn alatheiai* can be taken more naturally with *hymnēsei tis* and the translation will be: "With truth (with unforgetfulness) a man will sing the recompense of fair deeds made by the honey-voiced Kean nightingale." Either way the *kai* of l. 97 is a deprecating sound of artful modesty. (The older way of reading the line must certainly be given up, for it provided nothing at all as *kosmos* for Hieron: e.g. Jebb, "And along with thy genuine glories men shall praise also the charm of the sweet singer, the nightingale of Ceos"; Edmonds, "So there shall be a true tale of things well done and along with it men shall praise the grace of the honey-tongued nightingale of Ceos"; Lattimore, "And with his honors here remembered, men shall sound out the exquisite grace of me, the honey-tongued nightingale of Keos"; Gentili, "con la vera tua gloria si canterà anche la grazia del dolce poeta"; Fagles, "They will resound with your splendor of truth and resound too the rolling finesse of the honey-tongued nightingale of Ceos".)

6. THE CUT OF THE MYTH

1. Simonides knew the work of Stesichorus (or at any rate his name, 564.4 *PMG*) and Pindar and Bacchylides evidently knew a common epinician tradition that preceded them: there are many paths of song that they may follow (e.g. P. *I.* 4.1). This would seem to mean either that older songs were circulated within the profession (in writing or orally), or else that some of the early choral compositions had been adapted for single performance and so given a prolonged life. Perhaps both of these suppositions are correct.
2. Cf. *O.* 10.91 ff.; *P.* 3.114–115; *I.* 4.45; *N.* 4.6.
3. Phalaris, at P. *P.* 1.96, is a monitory example, but not the hero of a fiction comparable to a mythic narration.
4. See the discussion of A. Lesky, "Der Mythos," *Gymnasium* 73 (1966) 27 ff.
5. The marvel of the *Partheneion* was that three should kill so many; that of Simonides' Danaë song was much subtler and more wonderful—physically, that Danaë should survive; psychologically, that the baby should feel no fear, spiritually, that Danaë should be able to pray. Stesichorus took his listeners to the marvel of the three-headed, six-legged, six-armed Geryon and his death, but whether or not he stopped his song there we do not know (see S 7–87 *SLG* and D. L. Page, "Stesichorus: *The Geryoneis*," *JHS* 93, 1973, 138 ff.). In the same way, we do not know whether the song that told of Telemachus' visit to Sparta (208–9 *PMG*) stopped with the portent, since the *Nostoi* may have been long, or it may have been a series of short songs. For *thaumata* in epinician, note the explicit labeling of such at P. *P.* 9.31; P. *O.* 3.31; B. 9.31. For examples of other emphatic moments of marveling see, *Il.* 24.629–31; *Od.* 8.429; S. *El.* 897; P. Oxy. 213, fr. 1 (Niobe? Andromeda?) = 574*PMG*. See also A. Turyn, *Studia Sapphica* (1929), p. 33.
6. On Bacchylides' lifespan and the dates of the odes, see A. Körte, *RE* Supp. IV. 64, 26, and "Bacchylidea," *Hermes* 53 (1918) 140 f., also A. Severyns, *Bacchylide* (Liege, 1933). If, as Jebb thought, Bacchylides was born ca. 506, then he was only twenty-one when Ode 13 was composed; others follow Körte in making him a closer contemporary of Pindar's, whose birth was in 518.
7. On the developing iconography of the encounter with the lion see F. Brommer, *Herakles* (Münster, Cologne, 1953), pp. 8–11 and 81–83; Brommer adds to the listing of 369 vases offered by S. B. Luce, Jr., "The Nolan Amphora," *AJA* 20 (1916) 460–72; see also Roscher 1.2195 and *RE* Supp. 3.1028. The earliest known representation is on a geometric stand from the

Cerameicus (Brommer, taf. 4a) and shows an armed, helmeted warrior, aiming his lance at the lion's open mouth; on a seventh-century shield decoration from the Peloponnese, however, Heracles stands naked, holding the lion with an arm-lock around his neck (Brommer, ab.2). The black-figure painters continue to show sword or club but the favorite early archaic schema is like that of the shield decoration; then, towards the end of the sixth century, the weapons almost disappear and both Heracles and the lion sink to the ground to wrestle. With a few archaizing exceptions this is also the red-figure version; in high red-figure depictions Heracles seems to throw himself unarmed upon the lion. Especially notable is an early fifth-century white-ground lecythos from the Louvre (MN 909 = L 31) where the sword, belt, and cloak of the hero have been carefully hung in a tree and the club lies on the ground behind a Heracles who is on his knees, wrestling with the lion.

8. Wilamowitz thought this was the nymph Nemea; Jebb believed it to be Athena. All that is certain is that the speaker makes this prophecy at Nemea (*taide*, 55), and that she is someone who can decree or at least powerfully foresee the future contests there (*phami*, 54 ff.). The fact that Athena is mentioned at 195 may suggest that it was she who spoke earlier and such a supposition is greatly strengthened by Athena's frequent presence beside Heracles in the vase-painting scenes of the struggle with the lion (Luce, "The Nolan Amphora," found her in 128 of 302 black-figure examples and in 9 of 28 red-figure examples), and especially in the one that is closest to Bacchylides' account (Villa Giulia M 472). No other strong candidates suggest themselves.

9. To understand what might have been done in the way of concrete physical detail one has only to look at [Theoc.] *Id.* 25, especially 148–9, where muscles swell and strain.

10. This is the earliest direct literary reference to the lion's invulnerability, though Pindar refers obliquely to the magic powers of the skin that Heracles wears (*I.* 6.47), and the account in [Theoc.] *Id.* 25.162 ff. is entirely shaped by the notion of the unpierceable pelt (230; 255) which the hero cannot even cut from the corpse with metal—he must use the beast's own claws to tear the skin. It is usually assumed that this motif was late to develop because in early black-figure scenes Heracles may use sword or club as well as his hands, but Brommer (*Herakles*, p. 11) supposes that the variety of means may reflect a tale in which the hero tried first one weapon and then another before resorting to his hands. It is notable that when he uses his sword or lance, Heracles often tries to thrust it down the lion's throat, perhaps because he found the skin impermeable (e.g. the Cerameicus stand and the black-figure amphora at Kassel, Brommer, taf. 5). The bent sword can be seen on an Etruscan black figure amphora (Villa Giulia M 472); see Beazley's review of *CVA Robinson, JHS* 54 (1934) 90, and *Etruscan Vasepainting* (Oxford, 1947), p. 140. O. Berthold, "Unverwundbarkeit 2," *Relig. Vers. u. Vor.* 11.1 (1911) 2 ff. does not take account of B. 13; his remarks on the Nemean lion are criticized by N. Terzaghi, "Uber die Unverwundbarkeit des Nem. Löwen," *Arch. f. Relig.* 16 (1913) 309–13.

11. For the useless weapon, see Stith Thompson, *Motif-Index* D 1414; D 2086; D 1841.5; D 20891; D 2072.0.1; J 621; and for the magic animal who is proof against weapons, see D 1841.52 and compare 1841.6.

12. Note that the invulnerability of the pelt, like the poison of the Lernaean Hydra, is taken over by the hero to become one of his own magic powers;

see particularly P. *I.* 6.47, where Heracles prays that Telamon may have a son whose skin is unbreakable, like the pelt that he himself wears.

13. Contrast the attitude of the hero in the Olympia metope where he stands, head in hands, looking down at the lion's corpse.

14. The verb employed here (*krainō*: accomplish, fulfill, ordain) is particularly associated with the actions of effective powers, whether fate, gods, or rulers, as they bring about conditions that are fated, necessary, divinely intended, or allowed.

15. It is to be remembered that the Nemean lion was, according to Hesiod (*Th.* 327–32), the child (or grandchild) of Echidna, the sibling (or nephew) of the Sphinx, and the protected favorite of Hera, who brought him up to be a *pēm' anthrōpois* (329). The lion was thus closely associated with the nearest equivalent to the Near-Eastern female chaos dragon that Hellenic tradition produced.

16. For the daughters of Asopus, see Paus. 5.22.6, and also 2.5.2; 10.13.6; cf. C. M. Bowra, "The Daughters of Asopus" *Hermes* 73 (1938) 213–22. Also see below, Chap. 7, note 7.

17. It is probable that they also requested the praise of the family trainer that comes at 191 ff. Some have supposed that elaborate contracts were drawn up between patron and poet, and the scholiast at P. *I.* 2.22 reports that Pindar got double his usual line-determined fee for lines that praised a charioteer. On these and related questions, see S. Gzella, "The Problem of the Fee," *Eos* 59 (1971) 189 ff., who tends to exaggerate the mercenary element, as does J. Svenbro (*La parole et le marbre*, Lund, 1976, p. 147) when he reads *syn dikai* at B.13.202 as meaning "dans les formes du contrat."

18. The vase-painters had a scene in which Ajax carried the body of Achilles from the field, but this is precisely what Bacchylides did not want; see J. Boardman "Exekias," *AJA* 82 (1978) 11–24.

19. In a phenomenon frequently seen in epinician, the narrative touches the point in time that it will reconstitute, then sinks a little deeper, so that it dips up a bit of the surrounding element with the moment it would catch. Here the singers touch the battle at the ships at 105, but only in a relative clause whose function is technically merely to define the object of *boasō.* Then at 114 the singers sink deeper and reach the time before, when Achilles was still active, with a generalized clause that uses imperfect verb forms. Next a specific act that is immediately preliminary to the moment being sought is mentioned in a subordinate temporal clause (*lēxen*, 22). Finally, at 144 ff., immediate actions which we are to regard directly begin to be recounted; they occur at exactly the moment which was passed by at 105, but only these finally specified actions are presented as belonging to a realized scene.

20. Achilles' presence is almost actualized in 118–19, but his actions there are not concrete, being presented in an indefinite time and in the optative. The equation of Achilles' absence to sudden fair weather may be compared with Simon. 508 *PMG*, which seems to be an example of the same figure.

21. It is natural for epinician poems to make frequent mention of crowns, but in this song there is in addition a particular emphasis upon flowers. The Muses of line 222, like the Aeginetan girls of 91, wear wreaths of red flowers (and the girls also dance up flowery slopes, 88); Pytheas, at 69–70, wears a crown that is made of flowers specified as *panthalea*, an epithet that is repeated in 229, of Clio. These specifically flowery crowns (reinforced by the violet crown of Thetis at 122–3) cause one to imagine flowers when a

simple crown is mentioned (55, 184, 197), and they also lend a sensuous actuality to the two passages that use flowers in a bolder, almost symbolical way. The first of these is at 58 ff., where "flowers of glory-bearing Nike" (*pace* Merkelbach, *ZPE* 12, 1973, 90, who would make Nike the subject) nurture fame for those who gain Nemean crowns, thus reversing the expected commonplaces: victory flowers forth in fame; poetry nurtures fame-flowers. The second is at 228 ff., where Clio drips honey into the poet's mind; this seems to be a complement to the image of the poet as bee carrying honey of song among men (10.10 ff.).

22. By pretending that his song is a return of like for like, a gift that repays hospitality (224–5), Bacchylides makes it technically an act of justice (cf. 202) and order. In fact, the poet playfully makes two pretenses here, first that his poem is freely offered and not a commissioned work, and second that as such it might be despised, since it praises his host's son instead of his host. (A contrary opinion is expressed by S. Gzella, "The Competition among the Greek Choral Poets," *Eos* 58, 1969–70, 19 ff. Gzella takes these remarks literally and concludes that Ode 13 was actually sent unsolicited to Lampon, who had already given the commission for his son's song to Pindar.) The translation here proposed for 226–7 is based on Snell's suggestions.

7. INAUSPICIOUS TALES

1. For the myth of Opheltes/Archemorus, see Apollod. Bib. 3.6.4; schol. Clem. Al. *Protrep.* 2.34 p. 306.25 Stählin; Hyginus *fab.* 74; P. *Nem.* hypoth. 2 (scholia iii Dr.), hypoth. 3, hypoth. 4; *AP* 3.10; Statius, *Thebaiad* 5; *Myth. Vat.* ii 141 p. 123 Bode (= schol. Stat. *Theb.* 4.740). These are conveniently collected in G. Bond, *Euripides Hypsipyle* (Oxford 1963), Appendix 5, pp. 147–9. Archemorus is mentioned by Simonides (553 *PMG*) but there is no trace of him in art before the mid-fifth century; for a red-figure sherd showing the baby and the snake, see A.D. Trendall, *Paestan Pottery* (London 1936), pl. XVIa.

2. The Nemean festival was the most frankly funereal of all the games; the judges wore mourning robes, and Pausanias was shown the grave and the altars for Opheltes (2.15.3).

3. On *elpis*, see F. Wehrli, LATHE BIOSAS (Leipzig 1931), pp. 6–14.

4. See also the discussion in chap. 4.

5. Compare *Il.* 14.435, where *pelasan chthoni* means to lay out a corpse.

6. The actual pinning of the opponent to the ground is in responsion with the description of the dragon's yellow glance: *ton xanthoderkēs*, 12; *gaiai pelasses*, 38.

7. On Asopus and his daughters, see C. M. Bowra, "The Daughters of Asopus," *Hermes* 73 (1938), 314–33. They had been treated in a poem of Corinna's, in *Berliner Klassikertexte*, ed. Wilamowitz, V. 2, pp. 49–52; Ibycus reported Asopus as flowing from Phrygia (ap. Strabo 6.271), Pausanias (2.5.3.) identified Asopus with Maeander, and there was also a Boeotian Asopus. The Phliasians dedicated a statue of Asopus with five daughters at Olympia (Paus. 5.22.6).

8. Farnell long ago announced that there was "no shadow of probability" about the hypothesis that there was worship of Artemis Hemera at Metapontum ("Archaeological Notes," *CR* 12, 1898, 343 ff.). Recently, however, a large number of sixth-century figurines representing Artemis (some

winged, some carrying animals, some wearing pointed hats) have been found in association with sixth-century walls near the spring of San Biagio. This is the only spring in the Metapontine region sure to flow even in summer, and is located a few km. west of the ancient city. Heavy usage of the shrine seems to begin in the late seventh century, but precolonial sherds have also been found, and these (along with the extra-city location) suggest that this was an indigenous cult place before the Greeks came. In a nearby grove an inscription naming Zeus Aglaios was also found, and it has been conjectured that he had a neighboring *temenos;* his otherwise unknown epithet might possibly derive from his association with the water of the spring. On the Artemis shrine, see P. Zancani-Montuoro, *RAAN* (1975) 125 ff.; G. Olbrich, "Ein Heiligtum der Artemis Metapontina," *PP* 31 (1976) 376–408; M. W. Frederiksen, *Archaeological Reports for 1976–7,* Supp. *JHS* 23, pp. 43 ff. For Artemis and water, see Farnell, *Cults* II, pp. 427 ff. There were stoups dedicated to her at Samos, Olympia, Athens, Paestum, Locri and Tarentum.

9. In general, for Artemis as healer, see Gruppe, 1273 ff., and for her connection with the Proetids, 1275. Her name by popular etymology meant "healthy" (*artemēs*); she had a shrine on the Alpheus (again in a context with Zeus) where lepers were healed; cf. her cult in association with Arethusa at Syracuse (P. P. 2.7) and her cult at Limnai (Paus. 3.169). At Paus. 7.19.2 she appears as healer of pest; cf. 2.7.7 and 8.22.5 where she is said to live at healing springs. For Artemis as healer of madness, compare the legend of the women of Rhegium (Aristoxenus ap. Apollonius, *FHG* II p. 282). See Roscher, *Lex.* "Artemis" I.584.

10. Farnell, *CR* 12 (1898), 343 ff.

11. See the discussion of J. Stern, "Bestial Imagery in Bacchylides' Ode 11," *GRBS* 6 (1965) 275 ff.

12. *CR* 12 (1898), 343 ff.

13. For a discussion of all the parts of the myth, see O. Meiser, *Mythologische Unters. zu Bacchylides* (diss. Munich, 1904). There seem to have been two "Hesiodic" versions, that of the *Catalogue* (fr. 132–33 MW plus a passage from Philodemus *peri euseb.* p. 54 Gomperz; cf. fr. 131 MW) and another (reflected in Hdt. 9.34; Diod. Sic. 4.68; Paus. 2.18.4) that Apollodorus knew (*Bib.* 1.9.12 and 2.2.2). *PSI* 1301 (=fr. 37 MW), might belong to either. In the *Catalogue* version the girls angered Hera with their lechery and were punished with disease which was later healed; in the Apollodorus version they were driven mad by Dionysus, in punishment of their refusal to be initiated into his mysteries. On the problems posed by the duplication, see J. Schwartz, *Ps. Hesiodeia* (Leyde, 1960), pp. 369–77; 545–48; I. Loffler, *Die Melampodie* (Meisenheim am Glau, 1963), pp. 37–39; F. Vian, "Melampous et les Proitides," *REA* 67 (1965) 25 ff.; A. Henrichs, "Die Proitiden im Hesiod. Katalog," *ZPE* 15 (1974) 300–301. See also, more generally, J. Mattes, *Der Wahnsinn im gr. Mythos* (Heidelberg, 1970), pp. 63 ff.

14. Cult statue, Acusilaus, 2F 28 Jacoby; claim of beauty, Servius ad Virg. *Buc.* 6.48; lewdness, Hes. *Cat.* (28–29 Rz = Suda *s.v. machlosyne;* Dionysus, Hesiod ap. Apollodorus *Bib.* 1.9.12 and 2.2.2; see note 13 above). At Aelian *VH* 3.42, it is Aphrodite who drives the girls mad.

15. Baldness, leprosy, Hes. fr. 133 MW; sexual parts (?), Hes. fr. 132 MW, *teren olesen anthos;* cf. schol. Hom. O 225 where the disease lasts ten years

and continues in their children; see R. Pfeiffer, "Hesiodisches u. Homerisches," *Philol.* 92 (1937) 6 ff.; kill and eat children, Hdt. 9.34; Aelian *VH* 3.42; Apollod. 3.5.2.

16. Apollod. *Bibl.* 2.2.2. Melampous is the healer in every known version of the myth except that of Bacchylides; he is even found in Pherecydes 3F 114 Jac., which otherwise repeats Ode 11; see Meiser, *Mytholog. Unters.* Pherecydes reports that the healing was effected by prayers; Apollodorus (2.2.2) tells of a chorus of young men who dance and shout and chase the girls to Sicyon, where their madness leaves them; at Ovid *Met.*, 15.322–28, the cure is effected by incantations and by a medicine that induces a distaste for wine.

17. For the death of one girl, see Apollod. 2.2.2, who also reports that the other two were married to Melampous and Bias; cf. Hesych. *s.v.* Agriania, on the Argive festival for the dead girl.

18. Other possible places were Sicyon (Apollod. 2.2.2 and the epigram found there, A. K. Orlandos, *PAAH*, 1952, 394–5), or a place on the Sutha river (Paus. 2.7.8). Other possible divine healers were Hera (Pherecydes Serv. ad Virg. *Buc.* 648, Apollo (Paus. 2.7.8), or Asclepius (schol. P. *P.* 3.96, ii 75 Dr.; schol. E. *Alc.* 1). It may be that there was already some traditional connection between the Metapontine shrine and that at Lusoi, but it seems equally likely that Bacchylides chose this among the possible scenes of the healing because it allowed him the pun (*Louson*, 96; *lussas*, 102) which was much repeated; see the epigram cited Vitruv. viii 21 (p. 200 Rose) = Preger, *IGM* 11.215; cf. Ovid, *Met.* 15.322. On the *temenos* at Lusoi, see Paus. 8.18.8; 25.6; Polyb. 4.18.8; Strabo 5.215; Callim. *h. Art.* 233 ff. The site was excavated in 1897–98 by Dörpfeld and Wilhelm; see *JÖEAI* Bd. IV (1901) 1 ff. For possible mention of Lousoi in the Pylos tablets, see G. Pugliese-Carratelli, "Aspetti e problemi della monarchia micenea," *PP* 14 (1959) 412.

19. In the traditional version of the story, Proetus was so distressed by the multiple sorrows that had come upon him (loss of daughters and loss of kingdom) that he named his late-born son Megapenthes (Eust. ad Hom. p. 1480.4).

20. Apollod. *Bib.* 2.2.1 says that the brothers quarrelled even in the womb; that Proetus was driven into exile, then reentered Argos with an army of Lycians and took Tiryns by force; cf. Ov. *Met.* 5.236, where Acrisius is the exiled brother. Schol.Hom. *Xi* 319 = Pindar fr. 284 and others make the cause of quarrel the fact that Proetus had raped Danaë.

21. For the walls of Tiryns, see Paus. 2.16.5; 2.25.8; 7.25.6; Strabo 8.372; Apollod. 2.2.1; schol. E. *Or.* 965; the Cyclopes were also said to have built the walls of Mycenae (E. *HF* 15, 944; *IA* 152, 265, 845, 1500; S. fr. 207 N²; Paus. 2.16.5; 7.25.6). In addition to walls, the Cyclopes were particularly associated with the making of arms and weapons; at Hes. *Theog.* 141 they "fashion" the lightning bolt that is Zeus' weapon (cf. Orph. fr. 179), and they made the first armor, for Euteuchius in Euboea (schol. cod. Ven. ad *Il.* 10.439; schol. E. *Or.* 965). In the Orphic *Theog.* (fr. 92 Ab=Procl. in Plat. *Tim.* 1.327D) they are the original artisans, the teachers of Hephaestus and Athena.

22. There is even a tertiary ring in the first of the Proetid sections (43–58), for here the sequence is: Departure (43–45), Madness (45–46), Cause (47–53), Madness (54), Departure (55–58). Within the large ring of the

Tiryns section the sequence offers a little ring, then proceeds in linear fashion: Settlement (59-63), Quarrel (64), Cause (65), Quarrel (66-68), Prayers (69-72), Zeus (73-76), Cyclopes (77-79), Settlement (80-81).

23. Farnell was scornful of the lack of continuity: "Having achieved this remarkable leap from the Pythian Games to the Arcadian city, he found it a light matter to bring in by the way the story of the foundation of Tiryns" (*CR* 12, 1898, 343 ff.). J. Stern (*GRBS* 6, 1965, 279) believes that the digression is here simply to "emphasize the theme of flight."

24. On the other hand the men are of course stronger; when madness strikes Proetus, somewhat as it had the girls (*plaxen*, 86; *peplēgi*, 45), the prayer of his men, echoing the prayer of the people at the time of the quarrel, can control his impulse to suicide.

25. There may have been a tradition in which the new cult was physically brought back inside the walls of Tiryns; at any rate, Callimachus specifies *two* new foundations made for Artemis by Proetus, one at Lousoi dedicated to Artemis Hemera, another (at Tiryns?) dedicated to Artemis Koria (*h. Dian.* 233 ff.)

26. The word *admatoi* (84) means literally "untamed" and the unbroken foal was a common Greek metaphor for a virgin girl; as a married woman she was more apt to be compared to a bovine creature who knew the yoke, and Hera here (46) "yokes" the girls' minds to madness, as the first step in their preparation for marriage. It is notable that Proetus (105) offers cattle who have not known the yoke (the equivalents of his girls) in sacrifice to the goddess who rules over the untamed world, and consequently over the processes of taming, in the same way that she rules over youth and consequently over the rites that end youth. Nor can it be accident that at the opening of the song Zeus has been saluted as *hypsizugos*, which familiar epithet may, according to *Et. Mag.* 712, mean one who holds all creatures in his yoke (this meaning is pointed out by Stern, *GRBS*, 6, 1965, 278); note also that the race of men whom Zeus would honor are horse-tamers (75). For the Proetid myth as a myth of initiation, see A. Brelich, *Paides e Parthenoi*, (Rome, 1969), pp. 472-3.

27. Because the poem concerns City and What Lies Outside City, it is tempting to look for a schematic Nature/Culture statement, and C. P. Segal concluded that the epithets of Ode 11 make a clear distinction between the two, while they yet "interrelate the various areas or 'codes' of civilization which madness disrupts" ("Bacchylides Reconsidered," *QU* 22, 1976, 99 ff. esp. 127). Whatever that may mean, it is obvious that the poem does not offer any simple binary opposition. To begin with, the major distinction is shown to operate differently upon the two sexes: for men, leaving the city equals war which can be replaced by the founding of a new city; for women, leaving the city equals madness which can be replaced by founding a new cult. Again, for men, the divinity of the city is Zeus; for women, it is Hera. Meanwhile, outside the city there is one divinity for both sexes—Artemis. Furthermore, the two places are not defined as being in any sense equals or polar opposites. City-space is more thoroughly described than non-city; at the same time, city-space is nondifferentiated, whereas two sorts of non-city space are delineated—plains close to cities 30; 70; 80) and uplands further away (55; 93-5). Taken as a whole, the song describes its cities as: honored by gods (12; 60 cf.; 120); holding (or held by) festival (12); containing pleasant halls (43-44) and (for women at least) sacred shrines (46); characterized by streets (58); having a population of warriors

led by a king (62–3; cf. 120 ff.), contained by walls (77); concerned with raising horses (114; cf. 75, though the city association is only implicit by Lynceus). Lands just outside such cities are consistently described as food-producing (*portitrophon*, 30; *polykrithon*, 70; *hippoboton*, 80) and to the horse associated with the city they add the cow. The upland part of this noncity space is characterized only by trees (55; 93) and water (96), while the single animal connected with it is the sheep (95; 111). All three areas are tame (though this quality diminishes as one gets further from the city) and wildness is represented only by the god-induced and temporary madness of the girls, for the only wild animal mentioned is the *thēr* in Artemis' epithet *thēroskopos* (107). Raw Nature clearly lies somewhere well beyond "sheep-feeding Arcadia," and the poem's myth concerns itself exclusively with its three areas of Culture. The City, associated with the horse, is made of stone, strongly masculine, and closely associated with Zeus, though it has a place for women and Hera. The tilled fields and meadows, associated with horse and cow, are earthy and lightly feminine (because of the heifers and the sense of nourishing and cherishing that arises from epithets deriving from *boskein* and *trephein*), and have no particular deity. The unhusbanded pasture area is forested and watery, sexless, and closely associated with an Artemis who seeks out wild beasts (107) but who is also *boōpis* (99) and on good terms with Hera (107). In the course of the tale the relationships among these three areas are subtly changed, as people (men and women) from the stone city go out into the watery place of flocks and build a *temenos* (110) there, like the one in town (48). They also bring cattle (104) into this place of sheep, and establish a festival (112) there, like the festivals that mark a city (12). The fiction thus describes the extension of culture as a mad crossing of boundaries that can nevertheless be sanctified and regularized, like so many dangerous actions. It also associates the ideas of marriage and the domestication of animals, since marriage is another extension of culture into what had been nature, and as an initiation fable this story shows girls who withdraw from the city for a period of sexlessness with the goddess of youth (a period spent as far-wandering sheep) before they make their peace with Hera and become like cattle who are enclosed at home.

28. Like many of the western colonies, Metapontum had two traditions about its foundation, one that was historical and one that was heroic. According to Antiochus of Syracuse (ap. Strabo 6.265), the city was first settled as a subcolony of Sybaris, as an Achaean balance to the Laconian Tarentum, but there was also a tale of foundation by companions of Nestor of Pylus, on their way home from Troy (Strabo 6.264; 6.1.15; Solinus 2.10) and the city held an annual sacrifice in honor of these heroic founders. E. Schwartz, "Zu B.," *Hermes* 39 (1904) 630 ff., assumed that a reasonable Bacchylides could only refer to the first of these traditions, but the men of Magna Graecia seem to have been able to accept both sorts of tales at once, and a reference to the time of the Trojan War might have been particularly suitable if (as suggested above, note 8) the cult at Casa had a precolonial history; see G. Pugliese Carretelli, "Culti e dottrini religiose in Magna Gr.," *PP* 20 (1965) 5 ff., and "Problemi della storia di Metaponto Arcaica," *Metaponto. Conv. Magna Grecia* 13 (Naples, 1973), pp. 51–52, who believes somewhat rashly that the heroic foundation legends reflect actual Mycenaean contacts with South Italy.

8. THE TRAGIC MUSE

1. When under the direct influence of tragedy, as he is in *P.* 11, Pindar can speculate about the motive that led to a particular choice of action (22 ff.), but he does not build his speculations into a scene, nor does he emphasize the moment of choice.

2. A major exception occurs when Pindar uses the figure of Neoptolemus, but neither in *N.* 7 nor in *Pa.* 6 does he ask his audience to look directly at that hero as he moves towards his negative destiny, and at *Pa.* 6.113 ff. he asserts that Neoptolemus' end was determined by the atrocity against Priam, which makes it an example of accurate justice and consequently nontragic.

3. The Pelops tale would necessarily become less allegorical, more tragic, if any reference were made to the episode of Myrtilus, but Pindar makes no such reference.

4. Perhaps Dithyramb 15, the *apaitēsis* of Helen, should also be mentioned, though it is heavily epic in style ("Say Muse, who was the first to speak on the side of justice," 45). There (after Menelaus makes a speech in which he finds the possibilities of *dikē, eunomia,* and *themis,* but also of *hubris,* in the present situation) the sons of Agenor evidently choose the way of *hubris,* and consequently the punishment that will follow. In this they are like the heroes of divine-punishment tragedies who reenact their fundamental error or crime in a symbolic staged version.

5. The most likely festival would seem to be the Theseia; see Deubner, *Attische Feste* (Berlin, 1932), pp. 224–26; H. Jeanmaire, *Couroi et Courètes* (Lille, 1939), pp. 227–383; H. Herter, "Theseus der Athener," *RM* 88 (1939) 244 ff. 289 ff.

6. Kenyon thought that Medea and Aegeus (each represented by a semi-chorus) were the characters in this exchange, but at 5 the initial speaker refers to "our land" in a way that Medea could not; see C. Robert, "Theseus und Meleager bei B.," *Hermes* 33 (1898) 130 ff. It seems natural to assume that the questioning stanzas here are sung by the chorus as a group of ephebes (that 13–14 represent choral self-description) and that the answers are sung by the choregus. There is, however, no certain choral example of a solo dancer who exchanges songs with the rest of the chorus and it is possible that the answering part might have been sung, like the questioning part, by a group (the whole, in an altered position and stance, unless the two parts were given each to a semichorus). The tragic parallels nevertheless seem to justify the supposition that the king's words are sung by a single voice (cf. e.g. Cassandra and the chorus at A. *Ag.* 1056 ff., Herald and chorus at A. *Supp.* 836 ff., Xerxes and chorus at A. *Pers.* 931 ff., Athena and chorus at A. *Eum.* 917 ff.) and consequently we seem to be in the anachronistic presence of that Aristotelian *hypokritēs* from whom the tragic actor grew. For discussion and full bibliography, see A. E. Garvie, *Aeschylus' Supplices* (Cambridge, 1969), pp. 115–16. Aegeus' parentage, incidentally, seems to be generalized at 15, for he was ordinarily thought of as the son of Pandion and Pelia (Apollod. *Bib.* 3.15.5); Creusa's name lends an air of greater antiquity and attaches the king more closely to Erechtheus.

7. R. Merkelbach, "Der Theseus des Bakchilides," *ZPE* 12 (1973) 56 ff. Merkelbach believes that this was a little dramatic performance offered as a prelude to a demonstration by the second year ephebes from the Isthmus, made before the Boulē. He would have all the geographic references point to actual garrison posts (Cenchreai?) and he even insists that there is

specific meaning in each of the mythic adversaries, so that Procrustes, for example, represents "eine Art Kasernen-Geist" (p. 61), the leveling military spirit that cuts all recruits to size! On the training and traditions of the Attic ephebes, see Ch. Pelekidis, *Histoire de l'ephèbie attique* (Paris, 1962), and P. Vidal-Naquet, "The Black Hunter," *PCPS* 144 (1968) 49–64.

8. Sinis, at Cenchreae, is the furthest from Athens (Apollod. *Bib.* 3.16.2 makes him the son of Polyphemus, Hyg. *fab.* 38 has him be son of Poseidon); the meadow of Crommyon is in the Megarid, and closer to Athens (cf. Plut. *Thes.* 25, where Theseus brings the Megarid under Athenian domination); Sciron is on the cliffs between Corinth and Eleusis (Paus. 1.39.6; 55.6); Cercyon is at Eleusis (Paus. 1.39.3), not half a day away. Procoptes (Procrustes) does not have a fixed place; for his mattock, see Hyg. *fab.* 38. At Plut. *Thes.* 11, Paus. 1.38.5 and Apollod. *Epit.* I. 4, he and Polyphemon are one and the same, but at Apollod. *Bib.* 3.16.2 and schol. E. *Hipp.* 977, he is the son of Polyphemon, which would seem to be the view of Bacchylides, since Procoptes has evidently inherited the mattock. The deeds on the way to Athens decorated the Athenian treasury at Delphi (ca. 510) and were also the subjects of the metopes of the Hephaestaeum (begun 449); see H. A. Thompson, "The Sculptural Adornment of the Hephaisteion," *AJA* 66 (1962) 340 ff. All are depicted together on a red-figure cup from the British Museum (E. 84) where they culminate in the adventure with the bull of Marathon. For Theseus' arrival at Athens, see the Attic crater from the Armitage collection (*JHS* 1936, 77–8), where he has two companions, as in B. 18.

9. Compare the costume of Jason, arrived at one of his crucial hours, at P. *P.* 4. 78 ff.

10. "Waiting for the Barbarians," C. P. Cavafy. *Collected Poems*, tr. E. Keeley and P. Sherrard (London, 1975), pp. 14–15.

11. It is not known when Medea and Theseus first came into contact; both Sophocles and Euripides wrote tragedies called *Aegeus*, and the Euripidean play, at least, seems to have followed the story told at Apollod. 1.4.6 in which Medea, as Aegeus' queen, tried to poison the newly arrived Theseus, whom she was first to recognize; cf. Pfeiffer, *Callim.* I. 227. On the vase-painting evidence see B. B. Shefton, "Medea at Marathon," *AJA* 60 (1956) 159 ff.

12. Simon. 550 *PMG*.

13. The paths of Time are as crooked (*dolichoi*, 45) as the paths up the Isthmus (*dolichan*, 16) and by inference they are as full of surprises and dangers; they lead to their appointed ends, however, just as the Isthmian road leads to Athens. This line of thought leads to the double conclusion: Athens equals destiny fulfilled, and also (implicitly) Athens equals crime punished.

14. Though the song so clearly specifies the absence of Apollo, there is no sign of its being addressed to Dionysus and it is nothing like the song of Philodamus that a Delphic inscription calls a paean for Dionysus (*BCH* 1895, 393 ff.). Blass and others have supposed that this was a prooimion meant to introduce a dithyramb, but however that may have been, it is in itself a cletic hymn for Apollo; on the cletic elements of the strophe, see O. Meiser, *Mytholog. Unters.*, p. 25 f. The place must be Delphi, since the singers call upon Apollo to come where Delphic choruses sing paeans for him round his altar (8–12), and it is natural to suppose that the time is just before the

god's annual return. Presumably once the god is in residence, the music of Delphi will have a happier sound; cf. Alcaeus (307 [1] c V) where Apollo brings music and dance after Delphians have called to him, and Procop. *epist.* 68 p. 557, where it is imagined that the Delphians were silent in Apollo's absence. Every nineteenth year the return was postponed until the spring equinox (Diod. 2.147) and it is possible that the god was specially called upon in those years.

15. Wilamowitz, however, thought that this was merely the first triad of an unfinished longer song (*Bakchylides*, p. 18).

16. Hes. *Cat.*, 25 MW, had told how Daianeira killed Heracles by means of a poison applied to his clothing, but whether or not he attached this action to the stories of Iole and Nessus no one can say. B. Snell, "Drei Berliner Papyri mit Stücken alter Chorlyrik," *Hermes* 75 (1940) 182, maintained that Hesiod definitely did *not* connect the poison with the death of Nessus, but his is an argument from a fragmentary silence.

17. Note the holding effect of the final verb of the Heracles section, *melle* at 19–20, which catches Heracles with his act of sacrifice forever not complete, like the "freeze shot" of modern cinema.

18. The tale of the destruction of Oechalia was well known and had been given an epic treatment by Creophilus of Samos (Kinkel, p. 60; cf. Callim. *Epigr.* VI Pf.[2]). It was an episode in a myth in which a cultural advance (the bow) invented by a god (Apollo) was misused (by men who were in some sense black) and the misuse was punished by the god or his agent, using the new invention. Apollo taught Melaneus and Eurytus, kings of Oechalia, to use the bow (Paus. 4.2.3; AR I. 88; schol. *Il.* 5.392); then the story took one of two alternate forms: either Eurytus claimed greater skill than the god and was killed by him (*Od.* 8.221; AR I. 88), or else Eurytus offended Heracles, who carried Apollo's bow, and Heracles killed him. In the second case the punishment included the siege of Eurytus' city, Oechalia, and the story might also encompass Eurytus' broken promise to give his daughter Iole to anyone who could defeat him in an archery contest (S. *Tr.* 260; Apollod. *Bib.* 2.6.1; schol. *Il.* 5.392; schol. S. *Tr.* 266; schol. E. *Hipp.* 545; cf. Diod. 4.37) Oechalia was usually located in Euboea (Hecataeus *FGH* 1.28; AR I. 88; Strabo 10.1.10; cf. Paus. 4.2.2–3) but Messene, Thessaly, and Arcadia also claimed the city (Paus. 4.2.2–3; *Il.* 2.595; 729 ff., Thessaly; Pherecydes *FGH* 3.82, Arcadia). See C. Talamo, "Il mito di Melaneo, Oichalia e la protostoria eretriese," *Contributions, à l'étude de la société et la colonisation Eubénnes.* Cahiers du Centre Jean Berard II (Naples, 1975), pp. 27–36. The large applicability of this mythic pattern (divine gift/mortal misuse/punishment) to the fate of Heracles is obvious, though in the sophisticated fifth-century treatments the motifs of mortal misuse and divine punishment were both given ambivalent expressions: Heracles both misused and used well his divinely given powers (particularly his bow), and he was given an end that was both an agonizing death and an assumption to a life among the gods.

19. Cf. S. *Tr.* 752, *aktē amphiklustos.*

20. Athena of course will take Heracles to Olympus and introduce him to the other Olympians. The scene was well known in archaic times from the decorations of the old temple on the Athenian acropolis, the tomb of Hyacinth (Paus. 3.19.5) and the throne at Amyclae (Paus. 3.18.11). For a fifth-century vase-painting representation, see for example, the Vulci pelike (Munich 2360) where Heracles, as he rises with Athena in her chariot, is

already rejuvenated and ready for Hebe. See C. Robert, *Gr. Heldensage* II, pp. 599–600.

21. For Athena Erganē, see Paus. 1.24.3 and Frazer *ad loc.*, who lists the locations of this cult; H. Perdrizet, *Mélanges Perrot* (Paris, 1903), pp. 259–267; C. Meillier, "La chouette et Athena," *REA* 72 (1970) 5–30. Athena supervised women's weaving and at the same time their thoughts and plans (e.g. *Od.* 2.116–118; 7.108–111), and at Hes. *Erg.* 63–4, she teaches Pandora the art of weaving. For Metis the mother of Athena as one who "wove" the future, see M. Detienne and J.-P. Vernant, *Les ruses de l'intelligence* (Paris, 1974), p. 134, and 286–7 on the notion of the woven trap.

22. The same phrase appears at *Od.* 19.326 where Penelope uses it with positive valence of herself.

23. We do not know when the figure of Iole entered the story of Oechalia; Wilamowitz (*Herakles*, p. 70 ff., esp. 77) thought that Creophilus of Samos had combined the tales of Daianeira, Omphale, and Iole when he wrote his *Siege of Oechalia*. An interest in human motivation, especially in female jealousy and revenge, evidently developed in the late sixth century (as witness the tales at A. *Ch.* 585 and the notion of Clytemnestra's jealousy of Cassandra—a figure parallel to Iole—that Pindar remarks on in *P.* 11) and if it were certain that the Creophilus who composed the Oechalia poem were the same one who wrote of Medea (schol. *Med.* 264), one might argue that the jealousy of Daianeira quite probably figured in that epic.

24. A comparison of the epithets applied to Daianeira at 16.30 with those applied to Althea at 5.137–9 (*daiphrōn, kakopotmos, atarbaktos*) leaves a strong impression that whereas Althea is shown as understanding the act she commits, Daianeira is shown making a decision that she does not understand. This impression is strengthened by the reference below to the "dark veil" of the future, but nevertheless it cannot be proved that this song shows a Daianeira who was deceived as to the nature of the philtre: it is just possibly the portrait of a woman knowingly deciding to use poison.

25. The reference to Iole forces us to understand *phthonos* as including sexual jealousy, but the epithet *eurubias* seems to encourage a second sense as well—that of the grander and more general *phthonos* of the gods, as it was concentrated in Hera. T. Zielinski, "Bacchylidea," *Eos* 5 (1898) 25–38, supposed that the jealousy belonged to Nessus and was felt by him against Heracles, but that is an excessively modern sentimentalization of the centaur. For the notion that *phthonos* does violence (i.e., is unjust) compare the passage at B. 13.199–200 (discussed above, chap. 4), where the word has its more primitive meaning of invidious envy.

26. Jurenka and Crusius thought that the daimon and the *phthonos* were one and the same; O. Meiser *Mytholog. Unters.*, p. 25, suggested that the daimon was Eros, because of the epithet *amachos;* Kenyon correctly equated the daimon with fate, *ta hysteron erchomena.*

27. According to S. *Tr.* 573–4, Daianeira took some of the blood from the wounds which had been inflicted by the arrows that Heracles had dipped in the Hydra's bile (cf. Apollod. *Bib.* 2.6.2). A later version had her take some of the centaur's likewise poisoned sperm (Diod. Sic., 4.36.3–5), and Apollodorus compromised by reporting the philtre as a mixture of blood and sperm (*Bib.* 2.7.6). Obviously this motif of the philtre/poison is linked to the motif of the poison-tipped arrow, and consequently it is dependent upon Heracles' use of the bow. Conversely, it will not have been present in versions of the Nessus tale in which he was killed with sword or club un-

less, as seems to be the case on a proto-Attic sherd from the Argive Heraeum (C. Waldstein, *Argive Heraeum* II, Boston, 1902–05, p. 67; Beazely, *Development of Attic Black Figure*, Berkeley, 1951, pp. 6–7), he was thought of as first shot and poisoned, then finished off with sword or club when he reached the shore. The bow can be part of Heracles' equipment any time after the end of the seventh century; its literary "inventor" was Stesichorus (Athen. 12.512, but see Strabo, 15.688, who says "Peisander or someone else") but it had appeared in art a few decades before his time; P. Zancani-Montuoro, "Il tipo di Eracle nell'arte arcaica," *Rend. Linc.* ser. 82 (1947) 207 ff.; C. Dugas, "La mort du centaure Nessos," *REA* 45 (1943) 17–26. The earliest literary reference to the Nessus tale that we know of was that of Archilochus, mentioned by the scholiast at AR 1.1212 (= Archil.288 W) and by Dio Chrys. 60.1 (=Archil. 286 W). Next is a fragment of song in the style of Pindar and Bacchylides (P. Berol. 16 = B. fr. 64S = P. fr. 341B) in which Daianeira groans while being ferried by a centaur and Heracles seizes his club. Snell, attributing the song to Bacchylides ("Drei Berliner Papyri mit Stücken alter Chorlyrik," *Hermes* 75, 1940, 177–83), argues that this is the older version of the tale; that the philtre/poison version was introduced by Sophocles; that fr. 64 was therefore an early composition and Dithyramb 16 a late one in which Bacchylides was borrowing from the intervening *Trachiniae*. This line of reasoning is, however, unacceptable. In the first place, fr. 64S is not certainly the work of Bacchylides; Bowra attributed it to Pindar, but the flow of the narrative does not seem quite like either poet and Simonides is another possibility. In the second place, myths did not develop sequentially and irreversibly; on vases Heracles could use his bow against Nessus almost two centuries before the time of Sophocles, while he could also continue to strike him with his club until the end of the fifth century (e.g. the Boston cylix of Aristophanes, Boston 00.344, and the stamnos by Polygnotos, BM 95.7–16.5). And in the third place, poets did not necessarily reproduce "early" versions of myths early in their careers, "late" versions later. Fragment 64S, if it is Bacchylidean, could as well be later as earlier than Dithyramb 16. Finally, since neither the dithyramb nor the *Trachiniae* can be dated, it is as reasonable to suppose Sophocles influenced by Bacchylides as the reverse, but it is far more reasonable to assume that both were working within a familiar tradition. In Dithyramb 16, the easy assumption that every listener will understand exactly what Daianeira received (and why, and how, and what she will do with it) proves that the story that made Nessus transmit the Hydra's poison was well-known everywhere at the time of the song's performance. If the whole story had been a Sophoclean innovation and Bacchylides were working a few years later than the *Trachiniae* production, could he have made such an assumption about his Delphic listeners? C. Del Grande, *Filologia minore* (Milan, 1956), p. 161, and Stoessl, *Der Tod des Herakles* (Zurich, 1945), p. 63, like Snell, argued that Dithyramb 16 was necessarily later than *Tr.*; for a rebuttal, see M. Pohlenz, *Die Griechische Tragödie*² II (Göttingen, 1954), pp. 87 ff.

28. An extreme skeptic might ask what indication we have that the *teras* received by Daianeira had any connection with the Hydra. The answer is that there is no explicit indication within the poem because this is its "secret," the truth it forces its listener to discover. The Hydra poison is, however, implicit in the situation as it is described, since in crude story-telling terms there would be no reason why the centaur's blood, as nature made it,

should kill. Only if he was himself poisoned could he poison in return, and he is poisoned only if he has been struck by an arrow dipped in Hydra's bile. Bacchylides has taken care that we should from the start imagine his Heracles as one who used the bow, by mentioning Oechalia (14), the home of the bow, and this means that when we picture the scene on the Lycormas we will picture a centaur who is struck by an arrow, an arrow that kills because it has a poisoned tip.

29. The story has a further appropriateness, of course, because of Heracles' special relation to Apollo. Not only did he carry an Apolline bow (and briefly even the tripod), but he was, according to Bacchylides (*Pa.* 4), employed as Apollo's agent in the removal of the Dryopes from Delphi to Asine; see W. S. Barrett, "Bacchylides, Asine and Apollo Pythaieus" *Hermes* 82 (1954) 421–44.

9. HERACLES AND MELEAGER

1. The ode refers to the Olympic victory of Pherenicus in the horse race, won in 476. Because Pindar's *O.* 1 was composed for the same victory, certain critics have assumed that Ode 5 was not commissioned, but was sent unsolicited by a poet not yet known to Hieron, in hopes of future orders. This was the view of Wilamowitz (*Bakchylides*, Berlin, 1898, pp. 18 f.), who thought he could detect humility in the poet's approach to the tyrant. This notion was taken up by W. Schadwaldt, *Der Aufbau der Pindarische Epinikion* (Halle, 1928) p. 23. See also W. Steffen, "Bacchylides' Fifth Ode," *Eos* 51 (1961) 19 ff., who takes 11 ff. to mean that the poet was unknown to Hieron and had to introduce himself; cf. P. T. Brannon, "Hieron and Bacchylides," *CF* 26 (1972) 197 f. It is, however, possible to suppose that Hieron called upon both poets (perhaps even upon others unknown to us) to contribute to his celebration; a much lesser patron may have asked both to compose odes for Pytheas of Aegina, if Ode 13 and P. *N.* 5 are meant for the same pancratic victory. Jebb, Severyns (*Bacchylide*, Liège, 1933, p. 87 and note 60), Gentili (*Bacchilide*, 1958, pp. 13 ff.), and Snell all assume that the commission of Ode 5 was a normal one.

2. The first triad is marked by certain irregularities in responsion, and an unusual frequency of *brevis in longo*, which suggested to Snell that it might have been composed at a different time from the rest of the ode (p. 37* of second ed.). Reinach had earlier supposed that the mythic section was an example of "ready-made" epinician material that poets carried about with them for inclusion in whatever ode they might be asked to write: "Cette magnifique ode, où le mythe est si faiblement cousu dans l'éloge, semble prouver que les poètes lyriques à la mode preparaient d'avance et gardaient en portefeuille des episodes héroiques" (*REG* 11, 1898, 24). Whatever the particular order of composition, however, the only fact of importance for the present study is that Bacchylides considered this to be a finished and unified ode, suitable for Hieron.

3. Probably Bacchylides was in fact unable to be present for the performance at Syracuse.

4. Note how like this motion is to the motion of Aretē when she is teeming with *doxa* at 13.176. A sense of the peculiarly Bacchylidean quality of this eagle metaphor can be gained by comparing it with the eagle of P. *N.* 3.80–82, a bird of prey that swoops upon a bloody victim as an image of poetic *kairos* seized. One should also compare the warlike Homeric eagles at

Il. 21.252–3; 22.310: 24.315–16 (Achilles); *Il.* 17.674–7 (Menelaus); see the discussion of Fraenkel, *Agam.* II, pp. 67–70. It is amusing also to compare Fielding's mock-epic simile in chap. 6 of *Tom Jones:* "Not otherwise than when a kite, tremendous bird, is beheld by the feathered generation soaring aloft, and hovering over their heads, the amorous dove, and every innocent little bird, spread wide the alarm and fly trembling to their hiding places. He proudly beats the air, conscious of his dignity, and meditates intended mischief."

5. Cf. e.g. *h. Cer.* 50f.; P. fr. 137S; Soph. fr. 719.

6. Cf. e.g. P. *O.* 9.35; for starting and stopping the chariot of song, see P. *O.* 6.22; *I.* 2.2.

7. The fact that Polygnotus, in the Hades scene that he made for the Lesche of the Cnidians at Delphi, introduced Meleager among the Trojans suggests that he was in the early fifth century a figure no hell could do without. The tradition of Heracles' descent is likewise already well established at the beginning of the century; Pindar composed a dithyramb entitled *The Catabasis of Heracles,* or *Cerberus* (70bS; 61B); he may also have made a song about Heracles' establishment of the Lesser Mysteries which included a visit to Hades (see H. Lloyd-Jones, "Heracles at Eleusis: *P. Oxy.* 2622 and *PSI* 1391," *Maia* 3, 1967, 206 ff.); in addition, the schol. at *Il.* 21.194 reports that Pindar had Heracles meet Meleager in Hades and there accede to Meleager's proposal that he should marry Daianeira (see 70b *249a S). There has been much speculation as to the older versions of the descent of Heracles; E. Norden, *Aen. VI Buch 2* (Leipzig, 1926), pp. 223–4, argued back from likenesses between Bacchylides and Virgil to an orphic Catabasis known to both poets (its contents reflected in Apollod. *Bib.* 2.5.12): C. del Grande (*Filologia minore,* Milan, Naples, 1967, pp. 145–48) assumed that this epic source was the *Minyad;* others have supposed it was the *Cerberus* of Stesichorus (206 *PMG*), and most recently N. Robertson, "Heracles' Catabasis," *Hermes* 108 (1980) 274–99, has proposed the *Aegimius* of Cercops of Miletus as the source of the Heraclean descent. It should be noted however, that Robertson speaks inaccurately when he says (275 note 3): "It is certain that in the epic catabasis the meeting of Heracles and Meleager led to mention of Daianeira as a bride for Heracles." The first *certain* meeting of the two occurs in B.5 or in the Pindaric song known to the *Il.* scholiast, whichever is older, and these are likewise the first *certain* mentions of Daianeira in this context.

8. Most critics have seen the scene in the opposite way, convinced that the superior number of lines in his speeches gives Meleager the primary position, and persuaded somehow that the passive Pindaric Heracles showed more "corragio e fortezza" than this active one does; see, for example, the remarks of A. Olivieri, *A Proposito di Teseo e Meleagro in Bacchylide* (Bologna, 1899), p. 22.

9. There is no syllable of evidence for the "panic," "disorder," and "folly" that Brannon reports as attaching to Heracles in these lines (*CF* 26, 1972, 236).

10. Meleager's tale occupies roughly one half of the mythic passage and one third of the whole song.

11. At *Il.* 9.527 ff. the Homeric poet seems to refer to a well-known epic tale of which there must already have been several versions. Phoenix hints that Meleager's death was achieved by his mother's curses (*Il.* 9.571), but Hesiod (*Cat.* 25.10–12 MW) reported that no mere mortal dared to fight

against Meleager and that he was killed by Apollo himself, during the battle with the Curetes. (The same version was evidently used in the *Minyad,* see Kinkel fr. 5 p. 216 = Paus. 10.31.3) Both Apollodorus (*Bib.* 1.8.3) and Diodorus (4.34.5) knew of a third version in which Meleager had simply died fighting. There were as well early poems that told of Atalanta as having had some part in Meleager's adventures, or at least in the boar hunt, for she was shown among the hunters on the Chest of Cypselus (Paus. 3.24.2 and 5.19.1) and also on the Francois vase; there is not enough left of Stesichorus' *Suotherai* (221-1 *PMG*) to establish her presence or absence there. The motif of the brand that is burnt to end Meleager's life is found first at the beginning of the fifth century, but its near-simultaneous appearance in three different authors of that time bears out Pausanias' supposition (10.31.3) that this variant was already well known; the passages are Phrynichus, *Pleur.* (fr. 6S) pre-470; Bacchylides, Ode 5, in 476, and A. *Ch.* 602-11, in 458. Robert (*Hermes* 35, p. 155) was ready to make Bacchylides the innovator; others have supposed that Althea's brand was the invention of Stesichorus (M. Croiset, "Sur les origines du récit relatif à Méléagre de B.," *Mélanges Weil,* Paris, 1898, pp. 73-80). Still others assume that because it is a popular motif it must be older than the Homeric story with its curse (J. Kakridis, "Meleagreia," *Philol.* 90, 1935, 1-25; cf. Gentili, *Bacchilide,* p. 45; H. Petermann, "Homer und das Märchen," *WS* 15, 1981, 57), while E. Bethe argued that no one who knew the brand version could choose the curse, and that consequently the poet of the Embassy knew only the curse, which therefore must be the oldest variant (*RM* 74, 1925, 7). For fire magic in general, see J. Kuehnert, "Feuerzauber," *RM* 49 (1894) 37 ff.; for the connection of man's life with a tree, J. W. E. Mannhardt, *Baumkultus* (Berlin, 1875) 23; 49 ff.; 221. Similar modern Greek tales are cited by Kakridis, *Philol.* 90 (1935) 1-25, and *Die alten Hellenen im neugr. Volksglauben* (Munich, 1967), pp. 46-56.

12. When Atalanta was first used as a romantic explanation for Meleager's quarrel with his uncles is not known; she is associated with Melainon on the Francois vase and the Chest of Cypselus (Paus. 5.19.2), and in epic she seems to have played only a secondary role in the hunt. Aeschylus wrote an *Atalanta,* and Sophocles wrote a *Meleager,* but there is nothing whatever left of the first and about the second we know only that the chorus was made up of priests and that Meleager's sisters in the end were changed into birds. For what may be a fragment of Euripides' *Meleager,* and a reconstruction of that play (on the basis of Apollod. *Bib.* 1.8.2-3; Ovid *Met.* 8.272 ff.; Hyg. *Fab.* 174; Diod. 4.34; Accius fgg. 1, 4, 5), see D. L. Page, "A new fragment of a Greek tragedy," *CQ* 31 (1937) 178 ff.

13. The boar is usually enormous and depicted in great detail, as on the Francois vase; cf. the fragment of a black-figure mixing bowl from about 570 (Schefold 61b), and the red-figure vase of the Codrus painter (Berlin 2538; *ARV* 1269.5); see R. Kekulé von Stradonitz, *De fabula Meleagrea* (Berlin, 1861), pp. 36 ff. and Roscher, *Lex. s.v.* "Meleagros" 2608.

14. Note that Pindar knows of the killing of Eurytion by Peleus in the fighting after the hunt (fr. 48 S), and compare the frequent naming of the participants in the black-figure representations of the hunt.

15. Cf. Gentili (*Bacchilide,* p. 34), who recognizes a "tono rassegnato e distacco" in these lines.

16. This is emphasized in the parallel verbs *bouleusen . . . kaie te* (139 . . . 140), each placed in prominent position at the beginning of its phrase. One addi-

tional action is specified in the participle at the end of the statement (142), but unfortunately we cannot be sure what it was. The papyrus gives *egklausasa*, which could mean "weeping over," but which should have an object expressed in the dative; Jebb proposed keeping the same meaning with *agklausasa*, "crying out;" Wilamowitz looked back to the *ek* in 141 and suggested *eklusasa*, "releasing" (the brand from the box); J. Wackernagel ("Zu B.," *Hermes*, 1905, 154) cited Hesych. *exausai: exelein*, and amended to *exausasa*, which, if correct, makes Althea's gesture echo (or rather prefigure) that of Heracles as he draws forth an arrow from his quiver.

17. The word had already appeared in the context of Calydon in the *Suotherai* of Stesichorus (222.9 *PMG*).

18. Brannon, *CF* 26 (1972) 242, supposes that even the daimon of 135 and the *daidaleas* of 140 belong to this system, but I am skeptical.

19. The word *proleipon* (154) carries the sense of betrayal, so that he is abandoning his youth as a coward might abandon a comrade in battle. Youth was evidently one of Meleager's principal attributes; cf. P. *I.* 7.32, where he is mentioned with Hector and Amphiareus as an example of one who "breathed out his flowering youth" in battle. This association with youth perhaps gives a last ironic turn to Heracles' desire for a girl "like him in form," since the ultimate bride of Heracles is not Meleager's sister but Hebe herself.

20. The epic usages of Ode 5 are thoroughly studied by M. Lefkowitz, "Bacchylides' Ode 5," *HSCP* 73 (1963), pp. 45-96, where, however, the author concludes that the ultimate tone of the poem is one of almost unrelieved pessimism.

21. Only in the satyr-drama *Cyclops* is there a "messenger speech" spoken by one who himself was a principal in the reported action (Odysseus reports the deeds done inside the cave, 382 ff.); in tragedy the nearest parallels are the report of the lyrical Phrygian at *Or.* 1369 ff. and that of the likewise musical charioteer at *Rhes.* 729 ff., but neither of these has been central to the tale he tells.

22. In addition, everyone in the audience knew the parallel scene in *Od.* 11, where Heracles played Meleager's role of resident shade to a visiting Odysseus (601 ff.).

23. The same question was put by Odysseus to Agamemnon at *Od.* 11.397, and there, as well, the answer was "a woman."

24. I cannot recognize the "silly Ionic" Heracles that Zielinski found here ("Bacchylidae," *Eos* 5, 1898, 28 ff.). Bacchylides' hero shows a touch of jaunty confidence, but there is none of the gross comic quality that some of the older traditions gave him, and that we find reflected in Phrynichus' *Alcestis*, Ion of Chios' *Omphale*, E. *Alc.*, Ar. *Ra.*, and a number of satyr plays (see F. Brommer, *Satyroi*, Wurzburg, 1937, pp. 43 ff. and 272).

25. W. Steffen, "Bacchylides' Fifth Ode," *Eos* 51 (1961) 19, finds in the Heracles figure a correction and reversal of the pessimism embodied in Meleager.

26. Brannon (*CF* 26, 1972, 252) somehow persuades himself that Heracles ought to be able to see into the future; he then complains that he "has failed to realize the import of Meleager's narrative," and concludes that he is being portrayed as a fool!

27. Cf Gentili, *Bacchilide*, p. 35.

28. It is the contention of J. Stern, "Imagery of Bacchylides' Ode 5," *GRBS* 8 (1967) 35 ff. that Bacchylides did subscribe to a total pessimism here (cf. *GRBS* 6, 1965, 275-82). This is also the conclusion of Lefkowitz, though

she recognizes "hope in a divine solution" in the poem's concluding words (*HSCP* 73, p. 92).

29. This epithet (*thelximbrotos*, 175) seems to be new and invented for the occasion.

30. Note the very different opinion of J. Peron, "Crésus et Méléagre," *REG* 91 (1978) 325 ff., who believes that all the actions in the mythic section have been morally condemned and offered as flattering contrast to the just actions of a Hieron who (unlike Meleager and Heracles) is a favorite of the gods.

31. Brannon incomprehensibly finds, in the word play at 183-5 (*Pherenikos ... pheron*), something that "makes it quite clear just how precarious and impersonal Hieron's happiness is" (*CF* 26, 1972, 263), and he believes that the final lines mean that the best a man can hope for is immobility. Because the singers allow Calliope (176) and Artemis (99) to share an epithet, Lefkowitz (*HSCP* 73, p. 88) discovers "pessimism" even in the poem's view of its own celebrations, but surely it is easier to hear this duplication as a proper honor paid to a goddess who is also, in the same phrase, called *kalykostephanos*, than it is to suppose that Bacchylides meant to attach the idea of "destructiveness" to his Muse!

32. This argument is stated most elaborately by Stern (*GRBS* 8, 1967, 35 ff.), who goes so far as to claim that when Hieron is brought *eudaimonias petalon* by Pherenicus (186), the phrase does not have its ordinary positive meaning, "the flower (or acme) of happiness," but instead a negative one, "happiness lasting only as long as a leaf." Again, at line 198, Stern reports "good fortune blooms from plant-like" (i.e. short-lived) "stems," which is a very unfair translation of *puthmenes thallousin esthlon*. The commonest meaning of *puthmēn* is "base, bottom, foundation" and consequently when it is taken over by the vegetable world, though it can indicate something as fragile as a stalk of wheat, its sense is of firmness and it more often denotes a tree trunk, a vine stalk, or a root (cf Lefkowitz, in *HSCP* 73, p. 74, "*puthmenes* ... connote stability and the possibility of renewal"). The poet says literally: "with my song at their base the stalks of noble deeds" (or possibly "of good fortune") "will grow and thrive."

33. Oeneus has apparently angered Artemis by failing to sacrifice, then attempted to placate her by a double offering of goats (her usual sacrificial beast) and of oxen. His action thus occurs in a situation where a sacrificial norm has already been established; see Farnell, "Archaeological Notes," *CR* 12 (1898) 343 ff. As Ovid tells the story (*Met.* 8.270 ff.), Oeneus had performed an exclusively agricultural rite, offering grain to Demeter, wine to Dionysus, and milk to Hera, while he ignored Artemis altogether.

34. The identification of Artemis with the woods is strongly made by Ovid, who places the boar in a forest whose various trees and non-cultivated plants are listed (*Met.* 8, 335 ff.); a tree wards off the first javelin (346); the boar saves itself by entering a thicket (376 ff.); Telamon is held back by a tree root (397); a leafy branch from a tree stops Theseus' javelin.

APPENDIX

1. This does not seem to be a strong possibility, and for the sake of convenience Snell's line numbers are here used.

2. For this sequence, see the discussion above, chap. 4, note 16.

3. Corinth could also be called The Gates, because of being, like Isthmia, the beginning (or end) of the Peloponnese (schol. P. O. 13.4).

4. Herodorus (*FHG* 11.38) makes Euxantius the son of Minos but does not mention Dexithea; Pindar (*Pa.* 4.35 ff.) has him be the son of an unnamed Cean mother and (by inference) Minos; Apollod. *Bib.* 3.1.2.5, gives Minos as his father, Dexithea as his mother.

5. The legend seems to establish a connection between Ceos and Miletus, since the schol. at AR I. 186 (= Aristocritus, *FHG* 4.331) calls Euxantius the father of Miletus and locates a clan of Euxantidae in that city. Perhaps Ceos, like Miletus, was famous for wool; in addition both Miletus and Metapontum claimed to have founders from Pylos, and since Bacchylides asserts elsewhere (11.20) that Metapontum was founded by his ancestors, one might conclude that Ceos shared a Pylian foundation legend with Miletus.

6. See E. Rohde, *Der griechische Roman*[2] (Leipzig, 1900), p. 538.

7. Nicander (*ap.* schol. Ov. *Ib.* 475) reports Macelo as one of the daughters of Damon, among whom is also Dexithea; in his story Macelo is killed by Zeus' bolt, among with her husband, while her sisters are saved. The Nicander reference was first associated with Bacchylides' poem by Wilamowitz (*GGA*, 1898, 127); R. Jockl, "Zu den *Aitia* des Kallim. u. dem ersten Gedicht des B.," *WS* 37 (1915), 142–56, argued that Nicander would have taken the story from an Alexandrian collection, which in turn would have had it from Bacchylides; see also O. Schneider, *Nicandrea* (Leipzig, 1856), p. 134 ff. Callimachus (*Aitia* III fr. 75.67) makes Macelo an old woman, the daughter of Damon but the wife of a certain Damonanax, and he reports her as having been saved with her daughter, Dexithea. Callimachus is presumably using a work on Ceos written by Xenomedes (*FHG* 11.43), to whom Müller would attribute a *Historia Telchiniaca* (cf. *Etym. Gudian.*, p. 257 *s.v.* thelgein, and *Et. Mag.* 425.8). The two versions of the story are discussed by A. E. Housman, "The *Ibis* of Ovid," *JP* 35 (1920) 301 ff.

8. Poseidon, at P. *Pa.* 4.41 (by inference); Apollo, at Nonnus *Dion.* 18.35; the schol. at Ov. *Ib.* 475 mentions only Zeus. Here in Ode 1 the later reference to Apollo (148) makes it likely that he was Zeus' companion.

9. Nicander (*ap.* schol. ad Ov. *Ib.* 475) identifies Damon as king of the Thelonii, whom Rhode (*Der gr. Roman*[2], p. 538) equates with Telchines. At Nonnus, *Dion.* 14.38, Damon is lord of the Telchines.

10. Bacchylides somewhere reported the Telchines as children of Nemesis and Tartarus and gave them names; Actaeus, Megalesius, Ormenus, Lycus (Jebb fr. 55 = Tzetzes *Theogon* 81). Perhaps this list occurred in the gap between Snell's 129 and 138, or possibly earlier, between his 83 and 111. Stesichorus (265 *PMG*) may have associated the Telchines with the Keres and with eclipses. Others made them sons of the sea (Diod. 5.55) or even children of Poseidon, whose trident they wrought (Callim. *Del.* 31). For their connection with Rhodes, see P. O. 7, where Telchines represent the sinister combination of *dolos* and *sophia* and belong to the time before Athena's cult was introduced. Diodorus, 5.55, reports that they fled from Rhodes, having been warned of a flood, and were scattered; Nonnus, *Dion.* 14.42 ff., specifies that they were driven out of Rhodes by the Heliadae because they had put a magical blight on the crops. According to Callimachus (*Aitia* III 75.64), they occupied Ceos for an epoch, between the Lelages

and the founding of the cities. The Telchines were magical craftsmen whose most famous crime was using Styx-water to make land barren (Nonnus *Dion.* 1446 ff.; cf. Lobeck *Aglaoph.* 1191 f.; 1198). See *RE s.v.* "Telchinen" 197–224.

11. For earthquakes at Ceos, see Pliny *NH* 2.206; Strabo 10.486.

12. The separation of women from men in the story causes a mechanical fictional problem, since the daughters of Damon cannot receive the visitors in their father's house without giving him a share in their hospitality. The same difficulty exists, of course, for a married Macelo. This I suppose is why Snell reports that the women have already been driven out by their father (p. 39), though there is no evidence either in the poem or in the tradition for such an episode. Perhaps they encountered the gods in the open, as the daughters of Celeus did Demeter, and in some way paid them honor. In K5 (=71–81) a female speaks in a fawning voice, saying something about a double-edged grief, and also about poverty. Blass thought that she was apologizing to the visiting gods for her poor accommodations (but why should magical smiths be poor?) and urging them to go elsewhere (*pheugete*, 81), but this is impossible; a hospitable person urges a guest to stay, no matter what the conditions (compare Admetus with Heracles, E. *Alc.* 539). Jockl (*WS* 37, 1915, 142–56), was probably on the right track when he supposed that the speaker here is Macelo, refusing to go with her sisters in spite of the dream command: if she goes with them she goes to poverty and loses her husband, but she urges them to save themselves (*pheugete* in an acceptable context). If the women are to find Cretan husbands at the shore it is important that only the unmarried should go.

13. The plural at 138 shows that there was a third sister involved, and Snell and others have found her in the -*sagora* who seems to appear at 49 and 72. If this is correct, it seems that the dream appeared to her, thus creating a story in which each sister had her own function: Macelo, to honor her husband: Dexithea, to be the mother of Euxantius; -sagora, to be the receiver of prophecy. Snell, however, makes the dream come before the act of hospitality, which seems to make the reward anticipate the good deed that earned it; this is because he, like Blass, reads K5 as a speech of reception.

14. The city would be named Koreso, and Bacchylides may have been punning on its having been founded where the *korai* received the Cretans; see N. Festa, "Per l'onore del re di Creta," *Miscellanea per nozze Rostagno-Cavazza* (Florence, 1898), pp. 5–11.

15. That the father had been specifically mentioned can be inferred from the fact that Bacchylides, at 138, refers to the women who were saved as "daughters."

16. See M. Detienne and J.-P. Vernant, *Les ruses de l'intelligence* (Paris, 1974), pp. 244 ff., who cite Suetonius, *Des termes injurieux. Des jeux grecs*, ed. Taillardat (Paris, 1967), p. 54 and pp. 133–36.

17. See M. Eliade, *Shamanism* (Princeton, 1972), p. 470.

18. On the connection between metallurgy, magic, and the foundation of dynasties, see Eliade, ibid., p. 473, where the Telchines are considered among the smiths who have shamanistic qualities.

19. Jebb supposed that there were Euxantidae at Ceos, related to those of Miletus, a clan that specialized in wool-carding. The preparation of wool certainly provides a perfect example of a *technē* that has been civilized and made harmless by having been passed down through a female Telchine, and

perhaps it is worth noting that Macelo, at 1.74, is given the epithet "fond of the spindle." A kind of parallel to this sequence in which Telchine craft is transformed to become women's art can be seen in the conjunction that Pindar contrives between the Telchines and the cult of Athena at O. 7.50 ff.

INDEX OF PASSAGES

INDEX OF SUBJECTS

Martin Classical Lectures